Playing the Bass
with Three Left Hands

Playing the Bass with Three Left Hands

Will Carruthers

ff

FABER & FABER

This edition first published in the UK in 2016
by Faber & Faber Ltd, Bloomsbury House,
74–77 Great Russell Street, London WC1B 3DA

Typeset by Reality Premedia Services Pvt. Ltd.
Printed in the UK by CPI Group (UK) Ltd, Croydon CR0 4YY

A CIP record for this book
is available from the British Library

ISBN 978–0–571–32996–0

2 4 6 8 10 9 7 5 3 1

Contents

On Being an Imaginary Viking

We are getting ahead of ourselves here. Very far ahead. Almost to the end, in fact. Time was neither a straight line, after all, nor memory an exact science . . .

I was standing next to a man who had burned a million pounds. This was a rare pleasure in itself. Having occasionally burned money in public myself, as an experiment in defiance and occasionally for my own amusement, I was well aware of the reactions it might provoke in people who could think of money as nothing but good. I had never been near enough to a million actual pounds to set light to them but I had practised on the odd fifty here and there and I certainly had respect for the convictions of anybody who could strike that match and live with the consequences. We live in a time and place where the idea of money is an all-consuming fever, with very few real challengers. To destroy the symbols of the idea of this material religion is considered the ultimate heresy. Literally. Heresy. Even to question the concept of money puts you on shaky ground. If poor people question the great green god they are generally accused of jealousy and envy. Nobody could accuse someone who burned a million quid of being envious. That was an act of war. I mean, it's not an act of war like a cruise missile or something (which also costs a million quid), but it certainly annoys people. Although money has no conscience, it can be a blank canvas upon which we may reveal our worst vices and trace the shapes of our desires and dreams. Money is the nothing that seems like everything when you don't have it. The problem is, perhaps, that people begin to mistake the way for the destination. Money and fame are not happiness in themselves and if you doubt that, ask the zombie hologram of Michael Jackson for its opinions on the subject. Regardless of the void in these idols, they have become popular ends in themselves and, as such, perhaps need to be destroyed occasionally if only to limit the power they hold over our lives. It is telling that the ultimate goal for anybody involved in the creative arts is to be remembered after their deaths, by which point, hopefully, one might imagine their priorities will have changed somewhat.

The man who had once (allegedly) burned a million pounds was explaining what it was that he was trying to achieve and why. 'I realised that recorded music had become trivial and meaningless when I got my first iPod,' he said. 'It just didn't mean anything any more, so I tried to imagine a world where no music existed and it had to start again from scratch.'

There was something eternally hopeful in his nihilism.

I too had fallen out of love with the idea of recorded music, although my personal epiphany had arrived on an easyJet flight. I was looking at the back of the seat in front of me and I saw a vibrant picture of a can of Coke and a bag of crisps. It was a flight, so it was perfectly acceptable for them to advertise this junk food at some extortionate price. Thrown in as an incentive to buy the crisps and Coke was ten free downloads of songs. Why would anyone want to spend their lives making something that was given away free with junk food? The worth of music itself had been challenged and debased and perhaps the only way to get people to appreciate it again was to withdraw it. Of course this was impossible, but it didn't mean it wasn't worth a try.

The man who had burned a million quid went on. He said, 'Music just didn't mean anything any more. So now, I only want to record the sound of the human voice.'

Relishing the obvious irony in the upcoming possibility of recording music (albeit only with the human voice) with a man who had just explained his belief in the pointlessness of recorded music, I nodded and agreed. I had occasionally entertained myself with the idea of a big red button that would eliminate all recorded music from the world. Miles Davis, Jimi Hendrix, Abba, and the Spice Girls, freed from overwhelming zombie culture to exist only as memory in the mind of musicians everywhere. No copyright. No restriction. No more just pressing 'play'. Only the possibility of musicians playing music. Would you press the button? Would you press it to save music? I can't remember who it was that told me to remember to forget.

'I was driving my Land Rover, listening to the sound of the engine,' he continued, explaining the concept further, 'when I heard voices from the back seats. There was nobody in the vehicle with me, but I could hear singing behind my head.' It seemed that our old friend, the drone, had manifested once more to weave its imaginary magic, like the musical equivalent of a random pattern of tea leaves in the bottom of your cup that might speak of the future to those who concern themselves with these things. 'It was very strange,' he continued. 'It seemed to me like there were three Vikings in the back of the Land Rover and they were singing along in tune with the engine.'

Then, while showing us the film of the recreation of his journey, he made some imaginary Viking sounds to better illustrate the sound of his vision. There he had been, driving through some unpopulated landscape in Northumbria, or the Scottish borders, or somewhere in between, and then . . . from somewhere between the sound of the engine, the wheels on the road, and his fevered and solitary imagination, three Vikings had sort of materialised in the back of the Land Rover to sing along with his journey. Being a curious sort, he had joined in with this unexpected choir rather than thinking he had gone mad. He now wanted us to approximate the sound of the (possibly) imaginary Vikings.

I was also standing next to an incredibly hungover and amenable Australian with a voice like a thousand late nights, who had, perhaps, burned a little money in his time but not in any way that had produced smoke and flames. There is more than one way to not give a fuck, after all.

We had been chosen purely for the quality, or lack of quality, of our voices, which were as deep and sonorous as old bronze bells housed in picturesque and decrepit towers. Although we were green with the verdigris of time and other intoxicants, we could somehow sing in tune with the hum of the sleek forces that keep the world from wobbling off its axis and flying through space at a tangent to time. Or something.

The producer played the actual recorded Land Rover sound and we began humming and omming along, in a low-sounding mechanical rumble that worked in sympathy with the engine and the Vikings. The drone was in the key of B, I believe. Everything has a key. Vikings, engines, lamp-posts, cats, you.

Ommmmmmmmmmmmmmmmmmmmmmmmmmmmmmm mmmm . . .

The man from The KLF sang along and I tried not to feel intimidated by his presence. Somewhere deep inside, a ghostly voice was echoing a memory of a dimly remembered bacchanal. 'MuuuuuumuuuuuuMUUUUUUUUUUUUUUUUUUUUU UUUUUUUUUU,' it sang.

I don't think it was a Viking.

Ommmmmmmmmmmmmmmmmmmmmmmmmmmmmmm mmmm.

Rrrrrrrrrrrrrrrrrrrr . . .

We went across the borders, imagining imaginary Vikings,

and embracing the sound of the engine that drove us and our marauded voices. We sounded like hungover and considerably road-burned musicians, standing around a microphone, impersonating Tibetan monks, pretending to be imaginary Vikings, in the back of a real (but now recorded) Land Rover, for a man who had once recorded a song with Tammy Wynette. I suppose I had reached that stage in my career where these things no longer seemed implausible.

I had finally become a proper session musician.

I was also going to be paid by a man who had burned a million quid.

The three of us ran through the 'song' a few times.

'I don't think my Viking is low enough,' said Bill. 'You two do one together.'

So the woken-in-fright Aussie and I gave it a run through until the engine of our voices was a dulcet dream machine and the Vikings had come into clearer focus.

Ommmmmmmmmmmmmmmmmmmmmmmmmmmmmmmm mmmmmm . . .

From the drone comes all manner of things.

From the one comes the many, and so, to the one, the many must return . . . to mire and mingle and throw forth tentacles of existence from the void once more.

I hadn't obtained this particular job through my many weird contacts in the music industry (after years of service), or through an agent or a manager. I got this job by spitting schnapps into a Brandenburg barbeque that had been warming me and three of my friends after we'd spent a pleasant day cycling around the nearby forests and lakes. I may have swallowed a little too much of the schnapps before I started spitting it at the fire but, regardless, my impromptu fire-breathing and howling at the moon had served to impress our German host rather more than one might have expected, given the fact that we were actually on his property and I was in something of a berserker state of mind.

'You have a very deep voice,' he had said, calmly and reasonably, after I had growled at some real or imaginary injustice before spitting another mouthful of schnapps into fiery oblivion. 'Would you be interested in doing some recording work?'

'How much?' I growled.

'Only a couple of hours or so,' he said.

'NOOOOOOO . . . HOW MUCH FUCKING MONEY?'

I produced another fireball, by way of punctuation, which produced a pleasing blast of heat and a solid whompfing sound. I looked at him slyly. 'And who is it for anyway?'

'It is for something I am recording with Bill Drummond in Berlin in a couple of weeks,' he replied, still remarkably unfazed by my werewolf act.

That name calmed me faster than a hand job and a couple of Valium.

'From the fucking KLF? Bill Drummond who burned a million quid?'

'Yes,' he replied.

I sobered up and acted normal. 'I'll do it for free,' I said. 'I like him.'

So, I had given our host my phone number, blown another couple of mouthfuls of schnapps into the fire to seal the deal and then retired to bed for the evening, expecting nothing more to come of it.

And there we were, standing in the Berlin morning, doing our best to lend convincing Viking overtones to a Land Rover engine in B . . . or B flat.

We took a break from the recording and retired to the kitchen table to drink tea. 'I gotta say, Bill,' I said, as calmly as my impressed inner fanboy would allow, 'you kept me fairly well entertained during the dark times of Britpop and New

Labour in the nineties. Thanks for that.' I didn't directly want to mention the burned money, or the crazed acid house singles, or the fact that they had deleted their entire back catalogue at the height of their career. I didn't even want to mention the forty grand he had nailed to a board for the future Turner Prize winner, nor the Echo and the Bunnymen tour he had booked in the shape of rabbit ears in order to appease an ancient and vengeful bunny deity. He looked kind of haunted for a moment and said, 'My kids think I'm an idiot.'

And then we both laughed for quite a while.

When he was satisfied with our interpretation of his imaginary Land Rover Vikings, we all said our farewells. He left, looking a little hangdog but with a twinkle in his eye and plans and schemes that were somehow in him and beyond him and that might leave his children wondering what the fuck was wrong with him, until they were old enough to know better.

I would happily have worked for free. It's not often that you get to pretend to be an imaginary Viking in the back of a Land Rover driven by a man who burned a million quid the hard way.

Part One

Gateway Drugs

Mind Yer Fingers

I left school at sixteen and went to work in a sheet-metal factory in Birmingham. My dad was an absent partner, so I suppose I had joined the family business. The factory was run by a father and daughter team who spent most of their time in the warm office drinking coffee. My dad had decided that it was better for me to start at the bottom and work my way up, so that's exactly what I did. Well, the first bit anyway.

Three people worked on the factory floor. Me and two lads from Birmingham called Wayne and Ray. Wayne had a wet-look, permed mullet, and one of those little moustaches that were so beloved of British football fans in the mid-eighties. He was a Birmingham City supporter and I didn't give a fuck about football, so there were no problems between us in that respect. Ray was a tattooed ex-borstal boy from Small Heath who had been given a bit of tax-free casual work from the old man to see how things worked out, while Ray was trying to go straight and get himself out of the world of glue sniffing and petty crime that had been his lot since he was a kid. Me and Ray got on well. We all worked in a long narrow corridor of floor-space between two lines of ancient and dirty machines. Standing stacked along each wall were work benches, hand presses, metal saws, spot welders, MIG welders, brake presses, guillotines, drills and all sorts of things that whacked, bent and cut metal into whatever shapes people would pay us to make. Set in a tangle of decaying Victorian buildings in the Jewellery Quarter of Hockley, the factory itself looked like a narrow unlit sweatshop from a Dickensian dream of industrial Britain.

There was no real heating system, so we stood on ripped-up pieces of cardboard while we worked to keep our feet from getting cold. When it was really cold, our fingers stuck to the bits of metal we were working with. The radio was always on and it tormented me daily with the endless production line of pop that we were being fed at the time. If they played a song I half liked I would jump for joy. That happened about four times in a year. Mostly, Radio One played Stock, Aitken and Waterman, Spandau Ballet, Duran Duran and all sorts of other forgettable eighties shit that could cut through the whine and clatter of the factory and the brutal whacking of the washer machine. Not a washing machine, a washer machine. That infernal contraption had a unique rhythm all of its own: 160 beats a minute and nothing else mattered while it hammered out the unhappiest of hardcore, stamping out metal washers the size of your fist from hand-fed strips of fourteen-gauge steel. Operating this machine was like being hit on the head with a heavy thing, quickly and repeatedly, which is perhaps not the most soothing way to spend Monday morning, freezing the balls of your feet off after a weekend of no sleep and intravenous amphetamine sulphate. Like many things I will try to describe in this book, I do not suggest you try it yourself.

The mundane and relentless twattery of the music and the mindless chatter of the DJs were ominously broken every morning, just in time for tea break, by the mournful violins heralding the beginning of 'Our Tune'. This was the mawkish low point of a show hosted by Simon Bates, which made a daily feature out of an awful sob story sent in by one of Mr Bates' depressed listeners. After reading the story out on air Bates would play some sentimental song chosen by his willing victims to soundtrack the memory of their beloved dead dog, or the time they had all contracted syphilis together.

Sometimes we would get so bored at work that we would

abuse the various chemicals that had been left on the shelves of the factory over the years. We had no idea what these chemicals actually were, crusted and rusting in their old spray cans and forgotten pots, but we were hopeless narcotic explorers and we hacked our way through the chemical undergrowth with glee. You might not be able to change the world but at least you can change your mind, right?

One day we were abusing the contents of some arcane tin by spraying the contents into a rag and inhaling it.

'Do you feel anything?' I'd asked Ray after we had both taken a good blast.

'Yeah,' he said, 'my feet have gone really cold.'

'Mine too,' I said, and we both laughed and laughed. Then we did it again, just to make sure it had really happened. We chalked that experience down as another victory for entertainment and then went back to the machines and the boredom. The fact that we would occasionally alleviate our boredom with a mid-morning snifter of feet-go-cold spray was pretty ironic given the fact that we spent most of the day standing around on squares of cardboard to stop our feet from getting too cold.

I suppose it is possible to interpret the fact that we were abusing solvents and odd industrial sprays as a sign that we weren't responsible enough to have control over our lives. To a degree that is true. To another degree, we were victims of our environment, which was sometimes so shit that it seemed better to risk the unknown and the dangerous, especially if it made your feet go a bit cold in an entertaining way. At least we felt we were in control of the spray. We did not always feel the same way about some other parts of our lives.

We did a lot of work on a machine called a brake press. When the foot pedal of this contraption was pressed, its two steel jaws would come together, accompanied by the hiss of hydraulics, a hum and a clunk, to produce a perfect fold in a carefully inserted strip of metal. Sometimes there would be thousands and thousands of the same strips of metal, all requiring exactly the same bend. The hypnotic mantra of the machine and the repetitive work would go on and on, sometimes for days, eating the countless crawling hours between tea breaks and the thirty minutes we got for lunch. The machine had no safety guards. Safety guards slowed down the work rate and, because we lived in competitive times, the guards had been disabled so that we could help the machine to bend metal more quickly. This lead to an interesting conundrum of human consciousness whereby, on the one hand, the person working the machine was completely hypnotised by the repetition and boredom of the work while, on the other hand, a simple slip or a mistimed foot could lead to a terrible situation in which bits of either hand could be suddenly removed without warning. Once, when I had been operating that machine alone for about two days, I started remembering dreams that I had *never* remembered. Dreams that were years old surfaced in my brain like phantoms from a life I had forgotten. It felt like recovering from amnesia. My mind would split, with one half taking care of the boring but necessary tasks essential for survival, while the other half of my brain desperately tried to keep the entertainment factor high enough so that I didn't give up the ghost entirely and put my head between the metal jaws as a quick way out.

Another time, when we had a job that needed to be finished really quickly, Wayne and I were working together at this machine. He was operating the brake press and I was sorting and loading the thin strips of aluminium for him. We weren't chit-chatting or abusing any of the many aerosols on offer, and we had reached the point where we were hardly aware of anything beyond the beat and the noise of the job at hand and our own thoughts.

Click, clank, whirr, chunk, click clack whirr, chunk, click clack whirr, chunk,

click, clank, whirr, chunk, click clack whirr chunk, click clack whirr, chunk,

click, clank, whirr, chunk, click clack whirr, chunk, click clack whirr, chunk.

It was a constant and reassuring sound that had been playing for an hour when it was strangely interrupted. Wayne said, 'Ouch,' and the rhythm stopped so that there was only silence beyond the low growl and the hiss of the resting machine. He hadn't said ouch very loudly. It was like he had just stubbed his toe or something.

I looked up from the aluminium strips to see why Wayne had stopped work. He had gone very red and he was wearing a weird, almost embarrassed smile. He glanced down at his hands and I followed his eyes until I saw the two crushed ends of bone poking through the flesh. I glanced away from his hands towards the machine and there, cradled in its resting metal jaws, were the ends of Wayne's two smallest fingers. They were crushed, mangled and broken, but they were still recognisable as fingertips. I looked back at Wayne's face. He looked at me and a strange, nervous laugh came out of him. 'What should I do?' he said, and then he made that weird, almost laughing sound again, as though he wanted me to find it funny and then maybe it wouldn't be real. For a couple of seconds I didn't know what he should do either.

'You better go to the office, mate,' I said in a thin voice. 'You'll be all right.'

He turned away and walked down to the office, past the long lines of machines and tools, and with every step he took he left behind a little trail of blood that made fresh dark stains on the dirty concrete floor. I didn't know what to do, so I just stood there and waited with the machine and the two ruined fingertips. The boss came up from the office. He had a tissue in his hand, which he used to pick up the pieces of flesh that had once been Wayne's fingers. There was no way anybody was going to be able to sew them back on. It hadn't been a clean cut. There wasn't much blood on the machine but he wiped it off anyway and then he asked me if I was all right to carry on with the job while he took Wayne to the hospital. I told him that I was able and then I started folding the little pieces of aluminium that I had previously stacked for my workmate. I worked very slowly. Much more slowly and carefully than I usually did. When Wayne and the boss walked past me on the way to the hospital, I noticed that Wayne wasn't smiling any more and that his face had gone a kind of pale grey colour. I carried on putting ninety-degree bends in the aluminium strips until it was time to stop work.

At five o'clock I washed my hands and walked round the corner to the George and Dragon on Albion Street. Inside it was noisy and smoky and the air was alive with clacking dominoes, laughter and relief, as the tin bashers and the jewellers, the watchmakers and the machine operators all gathered for a drink after work. There were a lot of metal workers in there. Birmingham had historically been a big metal-working city. The old tin bashers were lined up along the bar and I cast an eye along them. I looked at their hands, maybe for the first time. More than one of those hands, gripping those different pints along the bar, was not using a full fist of fingers. The more I looked at people's hands, the more missing fingers I saw. The meat seller walked through the door with a carrier bag full of bacon and he started handing out the unmarked plastic packets to the people giving him money. I sat and smoked and wondered what the future might hold for me if I kept on earning a living on the machines and in the factories of Birmingham.

After a couple of pints I got a taxi back to the pub I lived in. The Queen's Head was an old coaching house on Garrison Street in Small Heath. It sat between three train lines, underneath electricity pylons, on a largely deserted patch of industrial wasteland at the back end of the Leyland factory. When all of the surrounding factories knocked off for the evening the pub sat alone as the only inhabited island in a sea of empty buildings and lifeless storage facilities. It was run by a fierce woman called Nancy McCann, who ran the place with an iron hand in a black velvet glove. It said 'licensed proprietor Ann Dympna McCann' over the door but inside she was the queen and the head, and everybody knew it. It was a lively place that rarely closed before 3 a.m. despite the fact that closing time by law was eleven. Nancy was a canny woman and if the police came round to knock on the curtained windows at midnight, she would let them in and give them free whiskey. More than once, I'd look out of my attic window before leaving for work and see the coppers sleeping peacefully in their squad car on the road outside. There was a full and well-used jukebox in the Queen's Head that constantly played Irish folk songs and a few others too. It'd be playing 'The Fields of Athenry' or 'Maggie' or 'American Pie', and I would sit there drinking Guinness with the old men until I was too drunk to drink any more, or until I ran out of money.

After I had drunk my fill I would go up to my room, play the guitar and listen to Jimi Hendrix on my old mono cassette player. I only had one tape. It was *Electric Ladyland*, and I listened to it every night as I was going to sleep for about a year, until I knew every note of every solo by heart.

About two months later, when Wayne came back to work, he showed us the stumps of his fingers. One of the stumps looked exactly like ET, which we thought was pretty funny, because in the film ET points at space with his finger and says, 'Home. Home.'

17

Now, Wayne didn't have a finger, but he had a stump that looked like ET's face.

He received about two grand in compensation for his accident, which seemed like a fortune to us at the time. He also got two months off work. Me and Ray used to discuss which fingers we might be able to chop off for two grand and a couple of months' paid leave. I decided that I could probably stand to lose the little finger on my right hand, and one day I even got as far as laying it on the bed of the machine while trying to convince Ray to press the pedal. We were only half joking about it.

I would spend my weeks in Birmingham working at the factory, and on Friday night I would get the train back to Rugby and hang out with my mates.

A Piece of Cake

We made some small talk and then he glanced over his shoulder and said, 'Here, man. Do you want some space cake?'

I had managed to scrounge a couple of drags off a few joints at parties in the past, but I was by no means a hash smoker at this point, nor did I have much experience at all with illegal drugs.

The idea of a space cake sounded great. It was a cake with space in it. How dangerous could it actually be? I reached into the prettily decorated cake tin that he was holding and took out a piece of cake. It looked like normal cake. 'Thanks very much,' I said. 'What's in it?'

He laughed, and said, 'Hash mainly.'

I ate the cake, absent-mindedly, and looked out of the window. 'Delicious!' I said when I'd finished it.

'Do you want another bit?' he said, narrowly avoiding a slow-moving pensioner, as he offered the cake tin to me again.

Of course I wanted another slice of cake. I liked cake and it would have been rude not to. 'Thanks very much,' I said and ate the second piece without a thought.

There was some music playing on the car stereo. It sounded very familiar even though I had never heard it before. I listened to it for a while and tried to decide how something could sound both very old and very modern simultaneously. 'What is this music?' I shouted, over the top of it.

'It's the Velvet Underground,' came the reply.

'It's good, isn't it?' I yelled back, unnecessarily.

Then I went back to staring out of the window at the

Warwickshire countryside, while 'White Light/White Heat' began to imprint itself into my softening brain and the speeding silver car roared along the quiet country lanes on the way to the party.

It was a fairly standard teenage party. There was loud popular music and there was too much booze. I had drunk too much of it by the time the first space cake made its considerable presence felt. I suddenly felt very sick indeed and ran outside to throw up.

I wobbled back inside and propped myself up by a wall. Somebody asked me if I was all right, which prompted another wave of nausea and more throwing up. I was not feeling very all right at all, so I made my way into an empty bedroom and fell asleep curled up in the corner of the room.

At some point in the evening one of the girls who was throwing the party came over and shook me awake to see if I was OK. I repaid this concern by vomiting over her curtains as she watched in disbelief, then I went back to sleep again without an apology. I was not the life and soul of the party. I was discombobulated, disembodied, haunted by strange visions, and thoroughly crashed the fuck out, the two hash cakes having put me in a place that was far beyond the realms of normal sociability. The party carried on around me as I slept peacefully beside the unclean curtains. I woke up, sometime in the very early morning, with that horrible mixture of tiredness and physical discomfort that demands a solution even when you are in no fit state to provide for yourself. The night and the room had grown uncomfortably cold and I needed heat, so I stumbled around amongst the strewn and sleeping bodies until I found an electric blow heater.

I lay down in the corridor with my head directly on the heater and went to sleep again. When I woke up, it was daylight. My head was so hot that it felt like it had been cooked and the rest of me was freezing cold. I stood up and tried to regain an equilibrium that proved to be difficult with the combination of the heavy remnants of the innocent-looking space cake and an overly hot head. I took a little walk around, stepping and stumbling over the sprawled bodies of unconscious teenagers in various states of entanglement as I tried to encourage my blood to flow into the parts of my body it had been neglecting. It looked like the party had been some sort of fun. There were books down the toilet, broken windows, half-finished bottles of booze, and pools of vomit all over the place. It seemed that I hadn't been the only person who'd failed to be the perfect guest.

I walked into the kitchen and saw Pete Kember looking like he'd had a good night's sleep and a shower. He was sitting at the breakfast table, eating a bowl of Frosties, while two people snored under the table.

'Morning!' he said, sounding weirdly cheerful and looking abnormally together. Pete didn't drink. 'How's it going?'

'I think I cooked my head,' I replied, genuinely thinking it might have been the case. 'How you doing?'

He just laughed and carried on eating his Frosties.

This was my first adventure with Pete Kember. There were to be many more, but I didn't know that then.

The Trip

We were sitting in a fairly nondescript room, in an end of terrace house in Rugby, staring intently at the wall. I had become utterly fascinated by the taste of a match I had recently struck and I was trying to figure out why the main centre of my consciousness seemed to be located somewhere above my right kneecap. I was intensely aware of the pulsing of my own heart as it pushed the blood through the arteries and veins of my body.

The wall we were staring at seemed to be alive with vibrant shapes and shades that fell far beyond the commonly recognised spectrum of colour and ordinary reality. Primarily the wall was lit by the Optikinetiks projector which Pete Bain had borrowed for the purposes of the evening's entertainment from his bandmates in Spacemen 3 but, strangely, there were other colours and lights on the wall and in the room which did not seem to be emanating from obviously external sources. We each had our own internal lightshow working in perfect organic synchrony with the music and the blobwheel, and which was being powered by the tea we had drunk an hour previously that had tasted like the earth itself.

'We should go to the fair,' somebody suggested. This seemed like a pleasing idea, so we all wobbled, laughing, to our feet, and prepared ourselves for the short walk across town to the old cattle market.

Me, Pete Bain, Roscoe, Craig Wagstaff, Kate Radley and the other members of our funfair orientated gang, prepared ourselves for the unusually epic journey of actually leaving the house.

After a short stroll that may, in truth, have been much longer or shorter than we thought it was, we drew near to our destination. The lights of the fair seemed much brighter than usual, and the stars were positively beaming as we approached the distant noise of this temporary feast for the senses. Giant painted clowns and mountains of pulsating neon pink candyfloss loomed on the horizon, as the clattering fairground rides and the laughter of the people riding them called to us like a siren's song to sailors. We were wobbly and giggly and laughing at stuff that probably didn't exist for other people, but we weren't hurting anybody. Not even ourselves, really. We were merely thrill-seekers, looking to catch a ride on the big wheel and to catch a glimpse of the great beyond – in that, we were just like everybody else at the funfair.

After we had dizzied ourselves with the plunge and rise of the rollercoaster and scared ourselves stupid with the cartoon shocks of the ghost train, we decided to return to the safety of the house and the comforts of the blobwheel. Pete Bain and I were walking a little way ahead when we heard a commotion from the rear of our psychedelic caravan.

'Look at that! Look at that,' our friends in the rearguard squealed. 'What the fuck is that? Is it a spaceship? It looks like a chicken. Look at it!'

Pete Bain and I exchanged knowing glances. We couldn't see anything and, given the circumstances, we thought it was unlikely that our friends could see what they were seeing either.

We walked back towards them to try to see what they had seen.

They were babbling in a fairly high state of excitement: 'What do you reckon it was? That was fucking weird. You should have seen it. It was amazing. A big neon chicken, kind of zigzagging around in the sky.'

'Seen a spaceship, have you?' said Pete. 'Yeah, right.'

'I saw it too,' said Kate. '*It was really strange.*' She was visibly excited about it, even though she hadn't drunk the tea, which actually was strange.

When we returned to the house, unimpeded by more neon chickens or spacecraft, we settled into the ever-rotating colour wheel and the fabulously 3D music as we gradually made our way back through the night to something approaching consensus reality.

I had started visiting this particular house of ill repute in Rugby before it had truly become a house of ill repute. After the pubs closed at the weekend, a gang of merrymakers would dutifully stumble down to the house to listen to loud music and smoke hashish. I had become friends with Pete Bain (who was the bassist for Spacemen 3) and he introduced me into the circle and vouched for the fact that I was OK. I had met him through various after-pub house parties in the town, where the older crowd would gatecrash and I would sometimes manage to hang around them long enough for someone to pass me a joint. Every weekend for about two months I would go down to Winfield Street after drinking more lager than I could stand, someone would pass me a joint and then I would go outside to throw up. After a while, I stopped throwing up, and learned to keep myself together. We liked to get wasted, but we were still on the right side of the fine line between fun and outright self-destruction.

The people who gathered there, and who lived there, were a few years older than me. Roscoe (who was shortly to take over from Natty Brooker as the drummer for Spacemen 3), Pete Bain and Tim Morris (the original Spacemen 3 drummer) used to visit for these late-night smoking and music sessions.

Over the course of a year that house changed. The drugs of choice became less benign and the atmosphere became considerably harder and a little more dangerous. I stuck around when I should have been gone because I didn't know any better. I didn't know the difference and I didn't care to listen to any of the warnings I was being given at the time. It was all illegal, and it was all outside of a normality I didn't particularly care for. I was young and naïve and I had a taste for self-destruction that I barely recognised in myself. I really wasn't that interested in living a long and happy life anyway. It seemed impossible to me. I had run screaming into the jungle with a knife between my teeth and a desire to fight imaginary tigers. Barehanded if necessary. I suppose it was a kind of death wish, but at least I wasn't going down without a fight. The problem was, I was only going into battle with myself, and that's a fight that nobody is equipped to win.

Eventually the musicians stopped visiting. The recreational users of the kinder drugs stopped coming round after the pubs, and the students moved out. The hippies were given the boot and what replaced them was altogether more serious. The people that lived there now were older than even the older crowd I had been hanging out with. The visitors the house received were more serious drug users, petty thieves and dealers from the town. I was still working in the sheet-metal factory in Birmingham, but I was spending all of my weekends at the house.

We would listen to all the old punk records, David Bowie, Lou Reed, reggae, ska, the Rolling Stones while we laughed at the people that slept, as we raided the ashtrays for dog-ends, and played endless rounds of blackjack, waiting for the first TV programme of the morning. It was called *Wacaday*. The dayglo-suited idiot presenter would appear on the TV screen on Saturday morning and start screaming, 'WE'RE WIDE AWAKE!' And we were. We hadn't slept all night because we had been injecting amphetamine sulphate and grinding our teeth with boredom and pointless energy. I had started off snorting the stuff and soon moved over into injecting it. Snorting speed was like sniffing broken razorblades off a piss-house floor. Banging it was like taking the top of your skull off and pouring spacedust into your brain. I never thought about the risks or about the fact that we all shared the same old needle, week after week. When all of my money was spent, I would catch the train back to Birmingham New Street on Monday morning, put in eight hours on the machines at the sheet-metal factory and then go back to the pub in Small Heath.

After a few months of this, I suppose I started to unravel a bit. My dad sacked me from the factory. My mum had already kicked me out of her house in Rugby after she had found three thousand magic mushrooms drying under my bed, so I moved into Winfield Street and signed on the dole. I suppose I was a quick learner. In the course of a year and a half I had gone from being a complete neophyte, to hanging out and being accepted by some of the more serious elements of the Rugby underworld, even though I was so young. Nobody asked my age, because I had just been a fixture of the house when the rough boys had arrived. I was like a potted plant, or something. One time when we were all shooting speed in the kitchen, the mysterious powder had turned to jelly in the spoon as it cooled. While he drew the paste into the syringe and struggled to fire it into his reluctant veins, one of the gnarled old punks turned to me and said, 'How old are you, anyway?' When I told him I was seventeen he looked a bit freaked out.

Our dole cheques arrived bi-weekly and each of us received them on different days, so whoever got paid would take everyone else up to the pub and pay for the drinks. We would drink in the Blitz and sometimes down at a pub called O'Malley's, which was the hangout of choice for some of the more insalubrious and criminal members of our not so secret society. Once, there had been a serious fire in O'Malley's and it had shut down for a few days. The owners painted the entire place black, including all of the furniture, and then re-opened it within a week. It smelled a bit burned but it was still operational. Obviously our dole money didn't go too far, and there was always the problem of having enough to eat when all of the money had been spent. We began to shoplift from the supermarkets, sometimes immediately after we had spent all of our money on booze. I was an inept thief at the best of times, and being a drunk shoplifter didn't help matters at all. Finally, I was apprehended by the security team at the local Sainsbury's with a stolen bag of Maltesers and a clove of garlic in my jacket. I suppose I was nobody's idea of a master criminal, although the judge did see fit to ban me from every Sainsbury's in the land after he had found me guilty of the crime. I never had the heart to get any further into thievery than pilfering from the supermarkets. It wasn't my thing. For me, it was easier to be poor, and that worked in my favour in some ways, because my friends stopped giving me the speed I could no longer afford to pay for. I still had my guitar, but I didn't talk about that too much. Nobody was talking about making music at the house any more, and the general view amongst my friends in the house was that there was something a bit weird about the musicians in town. Eventually I moved out of the house of ill repute. When somebody had stolen all of the plug sockets and the carpets and there wasn't a clean spoon left in the house. When the bailiffs and the police had come round and broken the front door down one morning to cut the electricity off. When there was a plastic bag full of some old lady's sentimental stuff that some idiot thief had stolen and then thrown up into the tree outside when he realised he couldn't sell it. I would look up at that bag, caught in the high branches of the tree, and wonder about the woman's valued trinkets that had been worth stealing but not worth selling. To be fair to my housemates they had given the thief a good bollocking about it. They did have standards.

I was learning to live with the constant fear of arrest. Much has been written about the paranoia of drug users, but little has been written about the mental strains of being constantly under the threat of law. Maybe it isn't just the drugs that cause the paranoia.

My friend Rowley Ford, an old-school sixties' dropout from Rugby who had taken the trip to India and never quite come back the same way, advised me of a good way to throw the police off if you happened to be unlucky enough to get searched.

'Always carry something weird in your pockets, man,' he said. 'Nothing disgusting or stupid. Just weird stuff, like mad people do. They won't search too far if they think you are mad.'

I asked him what kind of stuff in particular, but he couldn't really be specific about it.

'Just weird stuff,' he replied, and after a while that stuff somehow found its way into my pockets without me being able to explain it or understand it either. I guess that is just the way that weird works.

By the time I left the house I was nineteen. I had lost my virginity, metaphorically and literally, and I'd lost a good chunk of my innocence too. I was using intravenous drugs before I lost my virginity, which is a very strange set of priorities for a teenager to have. Eventually, when it happened, it happened with a woman who'd once been the girlfriend of a man called Christopher Fitzgerald. He died of an overdose. If you look at the back of *Sound of Confusion*, the first Spacemen 3 album, it says, 'In loving memory of Christopher Fitzgerald.' I think he had been about nineteen when he died and his father had started a campaign in the local press to hunt down the drug dealers he held responsible for the death of his son.

It all got pretty messy when the television cameras turned up in town and started interviewing people who really didn't want to be on TV. His old man had taken out an advert in the local paper that said, 'A day in the wells of time killed my son,' because it was his coded way of naming two people who he held responsible for the death. We all understood that he was angry and sad, but the truth of the matter was that you could have arrested every drug dealer in Rugby and there would still have been another to take their place. He might as well have blamed the manufacturers of the little peach Palfium tablet which his son had injected on the night he died. The only person who had killed his son had been his son. All the rest had been supply and demand. I suppose no parent wants to think about the reasons for that, and neither did we.

The Graveyard Shift (or How to Play One Note for a Very Long Time without Losing Touch with Your Mind)

We loaded as much of the equipment as we could into stolen shopping trolleys, crossed the road from the flat, and entered the graveyard, making enough noise to wake the dead. It wasn't out of a lack of respect. It was difficult to be silent. The wonky wheels skittered on the trolleys, the reverb springs twanged, and the amplifiers crashed against the cymbals, while we laughed and joked as we made our way across the paths that ran beside the graves. Rupert Brooke, the First World War poet who died before he saw action, and who was consequently revered for his patriotic verse, is buried in that graveyard, alongside the countless dead from various wars and other, more natural, causes. Intricately carved headstones line the paths amongst the yew trees, standing in mute testament to the love of the living for their dearly departed. We, of course, were very much alive and partly possessed by that feeling of invincibility that youth carries briefly, even as it walks so close to death. I had started hanging out with the musicians. My career as a thief had been going nowhere.

We would arrive at the small rehearsal room in the old lampworks building and set up our borrowed and scrounged equipment. Natty Brooker would sit behind whatever tangle of drums he had managed to gather from hedgerows and junk shops, holding the noise together with his offbeat Beefheartian logic and his caveman stomp, while the rest of us played together, somewhere close by, lost in our own worlds but communicating distantly through rhythm, sound and noise.

Darren Wissen would hunch over his guitar in a reverie, producing haunted sludge from the depths of the mushrooms he was so fond of, while Roscoe and Steve Evans added various woo-woo guitar and flying-saucer frippery as we collectively produced a fairly haunting and primitive dirge with few obvious connections to popular musical forms.

I had been relegated to bass guitar, despite my initial reluctance and protestations. I was soon hammering away on those four strings, loudly, with enthusiasm, but with very little experience or technical skill. Somewhere there is a tape recording of my first ever change of key while playing in this group. In the recording, the rest of the band are desperately trying to alert me to the impending change by shouting over the clattering din of whatever bastard riff we were in the process of mangling. 'NOW,' they shout, many fruitless times, as I comically fail to count the bar correctly and move my fingers in time with theirs.

This particular band never had a name and never did a gig. We never recorded anything beyond mono-cassette copies of our rehearsal sessions, and we rarely changed key or had any lyrics. We didn't have titles for any of the 'songs' but we would go back to the same riffs, week after week, and hold on to them like a dog with a bone, gnawing at the same motifs for hours over hours. We were just happy to play and, even though we talked about doing gigs, we weren't really that interested or ambitious beyond the rehearsal room.

Although Rugby was a small town, and we were all vaguely aware of each other's existence purely because of proximity, we had become firmer friends through our patronage of one particular pub and, specifically, through the Reverberation Club, which ran occasionally in its back room. The Blitz was a fairly typical mid-eighties British hostelry. Named after the famous London club, while sharing nothing in common with it except for the name, the Blitz was a coked-up designer's mess of fake industrial pipes, neon lights, video jukeboxes and weirdly patterned carpets. This cheap recreation of last year's brand new thing was housed behind an old Georgian frontage that looked out onto the main street leading up to Lawrence Sheriff School where I had tried to avoid as much unnecessary education as I could. Given that Rugby was a small provincial town, the clientele who frequented the Blitz were a mishmash of vaguely alternative people and the usual weekend pub crawlers. Thugs from the surrounding villages, punks, goths, and townies on the piss all gathered inside at the weekend to get their small-town kicks in whatever ways they saw fit. Bubbling away in the back room were the stirrings of a music scene that would influence countless bands, span the globe, and continue to be relevant thirty years and counting into the future. Judging by the tiny number of people who actually frequented the Reverberation Club, nobody would have predicted that at the time.

A few months previously, before I took the full leap into the subculture that became such a large part of my life, I had been sitting in the Polish Club with my younger friends from school when I realised that I needed a sanctuary that was beyond the understanding of most of the people I knew.

I fled that teenage disco, running through the town centre in panic and exhilaration while dodging the drunks and my own hallucinations as I tried to get to the Blitz, where the Reverberation Club was in full effect for the night. It felt like going home. OK, so home now looked like a peculiar undersea grotto, decorated with imaginary deep-sea fish heads and psychedelic netting, but it felt a damn sight more reassuring than groups of drunk kids vomiting in the toilets and disco-dancing badly in the hope of maybe sticking their hands in someone's underwear later on. Of course I was interested in those things too, but on this particular evening, when the bright lights of the Polish

Club bar had done nothing to soothe my jangled sensibilities, and my friend's head had suddenly launched off his body, leaving me gazing at a vision of him with a wobbling bobble of a face on a fifteen-foot giraffe neck, I decided it might be time for a change of scenery. I realised that I needed to find people that might be able to understand my predicament more fully, and that all fifteen of them were probably in the back room of the Blitz listening to the Thirteenth Floor Elevators and the Red Krayola. When I arrived, I paid my fifty-pence entrance fee and walked into an undoubtedly weird environment that felt considerably less weird to me than my previous environment. I settled into the darkness and watched the old blobwheel push oozing colours around the walls of the undersea grotto as a strange trio of women emerged from the mandalas of the lightshow to dance in a soothing way to the groovy music. The people I knew here were unconcerned by my babbling about giraffe creatures and, as the Elevators turned into The Stooges and The Stooges turned into the Velvet Underground, while John Lee Hooker stamped his foot to some obscure psychedelic Nugget, then somehow it had all seemed very right and proper.

I started hanging out more and more with the musicians who ran the Reverberation Club, and I would spend time round at Gavin and Darren Wissens' flat, where we'd brew up the tea from the mushrooms that Natty picked on the same fields where Lewis Carroll had played rugby as a boy.

We'd sit there all night, mostly silent, watching the birds take flight from the entwined foliage of the William Morris wallpaper, while we listened to Kaleidoscope, The Incredible String Band, obscure garage punk, Hawkwind and Bob Dylan. When the dawn came and the first cars started to phase past on the road outside, we would gaze out over the graveyard and marvel at the strangely frosted yew trees and the spirits of the dead that seemed to grow through them and bring them to life as the day grew stronger. Around 8 a.m., the butchers in the shop downstairs would start work for the day. It was peculiarly unsettling to listen to the sound of someone chopping up huge joints of meat and bone. We would sit upstairs and try not to imagine the scene downstairs too clearly.

Natty had once turned to me after a particularly long night and said, 'Maybe he is chopping up dead people down there.'

And then he threw his head back and laughed his old pokey-toothed cackle.

Until you have seen a man turn into a lobster and then throw his head back and laugh at a joke like that, there is no way I can explain to you how it felt.

Walking back to my house alone, one wild and windy night after another cup of some strange local brew, I approached the entrance to the graveyard and heard distinct voices calling my name. 'Wiiiiiilllllll. Willllllllllllll. Willllllllllll,' they keened, and although I told myself it was the wind, or the tea, or a combination of the two, I didn't really believe myself. I just kept walking away from those voices, and they got quieter and quieter as I left the graveyard behind.

The Spacemen

I remember the first time I met Natty. He was sitting in the living room at Spacemen headquarters, which at the time was somewhere on Murray Road. I had gone round drunk with my speedfreak friends to have a little fun with the artists. They were into different things than we were. They played music and made art. We stole stuff and got into fights. In a larger town we would have never met, but Rugby was not a large town, so we did.

We were pissing in the front garden when Pete Kember arrived. He just laughed and waited at the door with us to be invited in. Natty was sitting on the settee. I think the first thing he said was, 'What month is it?'

Nobody really had an answer to that.

Through playing in the graveyard band with Natty and Roscoe, I began to spend more time visiting them down at the house in Oxford Street that they shared with Jason Pierce. Pete Kember spent more time at that place than he did at home. Spacemen 3 were recording *The Perfect Prescription*. It was 1987 and all we wanted to do was get stoned. From the outside it looked pretty normal. It was a run-down terraced house, rented out to three young oddballs who received a few odd visitors and who kept unusual hours.

There was a huge stack of records in the front room, which were the massed collections of the three residents and whatever Pete Kember brought down with him when he visited. The entire front room had been plastered, walls and ceiling, with a huge collage of magazine cut-outs and photocopied album artwork. It was quite an experience to sit there on mushrooms and follow Screamin' Jay Hawkins's echoing face into the Five Blind Boys of Alabama, while Iggy Pop looked on in mock horror at a toothpaste advert where Mom had been replaced by an alligator and the toothpaste tube was full of snakes. 'I can't find my mind,' someone had written over the door, beside some tattooed sideshow freak from a sixties cartoon and a picture of a distorted badger. It was quite an understandable thing to have written over the door because if you lost your mind in that collage you'd spend quite a long time looking for it.

The walls of the kitchen were painted in vibrating red and blue blobs, which ran over the walls and doors with little regard for any common rules of decorating etiquette. Everything in the kitchen that wasn't art was squalid and uncared for. There was usually a tower of plates and cups in the sink containing traces of food and drink in varying states of decomposition. The settee in the front room was old, scavenged, probably unhygienic, home to an ecosystem all of its own. I slept on that sofa quite a few times. Everyone was on the dole except for Pete, who always had a good lump of hash and who would sometimes pass along the butt end of the joints he would constantly roll and smoke.

He hid his stash in a gouged-out hole in the plaster of the wall, underneath a loose flap in the giant collage. If the cops had come round to raid the place, which was always possible, they would have spent a long time searching the peeling scraps and peculiar juxtapositions of images in that room.

We listened to Captain Beefheart, old blues records, gospel, the MC5, the Red Krayola, soul, all sorts of odd psychedelia, the Thirteenth Floor Elevators, The Stooges, The Cramps, the Folk Devils, and on and on. We listened to them religiously . . . literally. There might be four people sitting in the room, eyes closed in silence, listening to every note and every breath of every beat. Kate once remarked that, on the few occasions she visited Jason there, she found it unsettling to sit in the front room when everyone was silently stoned and meditating on some obscure Suicide bootleg, or something. The atmosphere was quite dense at times, I suppose. Pete might be nodding off, burning holes in the already ruined settee, and Jason might cop a quick nod behind a can of super-strength lager and a bit of Pete's gear, while we would sometimes turn up on speed, or drunk, and ruin the vibe by talking too loudly and laughing. This caused some problems. Heroin users and speedfreaks rarely see eye to eye. They are concerned with different things. Despite that, me and Pete Kember became firmer friends.

Natty never took heroin at all when I knew him. He drank, and snorted the speed I occasionally brought round, and we would sometimes do mushrooms together, either up at Gavin and Darren's flat, or down at his place, but he was fairly strongly opposed to the seductions of the opiate life and he tried, very subtly, to discourage me too.

I had gone down to visit him once and, as I stood by the front door, I noticed he had painted all of the glass in the front bay windows of the house with white emulsion. After a while of knocking and shouting through the letterbox, he let me in and we both walked into the newly decorated front room. The entire collage, that riot of surreal images and rock and roll iconography that had taken days and days of work to cut out and stick up, had been obliterated in a snowstorm of white paint. There was a single, white-painted chair standing in the middle of the newly painted white floor. It was facing the only thing in the room that wasn't painted white, which was a small photocopied Hells Angels insignia that said, 'Approved by the Hells Angels.' Natty had reclaimed his front room from the Spacemen.

The Acid Party

I had first seen an incarnation of the dreamweapon weaving
soporifically among the drugged crowds in the cavernous halls
and empty workplaces of an abandoned industrial building
underneath the railway arches somewhere in London. On that
evening, there had been blobwheels and trippy lights and a
mixed and addled crowd of goths and psyche freaks, rogue
mods, mini-skirted sixties Warhol wannabes and other oddball
creatures of the night, all looking for a way out of the vampiric
Thatcherite culture that was feeding at the soul of Britain. I
watched The James Taylor Quartet wrap their considerably
sharp-suited skills around 'Soul Limbo' as disenfranchised
psychobillies chicken danced their way backwards between
long hairs, short hairs, flat tops and backcombed fright wigs
alike. The assembled crowd of people grooved and stumbled
between stages in various states of self-inflicted discombobula-
tion. Bowl cuts and paisley, skulls and leather, wafting fabrics
and winklepickers . . . whatever could this glorious conglom-
eration of alternatives have been turning into? Nobody knew
and nobody cared. We were united in taking it all in and celebrating the rites of existence, because almost anything was
better than the mindless pap that we were being tube-fed by
the all consuming organs of the great and the not so good at
the time. At least this felt real. If it was a hopeful hedonism,
too indebted to the past and always bound to fade in the light,
it was still all cool (even if it wasn't), so most people in attend-
ance were tolerant enough of the different musical dishes on
offer to at least permit their existence.

A band called The Weeds summoned the ghost of The Doors downstairs as Sonic and Jason sat on stools one floor above and played around with modal tones and gentle melodies that oozed and melted into the omnipresent beanbag of drone. It was unusual. In fact, it was practically unheard of at the time, and that was just fine, because we were speeding and tripping and stoned and drunk and trying to figure out what it was that we actually wanted. We were also trying to figure out why the hell things weren't as good as we thought they had been in the past, even though those glorious times had never been quite as rosy as our record collections might have painted them. That stuff had been a *reaction* to the overwhelming glum and prevailing blah culture of its time, after all, so perhaps our own slough of despond was actually a fertile breeding ground for every dark-loving mushroom and aromatic vision that had been forced beneath the ground by the shock troops of greed and materialism. We were young enough to not accept defeat gracefully. Duran Duran's muse might have been Rio, who was poncing about on a big yacht and dancing in the sand at some heathen tax haven, but *our* muse was named Suzy Creamcheese and she was dancing in the sands of our mind, which were turning a pleasant shade of turquoise with every touch of her twinkling toes. We held the unkillable optimism of better dreams spawning within a country that had taken a sharp turn into a rat's nest of shallow ambition. The death knell for post-war optimism had been sounded and we were witness to the breaking of the social contract in favour of personal gain, war and hate. Despite this, we were somehow hopeful in our despair. I guess this was part of the beginning of the gathering of tribes that would eventually flower into the wordless hedonism and unity of acid house. After all, what was there left to say that hadn't already been said, and where had it got us?

Spacemen 3 were due to play a concert in the small hours of

this houseless acid party. The band had successfully blown my mind at Dingwalls in London a few weeks earlier and I had been hoping for a rerun of the celestial overtones that had left me peering in amazement at the roof, wondering where it all came from. At the party the sound that Spacemen 3 produced when they took the stage quickly made most of the evening's previous attempts at psychedelia and sixties revivalism look very pale indeed. The band played a song that roared, growled, grew fangs and drew blood. This was music taken beyond the realm of pastiche and imitation. Despite the fact that the riff was a straight lift from the MC5, and it did sound a bit like The Stooges and Suicide (and a bit like a few other things), it also sounded entirely *other*. It had taken the sum of its parts and become an entity beyond them. I was genuinely spooked at the power and ferocity, and it wasn't just the cheap speed that had put the wind up me. It was totally believable, it was totally ours, and it wasn't happening twenty years ago. The song in question, the one with the fangs, was an early version of 'Revolution' and it sounded like every indignation you'd ever suffered, pumped up on steroids, with a gun as long as your arm, and ready to kill everyone that had ever done it harm. It roared and it raged, while Sonic Boom hectored and spat like a man on a mission to redeem himself and lead a revolt against the very establishment that had nurtured him. I was further convinced of the absolute power of the band and submitted to the ecstatic maelstrom with gratitude and genuine awe. After the gently reassuring ebb and pulse of the earlier saz and guitar duet the fury of the full Spacemen 3 live onslaught had been a terrifying plunge into the righteous heart of the inferno.

Heaven and hell indeed . . . and all based around the same simple but effective formula. One note. One note. One note. One note. One note.

Playing with Fire

I was working nights in a factory that made bolts for the space shuttle. I'd walk into the filthy clouds of the shot-blasting room, unlock the doors to the machines, and pour the carefully measured bolts into the rotating drums. I'd set the timers to start the process, and the dirtiest washing machines in the world would begin to turn as the high-pressure ceramic nozzles blasted silicon carbide grit and wore away the microns of titanium necessary so that the fastenings might actually withstand the rigours of space travel. While waiting for the blasters to do their work, I would sit alone at my dirty desk and write down the waking dreams that stopped me from sleeping on the job. I was filthy with grit and fine metal dusts, and the dirt from my hands rubbed off onto the pages as I scribbled out the possibilities that had nothing to do with the job I was actually doing. Or maybe they did. I was so tired working the night shift it was hard to tell the waking life from the dreams sometimes and, with only the hiss of hydraulics and the grind of the grit to keep me company, I would drift off without even knowing it, only to be woken with a shake and a growl by my angry-looking foreman.

Once they had been ground to the exact specifications and checked with a micrometer by the man in the clean coat in the clean office, the titanium bolts would be tempered in the kilns, turning them cobalt blue and every shade of rainbow in the process. While they were still hot from the kiln, two young kids would dunk the baskets of bolts into an open bath of trichlorethylene that sat inside the shot-blasting room. It was a two-man job and when the hot bolts hit the cool liquid, both of the young workers would be enveloped in a hissing cloud of steam. Trichlorethylene is a heavy industrial solvent, and consequently those two kids walked around for most of the night wearing bemused and addled expressions. They would keep me entertained with their pickled observations and the hazy logic of glue sniffers. Every night, they would gradually turn into the village idiots of the night-shift factory floor and I didn't envy them one little bit, because even though they were laughing more than the rest of us, they were often laughing at things that the rest of us couldn't understand. Perhaps this was all part of the training too.

The graveyard band became even less interested in itself than it was in the beginning, but I was still eager to play music. Gavin Wissen asked me to join the Cogs of Tyme, a garage punk band that he was fronting, who often played with the Spacemen and who were regulars at the Reverberation Club. He had previously, and perhaps unwisely, invited me up on stage to sing with the Cogs of Tyme during a gig in the back room of the Blitz one night. They were about to perform the song 'Go Go Gorilla' and he wanted me to sing backing vocals. My first time on stage had found me unexpectedly singing the backing vocals to a song I didn't even know. In the absence of any kind of a clue as to what I was supposed to be doing, I made very loud monkey noises, gibbering, screaming and howling like a gibbon while beating my chest like King Monkey himself. This amused me and the rest of the band, although the audience were fairly silent on the matter.

I made my live bass-playing debut some time later in the back room of the Blitz, playing garage punk covers and a few of Gavin's own songs with the Cogs of Tyme. A second gig followed at a psychedelic club called the Sensateria in Birmingham and before long I was thoroughly swept up in music to the point where it occupied most of my waking hopes and dreams, even when I was loading dirty titanium bolts into machines and doing my bit to make sure that nothing important fell off a space shuttle.

I guess it was around this time that Pete Kember started to show an interest in my bass playing too. We had become friends and he would sometimes come round to the flat I was sharing in Albert Street to smoke hash and listen to records. One day, when he was visiting, he casually asked if I would be interested in joining Spacemen 3. Jason had turned up to a rehearsal of the graveyard band a couple of days previously. 'I like your bass playing and I like your banjo playing,' he'd said, when nobody else was around. Then he had smiled his wide thin smile and said his goodbyes. There was nothing too strange in any of that. We were a small group of musicians in a small town, occasionally people would drop in to other people's rehearsals. Jason had said nothing to make me suspect that I was being headhunted.

I loved Spacemen 3 at this point and obviously I was keen to join the band, but I wanted to check it with Pete Bain first. He was my friend, and even though I knew he and Roscoe had been having problems with the band, I had not expected to be offered the job.

I went down to Pete Bain's house and sat on the same sofa where I had experienced the sheer terror of listening to 'Frankie Teardrop' for the first time after a particularly strong pipe of Nepalese hash. I asked him what he thought about Pete Kember's proposal. Pete Bain was suffering from a crisis of ambition. On the one hand, he wanted the freedom to make his own music and to have his own band away from the rigid control of Pete Kember and Jason, who at the time demanded the fairly singular attention of any band members. On the other hand, he had done a lot of hard work with the group and he knew that Spacemen 3 were an excellent band who'd reached a level of popularity that none of our friends were even close to. Spacemen 3 had a record deal, they had made two studio albums, and they had toured Europe and the UK. Maybe Pete found some of his feelings about the contradictions inside himself difficult to articulate. It was a difficult band to leave even if you wanted to.

'Why not?' he said. 'Go for it if you think you can do it.' And then he looked a bit pissed off.

'Pete,' I said to him. 'If you don't want me to do it, I won't.'

'No, no. I'm fine with it', he said, with a tight smile. 'There are other things I want to do. You'll hate it in the end anyway.'

I didn't care to learn why he thought I might eventually hate being in Spacemen 3, despite some of the things I had heard and seen. I was just desperate to play and I had been given an opportunity to do so. That didn't mean that I didn't give a shit about anything else. In Rugby there was no getting away from the things that you'd done, either to other people or yourself. Despite Pete Bain's mostly silent misgivings, I left his house feeling pretty excited. He'd given me the go-ahead I thought I'd needed and now I was going to be a member of Spacemen 3.

I was twenty years old and I had only ever played two gigs in my life.

I passed the affirmative news on to Pete Kember as quickly as I could. The band had started on the sessions for *Playing with Fire* down in Cornwall and I was told that I was expected there for recording duties, and that arrangements would be made for my travel. Pete and Jason were commuting every week or so from the studio on the outskirts of St Austell, which was a four and a half hour drive from Rugby on a good day.

The only problem was: I had a job.

I went into the bolt factory that night and talked to my supervisor. After I had explained the situation to him, he looked sympathetic and agreed to give me the one-week holiday I was due so that I could go to Cornwall and record. I figured that if things didn't work out with the band, I could go back to my job. I worked the next couple of shifts in an endless clock-watching agony of excitement. I was so looking forward to the prospect of getting involved in a studio recording session with a band that I loved that I found it almost impossible to care about bolts any more, even if they were going into space.

It was arranged that Kate Radley would give me a lift down to Cornwall. I was pretty fucking pleased with myself when she arrived to pick me up. We drove down to her mum's house in Cheltenham, had dinner, and then drove the rest of the way to Cornwall. When we reached St Austell we found the road that took us out to the studio on the outskirts of town. We drove up the hill, until we reached the rough and bumpy dirt road that lead us towards the lights of the house. Jason opened the front door of the small cottage and let us into the front room that also served as the control room for the eight-channel tape machine and desk where the fledgling tracks for *Playing with Fire* had already been laid. It was a basic hippy house in the country with a fairly primitive recording setup, but to me it looked like paradise and a dream come true. I was about to wield a blunt instrument at the cutting edge of music, and things were never gonna be the same.

We said our hellos. Pete said hi to Kate, Jason was obviously pleased to see her, and then we were introduced to the owners. They were in a band called Webcore, who were part of the new age travellers' scene. I was told I was going to sleep on a mattress in the room next to the studio, and I was perfectly happy about it. I was perfectly happy in general, to be honest – just absolutely overjoyed to be off the night shift and in Cornwall, in an actual studio, about to do some actual recording. Perhaps a remote hippy cottage in Cornwall was not anyone else's ideal first choice, but somehow the arrangements had been made

45

and there we all were. The owners were friendly enough and Pat, the engineer, an older fellow of around forty, with dreadlocks and who smoked a lot of hash, seemed to be enthusiastic and friendly. We settled into the soft and tatty chairs and I opened the beer that Jason had given me while Pete chewed off a piece of his hash for me.

'Don't worry about food and beer and stuff,' Pete said. 'We have a budget for that and we'll make sure you get backwards and forwards from the studio so that it won't cost you anything. Wanna hear some of the new songs?'

I was all mellow smiles as I said that indeed I did want to hear the new songs.

'Yeah, it's been going well, man,' Pete said. 'Have a listen. I think we've got some good stuff down.'

He played the first song. A spectral and elegiac organ motif ushered in one of those classic Spacemen 3 waves of sadness, beauty and hope, and I was instantly hooked. It didn't sound like anyone else and it didn't even sound like Spacemen 3 had sounded before, but then that was how they had always sounded, with each new album working as a progression and a departure from the record that had preceded it.

'Wow, man, that's fucking great. What's that one called?' I said.

'Uh, "Honey", I think,' Pete replied. 'I think it's gonna come out pretty well. There's no bass on it yet. Maybe we can do it tomorrow.'

I smiled and nodded. Jason smiled and Kate smiled and Pete smiled. It was all good in the hippy-dippy hood as 'Honey' played itself out in a pleasant and lovely way. Next up was the backing track for 'Che', which was basic skeletal bones, a guide guitar, and a sparse click track, with a soaring wah solo over the top that arched and peaked and slunk back to a low growl around the constant drone. Bare as it was, it sounded

like another world of possibility and I began to get genuinely
excited at what I was about to become musically involved with.
I fucking loved music and I wanted to play. Maybe more than
I wanted to do anything else. The night blurred into hashish
and good-natured chit-chat as the basic click tracks and chord
structures for the songs played in the background. You gotta live
it, after all. You have to get so used to the stuff that it becomes
your bones, the meat of your marrow. You gotta dream it and
breathe it and wish it into being and, at that point, it all seemed
like a very possible dream indeed. By the time we had retired to
our respective mattresses on the floors of the various rooms in
the house, I was very happy indeed. I pulled the slightly washed
blankets over me and felt that I was truly living the dreams I
had painted in the dust during the long nights in the bolt factory
in Rugby. It seemed like a different life.

I woke up after a night of real dreams to find the sun catch-
ing the crystals that hung in the windows between the faded
curtains and rags, which kept out a little of the daylight. I
dragged myself to the edge of the mattress, sat up, reached
for my clothes and found a fairly well desiccated cat turd
crusted into the carpet beside my discarded belongings. It
was a bright and clear morning and I took a peek out through
the dirty windows into the garden beyond the overhanging
ivy that covered the house. One of the owners greeted me
from the kitchen and showed me where the tea-making stuff
was. While the kettle boiled, he explained that the house
had been an old tin miner's cottage, and in the surrounding
woods there was a warren of old mines that had been cut into
the pale earth by the people who had previously lived and
worked there. He told me that the nearby river ran like milk
when it rained because of all the chalk in the ground, and that
there was a cave in the back garden that glowed in the dark
with phosphorescent fungus.

'Glow in the dark mushrooms?' I said. 'Woah. I've eaten a few mushrooms that made everything else glow in the dark, but I've never seen one glow without eating it first.' We both laughed.

I opened the creaking front door and stepped out into the sunshine to drink my tea and smoke a cigarette while I tried to imagine what my first day in a recording studio might hold.

Pete appeared after a while with a mug of tea and a joint.

'Morning!' he said, in a kind of over-exaggerated and deliberately comic accent. 'Sleep well?'

I replied that I had indeed slept well. 'I like it here,' I said, looking out over the tangle of garden and woods.

'Amazing, isn't it?' he said. 'We'll go for a walk up the back later. There are some crazy rope swings up there.' He passed me the joint and we both sat in the sunshine, the black hash rising in heavy curls from the lit end of the spliff as we drank our tea.

Pete was an odd sort, really. He could be difficult, pugnacious, charming and funny by turns, and he had the temper of the devil himself. Any argument with Pete was total war, and in those days he would sometimes go to war over a perceived slight then forget to stop. I had never had any major problem with him myself, but he certainly had a reputation for speaking his mind and for knowing what he wanted and what he didn't. I think he regarded some of my previous antics under the influence of drugs he didn't use with a kind of amused and baffled detachment, but we got on well. I think he respected some sorts of crazy a little bit, and so did I.

We finished our tea and headed into the studio. Pat, the engineer, arrived around midday and we sat around chatting while smoking another joint. He threaded up the tape machine and fired up the desk and the outboard gear. He pressed 'play'. The tape heads clunked into place and the tape whispered across the heads, the unedited pre-take sounds from the various tracks fading into the fuzzed-out wah and descending guitar chords of 'Che'. It was a cover of the Suicide song but it didn't sound anything like Suicide. Jason appeared from upstairs, looking dishevelled and amiable and sat on the sofa smoking his first cigarette of the day. Pete asked me if I was ready to lay down a bass track. I was nervous but I nodded yes, and Pat set up a chair beside the mixing desk. The whole studio setup was part of the front room of the cottage. There was a waist-high wooden railing across half of the room, presumably to stop errant hippies from stumbling into the recording setup while work was in progress. I sat on the chair and gazed at Pat's back and beyond him to the confusing constellations of knobs, faders and flashing lights on the desk. It was completely new territory for me and I was a little bit in awe of proceedings. I still didn't have a bass guitar, so Pat had borrowed one from a friend of his. He handed over a nameless and headless contraption that was painted a vibrant shade of glittering red. Given the choice, it was not a bass I would have taken from the racks, but then I was not particularly fussy, and there was no choice.

'Errrrrrrr,' said Pete. 'That thing looks fucking horrible.'

Despite Pat's protestations that the bass had a good sound, Pete continued to take the piss out of it and he carried on making loud 'eeeeeeeewwwwww' noises as I plugged it into the tuner and started tuning up to 440.

'We always tune a bit higher, man,' Pete said. 'Tune it up to the farthest mark on the tuner. It sounds more . . . tense.'

Without asking why, I did what I was told, and then Pat plugged me into the desk while I played random notes until he had a good level and sound. I was totally transfixed by the job at hand, and my heart was beating like a Suicide rhythm track.

'Just have a few runs through, man, and see what you think,' Pete said in a reassuring way, like it was just every day that you got to lay down your first ever bassline.

Pat pressed 'play' on the tape machine and the song started up again. I knew that both Pete and Jason were listening intently, but they both made an effort to appear nonchalant and disinterested.

'Sounds good, man,' said Pete encouragingly as I made a few tentative runs up and down the neck of the bass, trying to find the shapes that fitted the holes in the sound. 'Keep going.'

Jason smiled and nodded encouragingly from the sofa, where he had been joined by Kate. Despite my absolutely over-whelming feelings of excitement and terror at being sat in a recording studio laying down my first bassline, I settled into it until I was lost in the music and the hash, testing notes and scales and playing by ear and intuition. I was still a frustrated guitarist, in some ways, so I always had an urge to stray from the beat and the groove into more decorative areas, but that didn't seem to bother anyone.

'I absolutely hate the sound of the open E string on bass guitars,' Pete said. 'So try not to play it.'

Mainly avoiding the bassiest of bass notes, I soloed and ran around the neck with varying degrees of success, while Pete, Jason and Pat made helpful noises that gave me the confidence to continue. I knew the sound and the feel they liked – we had all been getting stoned and listening to the same records for so long that it wasn't too hard to know what was required. Nothing that I was playing was from the Suicide song, but it didn't seem to matter. Pete would nod at the runs and riffs he liked and then make a face when my playing strayed beyond his taste. I kept on noodling as the song played through a few times, until Pete said it was time to start recording.

Pat pressed 'play' and 'record', and I was away, improvising around the themes I'd found. When I fucked up, or fell off the edge, they'd stop the tape, drop me in before the fuck-up,

and I'd continue until we reached the end of the song. At the
end of the take Pete and Jason looked really happy.

'That's great. Really cool stuff, man. But I don't know if
we can use that whole take. Lay another track down and see if
you can do it better.'

Pat armed another track and I laid down more improvised
bass that sounded the same as the last one but different. I had
no idea what I was doing. There were no vocals on the song
and no cues to hit, so I was fairly free to do what I pleased as
long as it got the nod of approval from Pete and Jason. It was
their band, after all, and I was still very much a novice.

This went on for a while until the two tracks of bass were
down as well as I could play them, with each better-sounding
take replacing the previous one. Pete and Jason were both
standing up at the desk by this time. They ummed and ahhed
about which track to keep and which one to discard. Tracks
were precious, as there were only eight of them, and one of
those was always occupied by the SMPTE code that would
sync up the primitive drum machines, click tracks and sequencers, if they were needed. That left seven tracks to record on
for the whole song. After a while of listening and pondering
they decided that they would crossfade between the tracks
and edit out the rough parts of my playing while bouncing to
another spare track. With Jason on one fader and Pete on the
other, they listened to the two basslines, decided which bits
they liked best, then crossfaded between them live as the third
track recorded. Bounce-downs were a staple of our recording necessities back then. When they were satisfied with the
bounced track they erased the first two and I sat and listened
to the song with the first bassline I had ever recorded mixed in.
I was pretty pleased with myself, I suppose. I had never heard
myself sound so good, and my new bandmates seemed more
than pleased with the results.

Hash Yoghurt and Hells Angels

The night before, we had mixed a big chunk of hash into a pot of yoghurt and when we woke up in the morning, me and Pete ate it for breakfast. While Jason was at the studio working on some backing tracks, we headed out for a ramble through the woods to find the rope swings.

Great scoops of earth had been mined from the hills behind the house, and these dug-outs had gradually softened and filled themselves in with trees and thick vegetation. It was a kind of paradise up there, really, and as the hash took hold we walked over soft cushions of moss and fought our way through thickets of brambles until we found the rope swing, which was a stick tied to a length of rope that someone had thrown over the high branch of an overhanging tree. Pete leaned over the void of the old mine, snagged the rope, and manoeuvred himself into a sitting position on the stick. He then launched himself off from the bank, swinging right out under the canopy of the trees and into green space, laughing, spinning round and roaring as he went. 'Oh, man. That's a fucking trip!' he shouted as he swung back in ever-decreasing circles. 'You gotta have a go.'

I was stoned to the bone as I climbed onto the swing and launched myself out over the gorge. The trees and the bushes spun into a kaleidoscope with the blue sky. I laughed myself stupid as the pit fell out of my stomach. I was still laughing as Pete pulled me back in, and I fell off the stick and landed on the ground. After an hour of making ourselves dizzy on the swings we made our way back to the house.

Jason had finished his work and Pete was going to lay down some tracks, so Jason and I moved out to the garden with a guitar and a bass and a couple of beers. We sat and chatted for a bit and he ran through a song he'd been working on. It was called 'So Hot' and we were both laughing about it because it actually was pretty hot in the garden. He showed me the chords and we ran through it a few times. It sounded great to me even though he didn't have all the words. He had the chorus and the basic melody, and it just sounded like sitting in the garden on a sunny day drinking beer and having fun. It's a melancholy kind of song, of course, but we were happy. After a while Pete called me in to lay some bass down on a song he was working on.

I sat down in the recording chair and listened as the drone phased up and down and yawed into the void, before the church organs came in for a few bars and then settled back to the drone again. That one note sounded pretty damn comfortable with the back end of the breakfast we'd eaten earlier. I listened and drifted off with my eyes closed while Pete took the bass and played a simple two-note repeating refrain over it, to show me what he was after. After a couple of bars he said, 'I might as well put this down myself.'

So he did, and then he gave me the bass and asked me if I had any ideas. I played a few tentative notes until he nodded his head and then I found the runs and spaces between the notes that seemed to fit with the melancholy sound and the yoghurt for breakfast and it all started to make a mellow kind of sense to us.

'That's cool, man. That's cool. RECORD IT, Pat. Not that. Play that run again.'

So, the bassline started going down for what was to become 'Let Me Down Gently', and it was all so mellow that I was a million miles away, even as I was playing. The front door opened and in walked four travellers with two dogs and a baby. They walked past me as I was recording. 'All right, Pat,' one of them said, as they smiled and nodded at me and Pete on the way to the kitchen. We just kept on recording.

But this did not sit well with Mr Kember. 'Man. It's not cool them just walking in here like that,' he said. 'We are trying to make a record here and we've paid for the studio. How are we supposed to record with people just walking backwards and forwards in the studio with dogs and babies and stuff like that?'

Pat just shrugged. I guess it was normal in that place.

Spacemen 3 were no longer recording in the seclusion of VHF down at the Arches Lane industrial estate in Rugby. This was a whole hippy-dippy different kettle of fish and it was bound to cause problems eventually.

Regardless of any differences we might have had, we continued working. We'd lay the various tracks and get stoned and listen to them for hours on end. Then there might be a bit of tweaking and a drone added, and maybe Jason would add some guitar, then maybe Pete would lay some organ, and everyone was working together as far as I could tell. There were no arguments and the atmosphere was fine.

Jason and I decided to take a trip into town to get some supplies from the supermarket. We walked down the hill, in the sunshine, chatting about nothing much and everything in particular regarding the music and the weather. We were cracking jokes and feeling good.

As we got down towards the town, which was a walk of about a mile, we passed some houses and Jason pointed at a particularly rough-looking house on the corner. 'That is where the Hells Angels live,' he said. 'That's the Cornish chapter house.' We walked past and peered into the garden at the old settees and the bits of motorbike that were lying on the

HASH YOGHURT AND HELLS ANGELS

unkempt bit of grass at the front of the house.

After we had been to the supermarket and stocked up on beer and breakfast cereal and crap pizza (and whatever else we thought we needed), we decided it might be easier to wheel the shopping up the hill in the trolley rather than carry it all in plastic bags. It was a hot day and we were both feeling lazy. We took it in turns pushing the trolley up the hill towards the studio and, as we got closer to the Hells Angels' house, we saw a bunch of bikers sitting outside drinking beer. Both of us knew the drill for not attracting violent attention. Don't look over, eyes front, and keep walking.

As we drew level with them, they started shouting over to us. 'Oi. Where do you think yer goin' with that, then? Bring us a beer.'

These were fairly gnarly-looking bastards, and there was no way on earth me and Jason were going to fight them. Nobody sane wants to get in a fight with the Angels and nobody sane wants to get in a fight with Jason either, especially if he's on your side.

'Just keep walking,' I said. 'Don't look at them.'

So we put our heads down and kept walking, while they kept on shouting and laughing as we disappeared up the hill away from them.

'Fuck. I'm glad they never came after us,' said Jason. 'They might have taken the beer.' And we both laughed and kept pushing the wonky shopping trolley up the hill.

The next day, Pat arrived to start work and told us that we had been asked to go down and see the Hells Angels at their house. We were not entirely reassured by the news. 'What do they want to see us for?' asked Jason. 'What have we done?'

'They didn't seem angry,' Pat said. 'They just said they wanted you to go down to the house. It's probably best if you do.'

We all stood around silently wondering what the fuck the Hells Angels might want us to go to the house for.

'All right,' said Pete. 'Tell 'em we'll go down this afternoon.'

And with that, he disappeared into the kitchen to make another space cake.

We had all eaten a piece of Pete's lovely space cake and we were feeling the effects of its special ingredients quite strongly when the time arrived to go down and see the Hells Angels. Although we were understandably reluctant to go and see what they wanted, there was no getting out of it. The three of us left the house and started walking, very slowly, down the hill towards what we thought could be certain doom. It was hard to know with the Hellys, really. As long as you were all right with them they were normally pretty friendly, but if they felt that you had transgressed somehow, things could get very ugly indeed.

'Do you think it's because we didn't give them any beer yesterday?' said Jason. 'Maybe they are pissed off because of that?'

We were stoned and a bit paranoid, I suppose.

'I'll do the talking,' said Pete. 'It'll be all right.'

So we walked down the hill and up to the rough-looking house with the stuff in the garden, stuff that nice people didn't buy from garden centres. The three of us stood at the door and tried not to look scared, as Pete reached over and rang the bell.

'Ding, dong,' the bell chimed and, after an agonising eternity, the door opened and the looming shape of a grizzled and hairy biker stood facing us from the doorway. He was wearing full leathers and colours. He was grim-faced, and so were we.

'Spacemen 3?' he said, with a serious expression and a raised eyebrow.

'Yeah,' we said.

'OPEN UP YOUR MIND AND LET EVERYTHING COME THROUGH!' he shouted, gleefully breaking into a broad smile. 'We fucking love you lot. Come in!'

To say we felt relief would be an understatement. We felt like we had narrowly avoided a possible maiming. We walked through the front door laughing. We followed the leader into the front room, where we were introduced to the group of Angels that Jason and I had scuttled past the previous day. They were laughing about the fact that we had practically run away from them with the shopping trolley. 'You didn't even give us a beer, you tight bastards,' one of them said, laughing again, as they handed over tins of beer.

We thanked them and sat down in a line on the sofa.

The Angel who had answered the door offered Pete a ride on his motorbike. Jason and I sat on the sofa drinking beer, looking through the Hells Angels' photograph album.

'When we have a party and someone falls asleep, they get their picture in here,' one of the Angels said, opening the album. 'Here's Harry at a party we had last month,' he continued, jerking a thumb at his friend in the chair opposite and then pointing a dirty fingernail at the photo.

Me and Jason leaned in and tried to focus on the picture.

It was hard to tell what was going on in the blurred photograph but it seemed to involve some fire and our new friend Harry looking a bit surprised.

'If anybody falls asleep, we set fire to their balls with lighter fluid and then wake them up and take a picture,' we were told.

'HAHAHAHAHAHAHAHA,' we all laughed.

They flipped through the family album and showed us the photographs of variously distressed Hells Angels waking up with their balls on fire. After a while, Pete got back from his Angels' guided tour of St Austell and we all said our thanks and goodbyes and left. We were pretty pleased that the Hells Angels liked us but, as we walked back up the hill to the studio in the woods, we joked about how we probably wouldn't be attending the party we'd been invited to.

Wide Awake in a Dream

After a week down at the studio, I got a lift back up to Rugby with Pete, while Jason stayed behind to work on his songs alone. On the ride back to Rugby we got to talking about drugs.

'Do you still take speed?' Pete asked.

'Sometimes,' I said. 'I have some with me, but I haven't used any for a while.'

He was watching the road with a disapproving expression.

'It's really not cool, man, you know,' he said. 'It takes more off you than it gives you, and it's terrible for gigs and stuff. I'd really rather you weren't taking that stuff when you are in the band, man.'

'OK,' I said, because being in the band was more important to me than taking drugs . . . ironically enough.

'But will you turn me on to some smack?' I said.

I'd asked Pete for it before, but he'd been reluctant to give it to me despite my protestations that I had already been doing bad things.

'Oh, I dunno, man,' he said. 'It's really not a good idea.'

'No,' I said. 'But I still want to try it. Just show me where I can buy some.'

I wound the car window down and threw my half a wrap of speed onto the motorway as a bootleg of the Beach Boys' *Smile* sessions played in the car and the mood swung from the jovial and the silly to the dark and the tragic, and back again, in the space of moments. From vegetables to surf's up, from colum-nated ruins, to she's going bald and back to a broken man too tough to cry.

We pulled up at Pete's parents' house in Dunchurch. It was a huge place, almost a mansion. He parked the silver MG Metro in the driveway and we walked up to the imposing front door. Once inside, we stopped in the hallway for a moment and I was introduced to his mum and dad, who greeted us both cheerfully and asked how the recording had been going. It was all very nice. His mum made us a cup of Earl Grey tea and then we both disappeared upstairs to his bedroom.

Pete's bedroom was actually two rooms, and they were both painted a vivid shade of postbox red. The small sitting room had a huge framed Lichtenstein poster with the word 'WHAAM' printed across it in a primary explosion of colours and jet fighters. There was a vast army of plastic toys and figurines marching across the windowsill, and a huge collection of desirable vinyl propped up against one of the red walls. I sat on the sofa while he disappeared into the bedroom and began to rummage around in a well-hidden corner.

When he came back he was carrying a syringe and a dirty spoon. He began to prepare his hit. I looked through the door into the bedroom and saw that the scarlet carpet around his bed was covered in long black cigarette burns where he had obviously nodded off and dropped his lit cigarettes. It was a good thing it was a good quality carpet or the whole mansion might have gone up in smoke. It was fairly intimidating being in there. It was such a nice place to be getting ready to take heroin for the first time, and everything.

The brown powder was in the spoon with a little pinch of citric acid, and Pete stirred the contents with the orange plastic sheath of the insulin syringe. Next, the lighter went under the spoon until the contents bubbled and then he gave it another stir. It didn't look very hygienic. Although there was a solution of some sort, there was also a dark scummy ring, and all sorts of floating bits and bobs sitting in the small puddle of the spoon. It looked like water from the canal, and it occurred to me that, no matter how wealthy the family you came from, when it came to heroin, it seemed like you just had to do the same illegal, stamped-on shit that all the poor people did too. Pete bit off a piece of cigarette filter, tossed it into the spoon, and then placed the point of the syringe gently into it and sucked the shallow depths into the thin plastic syringe. He stood the syringe up vertically, with the spike to the ceiling, tapped it to bring the air to the top, and then pressed the plunger until a tiny jet came out of the hole in the needle.

His sleeve was already rolled up, so he tied his arm off, pumped it, and slapped the crook of his elbow until what was left of his veins appeared. He licked the spike and slid it in amongst the scars and the soft skin.

After a little digging, a blood-red flower appeared in the head of the barrel and he began to press the plunger. When it was all the way in, he withdrew the plunger, flushed the syringe with blood and then re-injected it. He took the needle out, pressed his finger against the entry wound, and then laid his head back and closed his eyes.

When he opened them again, he handed the needle over to me and I repeated the procedure with a tiny bit of the heroin I had bought on the way. My tolerance was so low I would get off on a tiny dose. I rolled my sleeve up, licked the spike (like that was going to make a difference to anything) and then felt the first sharp touch of the blunt needle in the crook of my left arm. It wasn't my first time with a needle, but I had never learned to like the experience. I fought the urge to pull my own hand away and waited for . . . I don't know what. What I'd heard? What I'd imagined? I waited to feel different, because I knew enough about drugs to know that most people's descriptions were nowhere near to the experiences themselves, and that perhaps everyone's experiences are different anyway. How do

I know how you feel pain or pleasure? Eventually after a while of digging around in the crook of my elbow I hit a vein and I saw the flower of my own blood in the clear plastic of the insulin syringe.

I began to press the plunger and felt the heat of the liquid enter my bloodstream.

Afterwards, we both walked downstairs. I felt a bit sick, but I didn't really care. I could have thrown up on the carpet in front of his mum and I wouldn't have felt terrible about it. I would have felt bad . . . but not terrible.

We got in the car and Pete drove us down to my flat. I sat in a chair in the corner of my room, smoking a joint with a heavy feeling in the back of my head and a strange taste (that was almost a feeling) in my mouth. I closed my eyes and opened them again, after an hour, or a minute, and I focused on the large yellow poster over the gas fire. Martin Rev and Alan Vega looked out at me in monochromatic black on yellow, while the bold typeface proclaimed, 'Suicide.' Suicide. Suicide. Live Suicide. My head nodded back as though it belonged to another body and I fell into something not quite like sleep. Even though I was aware of where I was, and who I was, the colours of dreams lit up and I started to see things as I would in a dream, even though I was still quite awake.

The dreams I had have stayed with me until this day. I don't know why, because I slept this same sleep a few times afterwards but I have never remembered another single dream.

At first I had a vision of a clean white fridge standing in a vague light. I was standing in front of it – or my vision was, because I, as I knew myself bodily, was not in the picture at all. As I watched, the door of the fridge opened by itself and a surging tide of shiny, black, scuttling cockroaches vomited out of the cool white interior. In real life so many cockroaches could not have fitted into this fridge. The flood of insects kept on pouring out and I could not turn my head to look away.

I was discomforted by this, but not horrified, and I watched with a cool disregard and detachment, as though I were watching it on TV and not on the private movie screen of my own mind's eye.

The insect scene shifted and I found myself face to face with a disembodied head. A witchy crone's face regarded me with something close to malevolent humour. She cracked her lips to reveal broken teeth and a rotting mouth, and then she began to laugh at me. I could feel the derision in her mockery and in her bright and dark eyes. Her cruel laughter washed through me until I felt a chill inside despite the warmth of the drug.

I snapped my eyes open and looked around the room, feeling dazed and unsure of my reality. I lit a cigarette and watched the smoke kick and curl from the lit end.

It is the only opiate dream I ever had that I remember, and I can still see it as clearly as that night twenty-seven years ago.

Isn't that strange? I know that some of you will be wishing I'd shut the fuck up about this, and part of me really, really, wants to – but then, the culture of silence and shame around this subject has killed a lot more people than any discussion ever has. Consider that, and then consider it again, and then consider if my talking about this in any way glamorises the truth of it. If it does, think about that wave of insects again and the fact that I lacked the sense to be as spooked as I should have been by the vision.

Back to the Bolts

I went back to the bolt factory and talked to my foreman about the situation I was in. I was going to need more time off work to go and be in Spacemen 3 and there was no way that the factory could let me go for four weeks. I had to choose between my job and being in a band. It was no contest.

At the time in Britain, the government had just brought in a law that meant that if you walked out of your job without another one lined up, you would not be eligible for dole money for six months. I believe they are called benefit sanctions these days. Being unable to claim benefits was quite a strong disincentive for quitting any job, and it wasn't like jobs were that easy to find. I explained this to my boss and he was sympathetic. I couldn't just quit. He had to give me the sack, which would improve my chances of receiving money from the state. He agreed to concoct a story about my bad timekeeping and my inability to stay awake while I was at work, even though I had never been late for work in all the time I had been employed there. We agreed that I would work one more week, then I could leave and he would give me the covering letter saying that I had been asked to leave by the company. I thanked him and he wished me luck in my new career. I left his office and went back to my last few days tending to the titanium bolts. They would just have to go into space without my help from now on.

When the week was finished, I got my notice of termination and went down to the dole office to sign on. I filled in the paperwork and made the arrangements for getting the small amount of money from the state that would cover my living costs and rent. I was now a full-time musician and there was no job for me to go back to. I didn't have a care in the world.

It was time to head back down to the studio and the little bubble of *Playing with Fire* in Cornwall. Pete was driving down, so I snagged a lift with him. Although he was a proficient and able driver, Pete piloted his vehicle like a fucking maniac at times and he seemed to take pleasure in cutting things as finely as possible regarding blind bends and overtaking. I rolled the joints and he shouted at the other drivers as we somehow avoided collisions with other road users and inanimate objects. Miraculously, we made it as far as Cornwall and it was dark by the time we drove through St Austell. On the journey down I had accepted certain death so many times that the inevitability of it was no longer a matter of so much concern to me. As Pete was rallying the car up the dirt road towards the house of the hippies in the pouring rain, he turned away from the windscreen and informed me, with some gravitas, that he could no longer see anything and that he was probably about to crash the car. I looked out of the window and tried to think about something else as the Beach Boys sang and played out the fractured genius of *Smile* for the hundredth time on the journey. 'Eat a lot, sleep a lot, brush 'em like crazy,' came the advice from the weirdest of California as death drove past in the opposite direction and we pulled up, surprisingly in one piece, outside the cottage.

In the morning, Thierry, the drummer from France, arrived to record some live drums and to rehearse for an upcoming show in London. Pete immediately started to torment him. Thierry's English, although much better than our French, was not perfect. He was often left struggling in silent incomprehension as we chattered and yammered away in street slang and Midlands dialect while he struggled to keep up. Pete noticed that he was listening, and so began to use the phrase 'in theory' a lot in his conversations, taking great pleasure in the fact that Thierry would perk up and start paying even more attention thinking the conversation was about him in some way. Not only was Thierry more stoned than he had ever been in his life, he was also being mind-fucked by a master. It did little to relax him into the alien situation he had volunteered for.

The first call of duty for him was to drum on a song called 'Suicide'. 'Suicide' is not an easy track for any drummer, requiring immense stamina, accuracy and concentration throughout its sometimes interminable length. It is hard work.

Thierry started off pretty well, keeping it steady with the click track and the guide organ riff but, after three or four minutes, his tempo would start to lag, or he'd lose the bass-drum pattern, and he would be stopped and told to start again, with increasing exasperation and frustration on his part. That didn't help his playing at all. It was too tricky to get the drop in right, and this was long before anybody had access to a digital editing suite, so it had to be one perfect take or nothing. As the afternoon wore on, Thierry's efforts to get it right became more and more wrong, despite his heroic efforts and the sweat on his brow. After two or three hours they recorded a take just to make him feel better, despite the fact that it was obviously not working.

'Yeah. That's cool, man. Nice one,' Pete said, while pulling faces and exchanging dubious looks with Jason and me. 'We can fix it afterwards.'

In the end, the drums on 'Suicide' were sequenced and played by hand from drum machines. Thierry managed to play the maracas on 'Che', and that was the end of his recording career with Spacemen 3.

The upcoming gig was a different matter. With only a couple of days to go there were no options. Thierry was going to be the drummer for the evening, and that was that. We set up the equipment and began the two days of rehearsals that would see us fit to play our first headline show in London together. Spacemen 3 were never the most diligent band when it came to rehearsals. I don't think anybody enjoyed the process, but it was necessary, so it was done. It was the complete opposite of the graveyard band I had played with for a year and who had never done a show. Spacemen 3 was a military operation by comparison. There were songs and cues and strict endings, and starts and woe betide anyone who missed them. Pete was a fairly serious taskmaster when it came to matters of musical precision on the part of his bandmates. I guess the fruits of that are partly evident in the music we left behind, even if it was sometimes a nightmare to be involved with. Luckily, I was focused on music and little else and was content to set my ego aside and endure the pain of repetition in order to serve the greater whole. We were going to play an old set of Spacemen 3 songs, and I was familiar with all of them. The parts had been written – I just had to learn to play them. They were all fairly straightforward and the only real difficulty was endurance and persistence. I suppose I am a fairly stubborn bastard in some ways, which has served me well in my musical career, even if that only means I can play one note for a very long time without losing touch with most of my mind.

Over the course of the two days we sweated and worried ourselves into as precise a band as was possible, given the limited time we had to do the work. Thierry and I were mostly functional as a rhythm section, and Jason and Pete knew the territory well enough to carry the band if we stumbled and fell mid-song.

The day of the show approached and I was reaching a state of high terror. I had only played two shows in my whole life and the prospect of playing a headline gig in London filled me with dread. A van was hired and we packed the equipment and ourselves into it and set off for the capital city.

We arrived at Dingwalls in Camden, unloaded the equipment and set it all up on stage. It was the first real soundcheck I had ever done. I had no fucking idea what I was supposed to be looking for or asking about, so I just nodded and mumbled my way through it while I did what I was told and stood where I was told to stand.

My Bloody Valentine were the support for the evening and they were standing at the front of the stage listening to the soundcheck, with their equipment in a little pile beside them. We left the stage to give them a soundcheck, and I wandered off and sat by the canal to try to calm myself down a little bit. I was absolutely shitting myself, to the point where I was tempted to run away and pretend that I had never wanted any of this in the first place. I was underprepared, under-rehearsed and under a cloud of fear and apprehension that was increasing as time ticked away. I smoked many cigarettes. I tried to think about something else. I failed. BONG, BONG, BONG, BONG . . . my heart thumped and fear had its horrible way with me, as I chickened out mentally and ran away to a place in my mind where there was nothing but more fear.

I went for a walk, which helped a bit, until I saw the crowds arriving for the show. It didn't occur to me that even if I fucked it up nobody would know it was my fault. At this stage, my inexperience meant I was unaware of the secret immunity of bass players. Nobody sees you and nobody blames you. Drop a horrendous clanger and most of the audience will pull a face at the singer. Anyway, I kept on walking around Camden, looking at stuff that wasn't related to music and my imminent failure as a potential rock star.

When I returned to the venue I wandered amongst the crowd like a man who had been hit on the head and had temporarily lost his reason. My Bloody Valentine played their set, but it was impossible to enjoy them in any meaningful way because with every passing song my personal moment of doom drew a little closer. I went outside for a cigarette. There were people fucking everywhere. There was no escape, even though nobody knew who I was or gave a fuck anyway. I found a little stairway, climbed it, and hid behind a low wall while I smoked another cigarette. Pete came and found me, sitting up there, biting my nails and drawing on a cigarette that had a one-inch burn going on. 'You all right, man?'

'Yeah,' I said. 'Bit nervous, you know . . .'

'It'll be fine,' he said. 'The rehearsals were good. You can do it.'

'Yeah,' I said, which was a massive lie. He passed me a joint and we listened to My Bloody Valentine while the crowd chatted and laughed in happy anticipation of the headline act which, inexplicably for me, was us.

My Bloody Valentine finished their set and an ominous silence replaced them.

It was ominous to me anyway.

'Come on, man,' Pete said. 'Let's go and do it.'

So we stood up, walked down the stairs, and entered the hot and sweaty club. My heart was like a wild animal in my chest.

I remember getting up on stage and standing there in the lights. I remember looking out at the crowd and then holding my plectrum in my hand and not being sure how I should hold my plectrum, even though I knew how to hold a plectrum. I moved the little triangle of plastic around with both hands while I was waiting for the last strains of 'Ecstasy Symphony' to fade out. I was just dumbly moving the plectrum around wondering why it didn't feel right. I heard the words 'thanks for coming' like I was in a dream, and then the slow and menacing introduction to 'Rollercoaster' started and it felt like the first stirrings of a trip in the pit of my stomach. The seconds stretched out to years, and all of my thoughts about the audience and whether or not I was going to fuck it up and look like a prick in front of everyone melted away as we all came in on time and the first note played itself, while what was left of me looked on in amazement. It seemed I did know how to hold a plectrum, after all.

I can't remember another thing about the set until we left the stage with the tail end of 'Suicide' feeding back into itself over the wavering backbeat and the flashing strobe lights.

The crowd were barely audible over the throbbing din, as Gimpy Pat played the effects on the mixing desk until flying saucers landed and civilisations crumbled while we made our way shakily to the tiny dressing room at the back of the stage. Thierry continued drumming as me, Jason and Pete lit our cigarettes. I was practically shell-shocked.

'That sounded all right, man. Well done,' said Pete with a smile.

I just sat there, dripping with sweat, wondering what the fuck had just happened. 'Thanks,' I said, and smoked like a man who had been given a last-minute reprieve on the gallows.

Thierry stopped drumming and came backstage in a blur of sweat and smiles. He shook my hand, grinning and emanating a palpable sense of relief and excitement. 'We did it, man. We did it!' he said.

I wasn't sure if we'd done it or not, because, to be honest, it felt like someone else had done it while I had merely been a bemused bystander holding the bass. 'Yeah,' I said, 'we did it. Well done, man.' And then I smoked another cigarette as though it was the air itself and I was gasping for breath.

After the noise died down and the people left the venue, I emerged from the dressing room and packed down my equipment. Walking out of the door, I bumped into Kevin Shields.

He shook my hand and said, 'Sounded great, man.' I mumbled a thanks, feeling like someone who had just blundered into something by accident and been applauded for it. He smiled. I walked past him and found the clear spot on the stairs, out of the way of the crowd, where the air was as fresh as London gets, and slowly brought my jangling nerves back to a gentle rattle.

Thierry went back to France, and the rest of us went back to Cornwall and carried on with the recording. Sometimes I worked with Pete alone in the studio, sometimes I worked alone with Jason. Sometimes they worked together. When all of the tracks were nearly finished and the time came to mix the album, there was a bit of a falling out. Ugly words were exchanged between Pat and Pete as we left the studio with the master tapes. Though I think there had been some background tensions between Jason and Pete about songwriting there had been no obvious arguments.

Playing with Fire was finished and mixed up at VHF in Rugby, where *The Perfect Prescription* had been recorded. VHF was a better studio in a lot of ways, but I wonder if those lighter moments on the album would have sounded the same without all of the greenery, that hippy house and the rope swings and the river that turned into milk when it rained.

We heard later, much later, that the house in Cornwall where we recorded *Playing with Fire* burned down. I don't know if it did or not.

Elvis Died for Somebody's Sins but not Mine

Every time I play this someone in my house gets angry at me. It's not fair.
YouTube comment on *Dreamweapon*

It had been billed as 'an evening of contemporary sitar music', which was perhaps slightly misleading in that none of us had ever seriously played a sitar, nor had we brought one with us. Ideally, Sonic would have brought along his saz, which is a Turkish instrument that reverberates pleasingly around drones and which can occasionally produce Eastern-sounding scales. Unfortunately, that particular instrument had been stolen from him by some music killer and nefarious shit. The Turkish saz was actually an intrinsic part of the Spacemen 3 sound. Get hold of one and play some ascending one-note scales if you don't believe me. Perhaps it was playing the saz on a teenage visit to Turkey that had first convinced Pete Kember that it was not necessary to be some twiddly-fingered virtuoso in order to produce a convincing and spiritually reassuring sound. Minimal is maximal sometimes, so if you can make it sound good with one finger and a bit of careful tuning, then why not? You don't get points for unnecessary embellishment and random jazz chords that only impress your muso friends. Keep it simple, play with conviction, make sure you are in tune and let the technicalities present themselves in the glorious overtones that only ever ask that you get out of the fucking way a little bit. Soloing over complicated chord changes is a trial sometimes. The mind has to be constantly aware of the shifting harmonic ground and cannot truly free itself into careless improvisation and inspiration. When you are sure of your footing, your eyes can scan the heavens. When you know where you are melodically it is sometimes possible to give free reign to the imagination, and from there perhaps even to find a spark of the divine itself. Keep it simple, stupid. It's a good rule. Our limitations can be liberating if we choose to explore them and give them time to reveal the secrets they hold.

Drones, and the multitude of melodic and modal possibilities they allow, had somehow fallen out of favour with the Western musical tradition around the Middle Ages. The resurgence of interest in them could be traced back to the 1950s, wherein the seeds were sown for the revival of the one-note bed as a place of possibility rather than limitation. Perhaps it is no accident that the resurgence of interest in the mystical drone coincided with a renewed exploration of the mind-expanding properties of certain plants and their chemical derivatives.

Had we, as musicians and careless chemical guinea pigs, inadvertently stumbled into an age-old tradition through the recreational use of age-old plants? Maybe it wasn't an accident, after all. Maybe illegal religions have always popped up as a welcome laxative for systems made sticky on an unrelenting diet of white bread and circuses.

Anyway, I presume that the bright spark or cunning entrepreneur who had booked this 'evening of contemporary sitar music' had somehow seen (or heard about) Sonic and Jason's previous excursion into drones and 'sitar' music at the acid party in London. During that particular *Dreamweapon* set a suitably inebriated person might easily have been ecstatically transported to the banks of the Ganges, and it might have been quite possible for that person to imagine they were hearing some fabulous type of 'contemporary' sitar music, especially if they had never seen or heard a sitar before – contemporary or otherwise. People didn't play drone music at all at this time, so anyone could have been forgiven for thinking it was something it was not. Anyway, *somebody* had pitched the upcoming evening at Watermans Arts Centre in Brentford, west London, as something it really wasn't, and the artistic overlords who ran the venue were satisfied with what they thought they were going to get. What they were going to get was not anything that any scholar of music would consider to be sitar music, whether it came from today, yesterday or sometime in the future. We had drones – at least something in common with sitar music – but we had no sitars. We sat . . . but we did not sitar. It could have been billed, just as accurately, as an evening of contemporary hurdy-gurdy and bagpipe music, but that might have understandably scared some timid souls away. Anyway, you get the picture, we were there, we had some nice guitars and we were going to play and get paid, which was fairly high on our to-do list at the time. If the price we had to pay was our playing one note for a very long time in order to accidentally entertain the cinema queue patiently waiting for the start of *Wings of Desire*, and the fifteen people who had actually come to see us, then so be it. Did I mention we were getting paid and that we didn't have a sitar? Perhaps none of it mattered. We were playing in an arts centre, after all.

Were Spacemen 3 art? Maybe that is not a question a simple bass player should be expected to grapple with. It has too many strings, and I am by no means an expert in these matters. Regardless of whether or not it was art, Spacemen 3 were certainly not something you would expect to encounter at a serious-minded arts centre in the late eighties. It was too far ahead and behind its time, I suppose. Bands didn't really play at art centres, anyway, or at least we didn't. We generally played in windowless rooms that stank of stale ale, exhaled cigarettes and abandoned sweat, in which obvious art lovers were rarely to be seen obviously enjoying art. We played to drunk people mostly. Often, the only really drunk people at arts centres are artists, and the reasons for that are probably best left unexamined as well. Let's look at the ducks instead.

When we arrived at Brentford arts centre we were pleased to look out through the generous windows that ran along one side of the reception room. These windows looked out onto the River Thames and Kew Gardens, beyond the far bank. Bobbing merrily on the river were ducks. Happy ducks. I have played a few shows in my time, but at no point recall another stage that provided a view including a picturesque river and complimentary ducks. We were going to perform in this windowed room, which also served as a cinema foyer, the main entrance, a bar, and a place where people could relax and talk about art while looking at ducks. I think there were a couple of swans too. This event was obviously going to be different. Because it was art, we hadn't rehearsed. Pete and Jason would do their thing and the rest of us would play one note. There were no songs to learn, we didn't need a drum kit or a soundcheck, and we only had small practice amps with us. Easy. Get stoned, play the music, load the gear into Pete's car, and then make the hour and a half drive back up to Rugby.

'Just play one note,' Sonic had advised me and Steve Evans (who had joined us for this one-off show) as we travelled down the M1 to London. 'Keep it simple. One note. No fancy stuff.'

By 'fancy stuff' he meant two notes. Anything beyond that was pointless.

We could play one note . . . mostly. Anyone could do it. A monkey could do it. But could a stoned monkey do it with feeling and without losing its sense of identity in the glorious all-enveloping om? Only time would tell and, as time was going to be behaving strangely again, we would probably have to wait until later to get a sensible answer from that notoriously flaky taskmaster.

75

We set up our amps in a small semicircle in the middle of the room facing the ducks. After a quick line check to make sure we were all making the correct noises, we retired to the dressing room to smoke hash. Well, everybody except Jason, who wasn't smoking much hash at the time.

The dressing room had neither ducks nor windows, so at least we were on familiar territory there. The small room filled up with the heavy smoke as we stoned ourselves into a one-note state of mind. Some of our state of mind might have leaked out into the main room, and perhaps that was the start of the problem. An arts centre is no place for mind-altering substances – or at least this one wasn't.

'Could you keep the door shut, please?' a concerned patron of the arts told us, warily sticking his head round the door and being careful not to inhale. 'The smell of that . . . stuff . . . is getting out.' We fake apologised for the smell and continued as we were. We were fairly blatant and continuous in our usage of hashish at the time. To us it seemed to be no cause for concern, concerned as we sometimes were with more dangerous amusements. I suppose we considered marijuana like other people considered coffee, and it wasn't like we were shooting speedballs in the foyer or anything. We were much more discreet about that sort of thing. Other people were not so easy with our choices. We considered this to be largely their problem, except when it threatened to turn into a legal situation. Of course, the illegality of our actions wasn't going to stop us, it just made us a little more careful sometimes. We weren't criminals by inclination, we just liked drugs, and some drugs were illegal and some were very illegal. There seemed to be no logical reason why that was the case. At least to us, anyway. Marijuana is a great drug for passing time. Anybody who has ever been in a band will know how much time you have to kill waiting around to do a show. Like Charlie Watts, the drummer from the Rolling

Stones said, 'Being in a band is twenty years hanging around and five years playing.' It's not like we were actually bothering anybody beyond their warped opinions of how we should live our lives anyway. We stuck our Rizlas together in our chosen arrangements, licked and ripped our cigarettes to reveal the legal tobacco, laid it on the papers, and then warmed the hash with our lighters and crumbled it into the joints. A little lick, a deft fold, and a ripped and rolled strip of Rizla packet in the end and we were ready to be officially 'on drugs'. Actually, we were usually fairly protective of the Rizla packets because it looked incriminating to have ripped Rizlas. We cared, a bit, and we weren't stupid all of the time.

When time finally arrived at the appropriate place for the impending performance, we made our way out to the amplifiers and guitars. The band were facing the ducks, while the majority of the crowd were congregated in a seating area somewhere off to the side of our equipment. Behind us was a line of people waiting for the cinema to open. I think there were as many people in the queue for the film as there were to watch our performance. We tuned the guitars and plugged into our amps. Sonic played the first chord of the performance on his Vox Starstreamer using the built-in repeater and a heavy tremolo, so that the sound might be pleasing to people who liked that sort of thing.

The guitar pulsed out a regular rhythm all on its own, that phased and gelled with itself as he turned the dial on the tremolo. 'W a w a w a w a w a w a w a wow W a w a w a w a w a w,' it said, turning time into atomic uncertainty and mystical probability, as all focus settled upon the one, which was the two and three and the four in the wawawawawawawa wow-awawowawawa . . .

Steve and Jason began to play one note somewhere in time with the tremolo and repeater, which were phasing across each other as the drone started to congeal into itself and become more than it should. I moved my plectrum around between my thumb and index finger and went for the most inconspicuous E I could find on the fretboard. Nothing too low and nothing too high. I wasn't going to be faffing around sliding between octaves and running around the neck, so I started as I meant to go on . . . and on . . . and on . . . and on.

I locked into Steve's inconspicuous E within the blurring tempo and tried my best to find the natural mean between the inconsistencies. It sounded fine. I wasn't standing out, or ruining the drone. In fact, I was so in time and tune that I could barely hear myself. I kept myself in line with the tempo by using the feel and the audible click of the plectrum on the strings of my electric bass. Tick, tick, tick, tick, tick, wawawawawawawa wowawawowawawa . . . Twatwatwatwatotwatwatwa . . .

It melded perfectly into a seamless whole and the grand pulsating amoeba settled into its centre, content and undividing as it rippled and flexed gently within itself, occasionally stretching along its axis as the fluctuations in time and space lent tension to the eventual resolutions in synchronisation and harmony.

The many became one. The one became the many, and all we had to do was hold it together and let it do the work as the repetition made nonsense of what we thought we knew.

Let us pick a word.

Let's choose the word 'strawberry'.

Take a deep breath and say that word out loud rhythmically until you have run out of breath. Now do it again . . . and again . . . and again, until it stops making any verbal or audible sense to you. Do you notice the way the inflections change with repetition? Do you lose the coherent start, end and middle of the word? I used to do this as a child with this word until it made me laugh when it all stopped making sense.

OK . . . we've got that bit down. Now try saying that same word for twenty minutes . . . over and over again.

Perhaps as a further experiment you could invite some friends round and all do it together. Can you tell your voice from everyone else's? Unity has a funny way of fucking with your sense of what is yours and what is theirs, what was what, and even *if* what is . . . at all . . . mostly.

Now get back to me on the monkey and the marijuana question.

Is this making any sense at all?

Hopefully not.

That's the whole single point, really: to end sense through repetition of the familiar. To strip sense from the senses you have, and thereby open the world through limitation. Stop. Making. Sense. It is the musical equivalent of the zen kōan, which so perplexes the mind in its seeming contradiction that the mind itself, repulsed by its own lack of understanding, quantum leaps beyond the self-imposed boundaries and habitual perceptions of reality it has taken for granted as being correct.

Or maybe you do. Or maybe it and you do. Is it you? Are you you? Is the you you knew you? Or is the I you were you? Is this confusing? Who? Are you confusing it with you?

Don't worry . . . you'll get tired of caring about these things eventually and just get back to the womwomwowmwowm-wowmwomwomwomwamwomwomwom.

It'll be easier in the long run, and this is going to be a very long run indeed so you don't want to be expanding any energy on useless questions about whether or not you even exist or not. The show must go on . . . and on . . . and on and womwowmwowm-wowmwowmwowmwowmwowmwowmwowmwowmwowm wowmwowwmwowmwowmwowwmwowmwowmwowm-wowmwowmwowmw. Settle down now, breathe deeply, don't

79

grip your plectrum too tightly, hold the tempo that's sliiiiiiding across the millifractions of the moment . . . that's gone, that's gone . . . Do you wish you weren't so stoned? Do you think you should have got a proper job, after all? Do you look stupid? Did you lock the door? IS YOUR CAT HAPPY? Or is everything going womwomwowmwowmwowmwowwow? Is that YOU going TICKTICKTICKTICKTICKTICKTICK? Is it time to tock yet? Settle down, monkey mind . . . *you can do this. It doesn't matter how stoned you are.*

Settle down. You can do this for as long as you think you can . . . can't you?

Thankfully, at this point within our peculiar conundrum of unity and individual performance, our friend the virtuoso will arrive in the nick of time to add a little light and shade to the endless plain of womwowmwowmwowmwowmwowmwow-mwowmwowmwowmwowmwowm.

He will bring a reassuring voice . . . something to hold on to in all of this *space* . . .

A familiar refrain.

Jason Spaceman is asking you a question? But what is it?

There it is again. It certainly sounds like something you ought to understand, but then it changes . . . ever so slightly . . . urging comprehension of the previous question you somehow missed but thought you understood. It's like a nursery rhyme you heard once in a more innocent time, and it is oh so obvious what it was. Then it changes, but only just enough so that you can't remember what was different about it the first time. Anyway. Fuck it, it sounds nice and that's the main thing. The tone is pleasant . . . and now that the band is playing all together we are almost loud enough to drown out those two people talking loudly over in the far corner of the bar about how shit we are.

I wonder what the ducks think? Floating blissfully upon the Ganges as they are.

How does it feel?

The guitars fade back into themselves and the room, and everything else seems to be ending too. Perhaps the song is finishing? Do you know how long you have been playing? The repeater and tremolo slide up along the octaves and somehow your mind, which has grown so used to their company and repetition, goes with them and *actually listens*. It . . . them . . . it . . . and then it plays . . . a little snatch of the melody from 'Honey' for no good reason . . . once . . . and then it goes back to the womowomwowmwowmwowmwowm . . .

Did that happen? Did you hear that?

Then . . . the actual voice of God appears. 'Ladies and gentlemen, would you please take your seats for this evening's showing of *Wings of Desire*.'

What? We are already sitting down? What does God even mean by that?

Womwowmwowmwowmwowmwowmowmwowmw wowmw wowmw wowwow.

And then the refrain . . . and the questions . . . and the questions.

Womwowmwowmwowmwowmwowmwowmwowmwow-mwowwmowmwom.

Spectral shapes, motifs and melodic archetypes drift in and disappear, while the occasional mythical beast emerges from the ocean of drone, rising and submerging with barely a ripple. Imaginary colours pulse lysergically, and the drift of time is forgotten within the boundaries of limitless sound. How could so little mean so much? And what happened to all of those stupid and meaningless questions that seemed so important earlier? After 44 minutes and 17 seconds of this sort of thing our perpetual motion machine begins its descent back to what we will laughingly refer to as reality. The music ends and a smattering of applause greets the relief and disappointment of relative silence.

I looked up from my bass and tried to come to terms with not doing the thing I had been doing for nearly fifty minutes. I shook the blood back into my rigid and aching left hand and flexed the claw of my pick hand. I checked that the other musicians were finished and then reached down to switch off my amplifier.

I was quite surprised to find that it was impossible to switch it off.

It was impossible to switch it off because I had never switched it on in the first place. This was quite confusing and embarrassing until I realised that nobody, not even me, who had been sitting on my amplifier, had actually noticed that it wasn't switched on. A monkey could have done what I had just done. A non-existent monkey could have done it. The ducks outside could have done it . . . or a giraffe. I stood up and walked over to the bar to get a drink, leaving my bass guitar propped up against the amplifier ready for the next set.

I returned to the dressing room and was greeted by the reassuring aroma and the large and reassuring presence of Pat Fish who had turned up, guitar in hand, to lend weight to our note for the next set. We said our hellos and continued with the job at hand.

The door to the dressing room opened and a member of the arts council stuck his head inside. 'Could I, erm, have a word in private with one of you, please?'

Sonic stood up and followed him out of the smoke-thick room, after inhaling deeply and passing the joint.

He returned ten minutes later looking faintly surprised and wearing a smile.

'Hahahahaahahaa,' he laughed. 'It looks like we won't be playing the next set. The management said that our services will not be required.' He laughed again. 'But they are going to pay us for both sets.'

This seemed like a minor triumph on more than one level.

'I heard some bloke at the bar moaning about that wonderful music,' said Pat. 'He was moaning and groaning and then he turned to his friend and said, "To think that Elvis died for this."'

The laughter and the smoke escaped the narrow confines of the windowless room. When we had stopped laughing, we went back out into the arts centre foyer, packed up our equipment and went home. The live recording of that performance continues to sell, twenty-seven years later. To this day, I'm not sure if it was art or not.

The Nun Next Door

Somehow it had been decided that the band were going to have a rehearsal in my front room. I didn't mind, but I wondered if the neighbour might.

I had never met her, but I had heard her coughing through the wall, and even though she had never been round to complain about any noise, I thought that the sound of ripping feedback and a full drum kit might be a bit much for even the most tolerant of neighbours. I decided to go round and let her know what was going on.

I rang the bell and waited by the door at the side of her flat. There was no answer. I knew she was inside, because I had heard her coughing earlier. I rang the bell again and rattled the flap of her letter box. I saw movement through the frosted glass and eventually, after an age of unlocking, the door opened and I found myself standing face to face with an elderly nun. She smiled at me. 'Hello,' she said, brightly. 'Can I help you?'

I was a little surprised that my neighbour was a nun. She seemed friendly, despite the fact that I was obviously a long-haired ne'er-do-well and probably not a churchgoer. 'Ah, hello,' I said. 'Sorry to bother you. I live next door and I just wanted to come and tell you that we will be making a bit of noise later. We are having a band practice. If it's too loud please come round and tell me and we'll stop. It won't be a regular thing, I promise.'

'Pardon,' she replied, still smiling. 'You'll have to speak up. I'm a bit deaf, I'm afraid.'

Hiding my obviously selfish delight at hearing this news, I repeated myself loudly.

'Oh, lovely,' she said. 'What kind of music is it? Are you a bit like Michael Jackson?'

I smiled back and shouted that we were a bit like Michael Jackson.

'Well,' she said. 'It will be nice to hear a bit of life in the place. You play all you want to. Don't worry about me.'

I gave her my heartfelt thanks and shouted that if she ever needed her bins putting out or any help with anything, that she should come and tell me.

'Oh, don't worry about that,' she said. 'You just play your music and have a nice time.'

I was all smiles as I thanked her again and walked back to my own flat. Not only was my neighbour nice, she was also deaf. It couldn't have been better.

When the band turned up with all of the equipment I went outside and gave them a hand loading it into my bedroom.

'You won't believe it,' I said. 'The next door neighbour, who coughs a lot, is a nun – and here's the good news: she's deaf as a post.'

Jonny set up his drums in the corner of the flat, and we arranged the amplifiers and plugged in the guitars. The power was switched on and Pete produced an ominous wave of searing feedback. 'Maybe we should do 'Walkin' with Jesus' for her?' he said, and then we launched into 'Rollercoaster' and the whole house shook to its foundations.

Shortly afterwards I got the news from my flatmate that he was going to move out. It wasn't to do with the rehearsals – there was just too much Spacemen 3 business going on, and that always brought with it a certain amount of weirdness somehow. Around that time, I got a letter from the dole office regarding my claim. It said, 'The law of the land has decreed that you must receive the sum of thirty-six pounds per week as a legal minimum.' The next day, I got a letter from them that said I was going to get six pounds per week for the next six months because I had got the sack from my last job. I thought it was actually a joke at first, but when the first dole cheque came through I realised it wasn't. There was no way I was going to be able to survive on six pounds a week.

The picture on the back of *Playing with Fire* is taken from a photo session we did in my bedroom for the first interview I was ever part of. Pete did the talking, while me and Jason just sat there saying nothing. Pete handled the press fairly well. He talked about drugs quite a bit, and we were fine with that too. When the photographer took the photos, I was completely stoned on hash and wine. All the way through the photo session, the cameraman kept saying, 'Just try to open your eyes a bit more.' I suppose we looked a bit stoned.

After it had appeared in the *Melody Maker* I received a visit from my landlord. Because I had stopped working and because the dole were giving me very little money, I had fallen behind on the rent. He came into his flat that I was now living in by myself, and said he wanted a word with me. These were the words he had with me: 'You've got your money for your drugs, Willie, but you obviously don't want to pay me. I think you ought to leave the flat as soon as possible.' I suppose he had read the interview. I couldn't be bothered to try to tell him that actually I had *no* money for drugs or anything else for that matter. We were still mixing the album and it was sounding great, so I didn't really care about the fact that I had no money or that I'd lost my flat and my job. I thought it would all work out OK if I kept on playing. Nothing else really mattered to me at all.

Tiny

Being short on clean laundry and quietly proud of our recent achievements, I had foolishly chosen to wear a Spacemen 3 t-shirt while going for a lunchtime pint with a friend in Rugby town centre. I walked through the town centre, happily whistling a modulated drone over some low-note split-frequency Tuvan throat singing as I strolled among the unhappy shoppers. The sun was shining and it was almost possible to imagine the town as being filled with possibility and wonder. I met my friend at the clock tower. The clock tower in Rugby town centre is a large clock, in a tower, conveniently situated next to the Clock Towers shopping centre. There were a few sixteen-year-old goths surrounded by pigeons in the uncomfortable seating area. The mini-goths were crimped and made up to perfection, resplendent in black leather and carefully distressed rags. They were hanging on stubbornly despite the lateness of the decade. I greeted them with a nod and a smile. I met my friend and we both walked the twenty-five metres to the crossroads at McDonald's then turned right into the pedestrian lane that would take us down to the White Swan, or the 'Dirty Duck' as it was known affectionately by the locals.

We chatted as we walked and my friend asked me how the band had been going. I was feeling pretty optimistic, so I was probably bragging a bit and telling unlikely tales of far-flung gigs in glamorous locations like Hull.

We were about to make a journey to Paris to play at the Locomotive club which was next to the Moulin Rouge in the Pigalle district. It was going to be my first trip abroad with the band. I was really excited about playing my first gig outside the country. That's probably why I had the t-shirt on. It was luminous orange and yellowy green, and in the middle it had the triangle with the 3 in it. It was a fairly striking design.

We walked into the pub and I bumped into somebody I knew. I made the customary greeting, 'All right, Tiny?' as I approached the bar where he was standing with one of his mates. 'How's it going?'

Tiny was so named because he was not tiny, in the same way that the Dirty Duck was neither dirty nor a duck. He was a big and imposing character who I had got to know through our cosy network of ne'er-do-wells and miscreants. He was a sort of biker and he had a face that carried a few scars from some late-night glassing incident outside one of the pubs in town. Don't get me wrong here, I liked Tiny, and we had always got on pretty well. We weren't mates but we were on more than nodding terms. My greeting to him would have traditionally been met with a similar response, a bit of banter, and maybe a joke if you were lucky.

Despite the fact that it was early in the afternoon, Tiny was obviously a couple of pints into his lunch, and God alone knows if he had slept in the last two or three days. 'Huh?' he said, as he looked me up and down with disdain. 'You can tell he's an arsehole just by the t-shirt he's wearing!'

He said this fairly loudly to the man who was standing next to him.

Being sober and fairly happy, I wasn't quite sure if it was some sort of joke, so I shrugged it off and laughed. 'Yeah, I know. I didn't have anything else that was clean and it was free.'

He didn't smile. He took a couple of steps closer to me, sneered and said, 'Yeah, but only a COMPLETE arsehole would wear it.'

He stood there, not far from my nose, and waited for my reaction. Tiny was sort of smiling, but it wasn't a happy smile. It was one of those smiles that meant you might be about to get punched in the face.

I looked at him, realised it wasn't a joke, and turned away to go and sit with my friend, who had taken a seat close by. 'Well, you can't please everybody, man,' I said over my shoulder before I sat down. I turned in my seat and said, 'We're off to Paris at the weekend. See you there, mate!'

'I'll see you outside,' he said. 'And then we'll see what kind of man you are.'

This was a fairly clear declaration of intent for such an early hour.

'Nah, you're all right, thanks, Tiny. Bit early for me, and I've got to look after me hands.'

'Yeah, I fucking knew you were a wanker,' he said. 'Why don't you come outside and we'll see how much of a big man you are?' he said, still standing and facing me.

'I ain't looking for a fight, Tiny. Leave it out,' I replied. 'I'm just trying to have a fucking drink.' I wasn't smiling any more. I sat down and ignored him while he continued to throw boring insults at my back and pretended to laugh at his own jokes. I wasn't feeling so fucking optimistic any more, but I didn't really let it get me down.

Waves of Joy

As the ship pitched and rolled, low waves of vomit rolled across the toilet floor and broke gently against the unconscious figure of the recumbent drummer, who was snoozing peacefully in the unfresh tide with his head on his arm. Mercifully, he had somehow seen fit to keep most of his face away from the contents of other people's stomachs. When the ship pitched back to stern, the vomit rolled away from him, broke against the far wall under the urinals, gathered force and then made its way back across the toilet floor towards him as the ferry plunged into another huge trough of water. It had been a rough crossing, but not for Jonny Mattock, who was probably dreaming about something related to drums while being blissfully unaware of the fact that he was being freshly exposed to a gently lapping tide of partially digested food every thirty seconds. He was fairly well coated in the stuff, so it seemed that he had rolled over a couple of times in his sleep trying to get comfortable. I stood in the reeking bathroom, stepping over the rhythmic waves of puke, and considered the best options for both of us.

Jonny Mattock was not taking drugs to make music to take drugs to. Jonny was not very good at taking drugs at all. By our standards, he was a total amateur. I am not saying this in any way to disparage the man. He still remains the best drummer I ever played with, or at least the one I found it easiest to play with. Jonny's drug was drums, everything else was secondary, and he was possessed by a sense of enthusiasm unrivalled by anything except his own ability to drum with unusual precision, grace and flair. Despite this, he was shit at taking drugs and he

was from Northampton. People from there were understandably a little more jolly than people from Rugby, and although
we kind of mocked them for it we were probably a little envious of the fact that they could laugh easily without the help of
heavy narcotics and dinosaur wiggly pills. The first time I saw
Jonny he was playing a show in the back of the Blitz in Rugby
with a 'wacky' Northampton band called Apple Creation. I
remember this incident not because I got chatting with Jonny
or because I enjoyed his drumming. I noticed Jonny because
he was wearing a kaftan. 'Look at that twat in a kaftan,' I had
said, rather uncharitably. I had narrow tastes at the time and
they did not involve smiling drummers in kaftans. I liked The
Stooges, amphetamine sulphate and beer. Not the friendliest
cocktail in the world.

Anyway, there we were a few years later, and here he was,
conked out in a paddling pool of puke on a piss-house floor in a
ferry on the way back to Britain, and something had to be done
about the situation. I went back to report my findings to the
rest of the band, who had also been searching for him. 'He has
passed out on the toilet floor – and it's not pretty,' I said. 'He
looks comfortable enough . . . but he really shouldn't. Come
and have a look.'

The reasons for Jonny's largely comatose state were fairly
obvious. Prior to getting on the ferry he had approached me
and said, 'I've got this lump of hash that someone gave me.
What do you reckon I should do with it?' Jonny didn't smoke
a lot of hash, but we had led him astray a little bit, so now he
did, but not very often.

'Don't take it through customs, man,' I advised him, but
perhaps I should have been a little bit more specific, because
ten minutes later he came up to me and said, 'I ate it!' He
laughed like a maniac, which he often did anyway.

'The whole thing?' I said, in a slightly disbelieving tone.

'Yeah,' he said, looking a bit worried but still smiling.

'You are gonna be fucked up, Jonny,' I said. 'That's nearly a sixteenth. You'd better find somewhere comfortable to sleep on the ferry.'

It was a rough crossing. The ship rolled and wallowed in the stormy seas and most of the people on board lost their lunch in the process. One puker would cause a chain reaction of puking from queasy passers-by, until it had become a veritable festival of reckless regurgitation. I have never seen so much vomit in my life. There was a group of schoolkids on board and I saw most of them throwing up in the toilets and along the carpeted corridors with youthful abandon. It was quite a funny spectacle, if you had a strong enough stomach. During all of the entertainment on offer we had somehow lost track of Jonny. He'd crashed out in a chair for a bit, nearly been sick on the manager's wife, Tracy (who was on her first and last trip away with the band), and then gone walkabout. That was how I came to find him on the toilet floor.

Jason and I looked down at Jonny from a safe distance. 'Errrrrr,' we both said. 'JONNY!'

No answer.

We poked him with our puke-covered boots. He stirred but he didn't wake up, so at least we knew he wasn't dead. It would have been most careless for a drummer to choke to death on someone else's vomit, although it might have improved record sales briefly.

'Shall we pick him up?' I said, with absolutely no enthusiasm whatsoever.

Jason shared my lack of enthusiasm for picking up the sick-sodden drummer. 'He looks pretty comfortable and we are nearly at the harbour, let's come back and get him when the ferry docks,' he said.

We both nodded and left him where he was.

When the boat finally docked, Kate Radley and I volunteered to go and help Jonny from the boat. He was still serene in the pool of now unwaving vomit. Kate started laughing and wrinkled her nose, as we both steeled ourselves for the unpleasant task of helping our stinking friend to get off the boat and negotiate customs.

I reached down and looped an arm under his, while keeping my face as far away from him as possible. I hauled him to his feet and Kate looped her arm under his other shoulder. Eventually we managed to get him into a kind of upright position, and he even started making a few noises that suggested he might be approaching wakefulness in some small way.

'ERRR, EEEE, OOOOO, AAHH,' he sort of said, as we encouraged him to put one foot in front of the other while the two of us supported his weight. I tried very hard not to think about vomit and how much of it was getting on me. What are friends for anyway?

Jonny was becoming more awake. We managed to get him out of his temporary bedroom and into the hallway.

'Eeep,' he said, and then smiled and staggered a bit, while Kate and I laughed and gagged and tried not to drop him into the little puddles of stuff he was dribbling onto the carpet. Staggering and laughing and with very little help from him, we eventually bundled Jonny into a seat in the most isolated corner of the van so that he could sleep off the last remnants of his foolish indulgence as far away from everyone else as possible.

Mercifully, we were not stopped by customs on the way off the ferry, and Jonny didn't have to answer any questions he was in no condition to deal with. Many people were leaving the ferry in similar states of discoordination anyway and it was almost impossible to tell if any of them were drug related.

We drove Jonny back to Northampton and dropped him off at his mum and dad's house, telling them he had been suffering from a touch of seasickness. He was fairly coherent by the time we dropped him off and his mum didn't seem too concerned about the fact that we had returned her only son to her in a state of considerable inebriation with sick in his hair. Of course, he was still smiling.

Part Two

The Key to the Door

The Autist Turns Twenty-One

To understand the limitation of things, desire them.
Lao Tzu, *Tao Te Ching*

I moved out of the ground-floor flat and into a small room at the top of the house in an effort to save money and to keep my spiralling debts from spiralling more quickly. A few of my other friends were renting rooms up there from the same landlord who had presumed that I was spending all of his rent money on a lavish lifestyle of drugs and paddling pools. I had moved into the small spare room at the top of the house without telling him.

One of the people that shared the house was called Sid, an old-school punk and reggae skinhead who would sometimes decorate the house in the grip of a late-night fever. On more than one occasion I had come downstairs after sleeping through a night of noisily shifting furniture and hammering after he had taken the quick road to the long night and been inspired to make the place look nice along the way.

Sid had a girlfriend who would sometimes threaten to kill herself if he did something she didn't like. He had gotten sick of her threats, so one day he had taken a sturdy rope, tied a proper hangman's noose in it, and slung it over the banister for her.

'If you are going to do it, just fucking do it,' he said.

In the morning I had come downstairs to find the noose hanging in the stairwell near the front door.

That noose stayed there for about three weeks and his girlfriend never used it, which was quite a relief for everyone. I suppose it was a bit weird, having to walk past a beautifully tied noose every time you went to get a pint of milk and some cigarettes, but nobody complained about it. Eventually, it became one of the fixtures of the house, like a potted plant or a picture on the wall – a unique and striking hallway feature, which seemed fitting in some weird way.

It was my twenty-first birthday and I wasn't really celebrating in any joyous way.

We had recently played a show down in London and we had received a review for it in one of the music papers, which we read religiously because we were sometimes in them. It was kind of strange and exciting to be mentioned in the national press, and I suppose we felt like we were important in some ways. It is pretty seductive to see your name in print or to see a picture of yourself staring back at you from the racks in the newsagent, even as you are wondering if you can afford a packet of cigarettes. This is particularly the case when you have a feeling that most of the people in your hometown don't like you. It is revenge in a way, like a big 'I told you so.'

It is also a complete illusion, but I didn't know that then.

On the morning of my twenty-first birthday I walked down to the shops to buy a copy of that week's *Sounds*, eager to give my wonky self-esteem a little boost with another dose of ego gratification. I wasn't expecting a photograph of myself or any kind of personal mention (only being a bassist and everything), but I thought I might be able to catch a little buzz of association. I was in the band, after all.

I bought the paper, treated myself to a fresh packet of Embassy Number 1 for my birthday, and went back to the house to see if there was any sniff of printed validation for my increasingly precarious existence. I walked up the stairs past the noose, and I suppose I was feeling all right. I didn't have any money and I was sinking further and further into debt but I was in a band that seemed important to me. Of course that band was in the process of falling apart but I wanted it to be so all right that it blinded me to the reality of the situation. The music was good. What else mattered, really? I sat down on the settee, lit a cigarette from the fresh pack, and flipped through the pages of the paper.

It was a fair-sized review. Half a page, or something, with a blurry photo of a mysterious shape intended to alert the casual reader to impending drugs, or something. I read on eagerly.

'Stone bored,' the title said, 'written by Felix Taint.'

I read on.

'This band are truly awful and the hirsute bass player best exemplifies what it is that is truly awful about them. He shuffles onto the stage like an autistic sloth and plays the bass guitar like someone stuttering to speak. He looks, and sounds, like a twat.'

Despite the fact that I had never been mentioned in a review before, it was not quite the validation of my ego or the birthday present that I'd been hoping for. The review continued: 'Dressed like a casualty from a church jumble sale granny fight and looking like he still lives with his mum and dad, he was noticeable only by virtue of the fact that he is the most boring member of a fantastically boring band. I hate this band but most of all I hate him and everything about the way he stands.'

I looked up from the newspaper and took a thoughtful drag on my half-finished cigarette. The author obviously hadn't realised one of the golden rules of music. If the band is shit, it is never noticeably the fault of the bass player. We are the invisible members of every band. Victory and defeat are the same for us. We pass by, in the shadows, grimly waiting to take out our frustrations on the world as soon as somebody pays attention.

'Fucking wanker,' I said to myself and the empty room, and then I read it again just to make sure he was a wanker.

Pete Kember came round to the house later on.

'Hi, man. Happy birthday,' he said, sitting down to roll a

joint. 'How's it going?' He looked at me warily, trying to gauge my reaction.

'Have you fucking read that review?' I said, knowing full well that he would have. 'It's my fucking birthday,' I added, self-pityingly.

Pete looked at me and immediately took the no indulgence route. 'Man, you can't take that stuff to heart, you know. It doesn't mean anything anyway. It's just his opinion.'

I was less than convinced by his wafting away of the fact that I had been roundly print-fucked in a national newspaper on my birthday. At least the reviewer hadn't mentioned my name, presumably because he couldn't even be bothered to find it out. I tried to decide if this was worse or better.

'Just ignore it, man. Don't let it get you down,' Pete said, which was easier said than done.

'Fucking wanker,' I said. 'I hope I see him sometime. I'll smash his fucking face in.'

And then we smoked the joint and I stopped caring quite as much.

Later that night a few of my other friends came round and we had a few drinks. At some point during the party, I took a trip to the toilet. On the way out, I spied the noose hanging in the hallway and decided to investigate it a bit more closely. I walked down the stairs, took the rope in my hands and inspected the finely tied knot. I would like to point out, at this point, that I was in no way suicidal because of the uncomplimentary review. I was just bored and drunk and fascinated by the noose because – oh, I don't fucking know – it was unusual? I realised that if I stood on a certain step I could actually slip the noose over my own head, so I did, just to see how it felt to have a noose around my neck. How many times does that opportunity present itself in one lifetime? I tightened the knot up to my throat and tested my own weight a little bit to see how that felt and then, holding the rope above my own neck to take some of my weight, I swung out into space. Just to see how it felt. Maybe I thought it would be funny to call someone out of the room and freak them out and I was actually laughing at the thought, even as I was hanging in the hallway. When I tried to get back onto the step, I realised that although I could maddeningly brush the lip of the step with my toes, I was too far out to get back on to solid ground. It was an uncomfortable realisation. When I tried to swing back to the step, the noose tightened. It was a tricky situation and I was too drunk to find the urgent escape that I obviously needed. I started to panic. The rope around my neck made it difficult to call out for help. I swung there in the hallway making choking sounds, trying to hold on to what little breath I could force past my constricted throat.

While I struggled to breathe, I began to imagine the tiny headlines written in a future issue of the *Rugby Advertiser*. 'Local man kills himself on twenty-first birthday after bad review.' Then I imagined that everyone would go and read the fucking review in the music paper that had lead to the tragic act. Luckily, at the moment when it seemed that I was truly finished, and I had accepted my absurd death would result in everyone reading about the fact that someone thought I wasn't a very good bass player, a friend of mine came through the door at the top of the stairs to visit the toilet. He was stoned and whistling until he turned and saw me hanging in the hall-way, turning purple and twisting helplessly at the end of my tether.

'Fucking hell, Will,' he shouted as he ran down the stairs towards me. He grabbed me by my body and pulled me in to the safety of the stairs again. 'What the FUCK are you doing?'

I was choking and gagging a bit, but I managed to get a few words out. 'It isn't what it looks like, Dave. I was just fucking around and couldn't get back to the step. I wasn't trying to kill myself.' And then we both started laughing.

I had a bright red rope burn around my neck for about two weeks.

When people asked what it was I didn't bother to try to explain it to many of them. It was too weird and nobody was going to believe me anyway.

Says a Lot to the Trained Mind

We were all sitting in the van at Dover, ready to begin a tour of Europe that would see us drive nineteen thousand miles and play thirty-two shows in six weeks. Along the way we would lose one tour manager and drive another one half-mad. Jonny would set Jason's hair on fire, the German promoter would dislocate his shoulder teaching us how to dive into German lakes. We would carry our pleasures across many of the borders of the then European non-union. We would record the album *Live in Europe 1989*, there would be fallouts, make-ups, dull stretches of autobahn, insufferable Bavarian bed and breakfasts, and there would be a man dressed as a nun, with swastikas tattooed all over his face, who would greet us at our first ever show inside the Eastern bloc. We didn't know any of this then. We were just sitting in the van getting ready to catch the ferry and then drive to the first show, in Amsterdam. The first show had been booked in Amsterdam for a reason. As we approached the ferry we were waved over into a customs bay by a uniformed official. We hadn't even left the country before being stopped.

'Good morning, gentlemen,' the non-uniformed customs agent said as he leaned into the open window of the van. 'What are you up to then?' he enquired. He seemed friendly enough, kind of scruffy. He looked like he might even smoke a little hash himself.

We were instantly suspicious.

'We are going on tour!' Pete offered, brightly and politely. 'We are in a band.'

'Oh, really?' our new friend said, with either real or fake interest. 'What's the name of the band, then?'

'Spacemen 3,' replied Pete.

The world-weary customs man came up close to the window, looked inside and gave us half a smile. 'Really?' he said. 'That says a lot to the trained mind.' He smiled more broadly as he gauged our reactions to what he had just said. But then he stopped smiling so much. 'OK. Let's have a look in the back, then, boys, if you don't mind.'

Like it mattered if we minded.

We all got out of the van and lined up at the back door, ready to unpack the stuff we had recently packed.

'Let's have a look at the guitars, then, lads,' our new friend said.

Pete, Jason and I hauled our guitar cases out of the back of the van, laid them on the concrete, and lifted the lids. Jason's all-wood Telecaster with the big '3' at the bridge, Pete's Vox Starstreamer and my Gibson Thunderbird lay exposed and gleaming in the grey Dover morning.

The assembled customs agents cooed and began to make appreciative noises. 'Mind if I pick it up?' one of them said, pointing at the Starstreamer.

'Be my guest,' Pete replied, looking as confused as the rest of us.

We were expecting a full shakedown, but it seemed that they just wanted to have a look at the guitars.

'Very nice!' the customs agent said, admiringly, as he gently cradled the teardrop and played half a chord. 'You've got some nice guitars.'

'Uh, yeah. Thanks,' we said.

'OK then, lads. Off you go. Thanks a lot and have a good tour.'

We fastened the cases and stashed them in the van. Once we

were a good distance from the customs point we all burst out laughing.

'Fucking hell,' said Pete, 'what was all that about? They could probably tell we take drugs just from looking at the guitars!'

We did carry sumptuous and bohemian-looking guitars.

Suicide

Every night before we played 'Suicide' Pete Kember would pause to introduce the song. 'This is a song for Alan Vega and Martin Rev,' he would say, and then, after a short pause for dramatic effect, he would say, '"Suicide".'

The last word always sounded somehow triumphant. The drone would begin from his keyboard, Jonny would kick the drums in with robotic precision, and Jason's scorching wah-fuzz guitar would begin its ascent as I started the rumble of the lowest and higher octave Es. At the unbearable peak of impending one-note doom and tension the keyboard would step through the descending figure to bring the whole band crashing into the simple two-note riff, which would then propel the song through its varying eternal lengths. Sometimes we played it for ten minutes, sometimes for twenty, and sometimes it seemed to go on for so long that time itself ceased to have any meaning. For a bassist this was agony to play, like running a marathon, and whether we were playing for ten minutes or twenty, after a while I would be internally pleading for it to end, my fretboard fingers cramped into claws, my pick hand feeling like it was being hit with a hammer. Despite the hypnotic and transcendent nature of the sound we made and the volume reached, playing 'Suicide' live was always a uniquely painful sensation that kept me firmly rooted in the material world. It was the last song we played. Always.

One night in Geneva we played this song to a crowd of around fifty enthusiastic fans, and during the performance we noticed another crowd of noticeably less enthusiastic people had gathered at the back of the room as we brought our set to a close. These newcomers were looking decidedly confused and intimidated by the ungroovy noise pouring from our stage. Presumably, they had turned up hoping to find some kind of après-ski disco and we were postponing their chances for any off-piste mating rituals. They didn't look very happy, which filled us with considerable glee.

Leaving the stage, after the usual ten minutes of maddening repetition and blistering noise, Jason and I left our guitars standing against the amps, feeding back into a huge and menacing drone with the notes that Pete had taped down on his keyboard. As we were squatting beside the stage, sweating with relief and exhaustion, it was suggested that perhaps the evening still held a little sport.

'Shall we go on and do it again to piss the skiers off?' said Pete, with a loud laugh. 'They didn't look like they were enjoying it at all.'

It was quickly agreed, with much laughter, that even though we were all tired it would probably be worth going through a bit more pain to annoy the people who wanted to have a good time without us.

We were difficult like that.

Jonny, who was still nailing the robotic Bo Diddley beat with superhuman endurance, played his last and triumphant cymbal crash and walked offstage looking like a man who had recently finished an assault course.

'We are gonna go back out there and do it again,' said Pete. 'Really go for it this time. Let's do a crazy one.'

Despite his obvious fatigue, Jonny smiled like a man in possession of the keys to the store cupboard of enthusiasm.

We waited for the drone to play out for another minute or two and then walked back out onto the stage. The assembled crowd at the front of the room clapped and cheered and looked pleased to see us. The people at the back of the room looked hugely disappointed. We picked up the instruments and started the interminably long build-up again.

'Hey, you lot at the back. Hope we aren't stopping you from skiing,' Pete remarked, sarcastically, into the microphone.

We played and we played and we played, mercilessly gouging the same riff into the patience of the unconverted. We played that same riff for another ten minutes or so, laughing throughout.

There is a recorded version. It sounds fucking great, but we were only doing it to be bastards, really.

After the sessions for *Playing with Fire* had been finished, the band were hoping that Alan Vega would provide a vocal for the recorded version of 'Suicide'. Phone calls were made and Alan agreed to do it. A session was booked, and we made the journey to London where we had arranged to meet the singer and take him to the studio after a show he was due to play.

Pete, Jason and I stood in the venue and watched Suicide play to a largely disinterested Siouxsie and the Banshees crowd. Music had progressed enough by this point that the crowd didn't actually hate them and nobody threw anything at the band as they played, which had happened earlier in their career supporting some of the first punk bands in Britain. Suicide were ahead of their time and they had suffered for it.

Suicide played a great set, and afterwards we made our way backstage to meet the band. Alan had mentioned over the phone that he had some lyrics together and that the working title was 'Suicide: It's a Way of Life'. This all sounded pretty hopeful to us, so we sat backstage in the small dressing room chatting to Marty Rev as we waited for Alan to appear. Pete was noticeably excited. After an age of waiting, and more than a couple of relayed messages, Alan appeared.

'Shall we go then, man?' said Pete. 'We've got the studio

booked and time's getting on. We don't wanna be late.'

Hearing this, Alan Vega looked a bit pained. He was sweating and he looked tired after the performance.

'Ahhhh, man,' he said, in his New York drawl. 'I'm kinda beat. I'm gonna have to say no tonight, man. It's too bad, but you know how it is.'

We were shocked.

'What?' said Pete. 'We've booked the studio. You said you were gonna do it. We've come all the way down to see you and it's all arranged. We've paid for the studio. This isn't cool, man.'

And it wasn't cool.

Alan started to get a little testy. 'Well, man, you know how it is. I'm tired and I just can't do it tonight. Maybe some other time, all right?'

We looked at him and he looked at us and we all knew it was never going to happen. He left the dressing room.

'That's not cool,' said Pete, looking absolutely crestfallen. 'That's fucked up.'

We nodded, left the dressing room, got back in the car, and drove back up to Rugby.

'Suicide' was going to remain instrumental, and it was never going to be a way of life.

Or Start Living with Your Mother

I was living with my mum again. The situation was far from ideal for me but at least I had somewhere that I could afford to live while I waited for the royalties to come through. She was pretty pleased that I seemed to be doing something positive with my life. She liked the music and she liked the members of the band. They were always polite when they picked me up or dropped me off, and the little container of citric acid she had found in my small bedroom was no real cause for concern. We had only been listening to records up there and citric acid was good for a hangover.

She wasn't so impressed with my Spacemen 3 t-shirt. When she used to hang it out on the washing line, she always made sure it was inside out so that the neighbours couldn't read the word 'fucked'. She said, 'Why does it say "for all the fucked up children" on it? It makes it seem like somebody *did* something to you?' I didn't really have an answer for that, or at least not one I was prepared to get into. My mum and I didn't see eye to eye in some ways, but we were gradually starting to understand our differences a little bit. I guess I was still only twenty-one.

'Revolution', as a single, had brought the band to a higher degree of public attention and popularity. Now we were reaping the rewards, in terms of publicity, for the positive critical reception and subsequent sales. We had even been on the telly. You really couldn't ask for a greater degree of acceptance than that in some people's eyes. The band had appeared on *The Chart Show*, which was a Saturday morning music programme that featured a ten-minute 'indie chart' section, and we had also been on *Snub TV*, another weekly music show that focused entirely on indie music. Imagine that, eh? Music programmes that didn't involve Simon Cowell with a face like a cat's arse lording it over a terrified bunch of hairdressers from Macclesfield singing tarted-up super-karaoke songs.

Before long Spacemen 3 were on the front cover of one of the weekly music papers. The *Melody Maker* sent Chris Roberts up to interview the band, which meant that he talked to Pete, who by now had become so much the leader of the band in the eyes of the press that the rest of us were reduced to shadows in the background of the photographs. Pete had taken the journalist on a little tour of Rugby, and nobody was any the wiser as to what they might have got up to.

On the day of publication I hadn't had a chance to buy a copy of the paper so I had, perhaps unwisely, asked my mum to grab one when she was at the shops. I caught the bus back to Bilton, walked across the green, and down past the school I had attended when I was a child. I walked up the street, past the lines of semi-detached houses, saying hello to the neighbours I knew as I went past. I walked down my mum's driveway and opened the door into the kitchen. She came out of the lounge and turned to face me, holding a copy of the *Melody Maker* in her hand. She did not seem overjoyed that her son was now so famous he could be seen lurking in the background of a photograph in the national press.

'Have you read this?' she said, with an angry look on her face. 'It's ALL about drugs!'

This didn't come as much of a surprise to me.

'It can't be all about drugs, Mum,' I said, trying to calm her down a bit. 'Let me read it.'

'WHAT ARE PEOPLE GOING TO THINK?' she shouted, understandably upset by the fact that we were all going to be found guilty by association of a lot of things we might not actually have done.

'I DON'T KNOW WHAT THEY ARE GOING TO THINK UNTIL I'VE READ IT, DO I?' I shouted back.

It was fairly hard to defend an interview I hadn't read.

She slammed the paper down and stomped off in a disappointed huff.

I picked the paper up, walked upstairs, lay down on my bed and looked at the front cover, which featured a larger than life picture of Pete Kember's face, set in stark half shadow. The words 'Spacemen 3 – from here to eternity' were written across the picture. I opened the paper and read on with a grim sense of anticipation.

'Pete Kember, aka Sonic Boom of Spacemen 3, takes me up to his sumptuous red room in the mansion he shares with his parents . . .' the interview sort of began. 'He sits me down, makes me a cup of tea, and then plays me a mangled cassette copy of what might be a Suicide bootleg. He then rolls me so many joints I forget why I have come to Rugby in the first place, although I do feel rather comfortable about the fact. After a short eternity of contemplation we go for a ride in his car. He takes me to the chemist and picks up his methadone prescription and then explains his current predicament and the ridiculous drug laws in Britain that are leading to innocent people being forced into intolerable and dangerous situations beyond the law, merely for exercising their right to choose which intoxicants they prefer . . .'

My mum was right. It was pretty much all about drugs. I wasn't in a state of shock but I was wondering how to spin this so my mum didn't kick me out of the house again. I was skint. I had nowhere else to go and I was in no position to throw any rock-star strops.

Of course, I completely agreed with most of the things that

Pete had been saying, and I couldn't see any logical arguments against his case for harm reduction and the resocialisation and medical treatment of people with drug problems. I also liked taking some illegal drugs recreationally myself, and they weren't really a problem for me as far as I could tell. This may have been partly because I couldn't afford to buy them any more. But how I was going to explain to my mum that it might actually be a *good* thing to open up some lines of communication about this taboo subject that didn't involve outright hysteria was a different matter entirely. It was going to be difficult. I briefly considered the options while smoking a joint. I was leaning a long way out of the window, but not far enough so that the neighbours might see me. It wasn't for my personal enjoyment. It was for the good of the situation. I was hoping it might make me a bit calmer if things got weird. I lay back on the bed and briefly considered not bothering to try to explain. But that didn't really seem to be an option.

After ten minutes, I took the long walk downstairs and tried to be as diplomatic and understanding as possible. My mum wasn't an idiot, but she knew only what she'd been told by the TV and the papers about the whole 'drug' subject, and that could sometimes leave people with large gaps in their understanding. The only problem was, because we were on drugs we obviously couldn't be trusted, and every word we might say was probably just some crafty way to get more pot, or something. I went downstairs stoned and got ready for the stony silence.

'Look, Mum, I'm not a junkie,' I said. I thought it was a positive and hopeful opening gambit, and it was true. 'We do these things, and I know it is hard for you to understand.'

She looked at me mistrustfully. 'What are my friends and neighbours going to think about it all? What am I going to tell them? What am I going to tell Aunty Yvonne? She wants to read it. I already told her you were in the paper.'

This was a tricky one. Aunty Yvonne was probably not going to understand, despite the fact that we got on pretty well.

'Look, Mum . . . he gets his methadone from the chemist. From a doctor. It's a way of making things a bit easier. It's dangerous buying heroin on the street. People are dying.'

The mere mention of the word heroin was enough to make her howl a bit, and it made me feel bad too.

'He seems like such a nice boy too, and with that good education!' she said, as though she had just found out Pete was an axe-murderer and that an expensive education wasn't, after all, an impenetrable shield against the problems of the world.

'He is a nice boy, Mum,' I said. 'You know he is. He's been round here a few times. Has there ever been any problems?'

'No,' she said. 'He's always very polite.'

'There you go, then,' I said. 'Just don't show the interview to anybody. I don't suppose any of your friends buy *Melody Maker*, do they? If they make any comments, just tell them that Peter has got a medical problem and that they shouldn't be so judgemental.'

She looked at me suspiciously.

'I don't like it, Will,' she said.

'None of us like it, Mum,' I replied.

We were now in the unenviable position of being semi-famous druggies who lived in a small, small town, during a time when the use of illegal drugs could send you to prison, and draw scorn and mistrust from people who used different drugs. Everybody in the band, except for Jason, was living with their parents.

Taking Drugs so Other People Don't Have to

'Taking drugs to make music to take drugs to.' This seems to be a phrase that people have taken to heart regarding Spacemen 3. It is fairly shocking, I suppose, and it certainly was at that point in the eighties when the overwhelming message being beamed at us loud and clear from every billboard and public information broadcast was: 'Just say no.' Just say no. Simple. Except, of course, it wasn't and it never had been. It was like saying, 'Just accept life is shit and get on with it' – at least for those us with the fever to change our minds and no idea how to do it any other way. Just say no. I love the 'just' in that phrase. '*Just* say no,' like it was the easiest thing in the world. Although 'just' saying no might have been an ideal, we were living in a far from ideal world. This was the height of the 'war on drugs' cooked up by Ronnie Reagan and his creepy wife Nancy one night after a couple of strong cocktails and some slimming pills. Margaret Thatcher loved the idea. It was war. It was tough on drugs, but mainly it was tough on the users of drugs. Fuck those hippies, beatniks and Rastafarians. It was 'just' like that upstanding paragon of human decency Richard Nixon had foreseen all those years previously. It had been his bright idea to wage war on drug users in the first place.

Making your natural opponents illegal was an effective way to make life difficult for them. Those druggies weren't going to vote for the joyless embrace of a solid career and boring sex in some miserably over-mortgaged fuck hutch at the edge of despair. *Just say no*. Pleasure was for the weak and this was the time of personal responsibility. If you had any problems they were YOUR fault and you should just bloody well sort them out and pull your socks up, or die and let the strong trample your broken body into the earth as fertiliser, or something. There was no such thing as society, or so we had been told by our swivel-eyed Iron Lady of the psychopathic stare. Unfortunately, we were in a band, which is a fairly social thing to do. We were understandably a bit confused about society, and we took drugs. We were never going to agree with our leaders.

We had been educated about drugs – in a way. There'd been Zammo, the stereotypical smackhead from our schooldays soap opera *Grange Hill.* Nobody wanted to be like Zammo who, in the course of about a month of episodes went from being a loveable character to a shuffling zombie. Why didn't Zammo put us off? I wonder why Zammo did heroin? Probably some evil drug pushers gave him some drugs outside the school playground and then he was gone. One of the less than human hordes who would nick your telly and stab your dog for a fix. We didn't want to be like Zammo and we didn't want to die of ignorance either, as the terrifying new public information films about Aids warned us with the weight of the crashing tombstone that ended that particular advertisement for life. It didn't stop us sharing needles with every thief, drug casualty and decrepit specimen in our small Rugby underworld. It didn't mean that clean needles suddenly became available either. What the fuck was wrong with us? There was quite a lot wrong with us, actually, and some of it was a direct consequence of years of disastrous policing and the attitudes of the people around us. Of course, we had personal problems too, but nobody wanted to talk about them. Just say no . . . to everything, including rational debate and harm reduction.

I would like to tell you it was glamorous and bohemian, but we did live in Rugby. I would like to tell you that we actually had some sort of deliberate plan for breaking into the subconscious to bring back messages of universal truth and understanding; that we chose to plumb the depths of the human spirit to return with the name of the demon that caused the malaise. But we just liked taking drugs because we thought that life was a bit shit sometimes and we felt better when we were on them.

We were kids when we got so deep into stuff that we might have been better leaving alone. Before we knew what we were doing, we were doing it, and after that there was no easy way back to the civilised society we now viewed with the same suspicion it reserved for us. Most of the alternative crowd were part-time outcasts and, to a degree, most of them were playing with rebellion. To go deeper, to go right down, was to risk being cast out by everybody – to enter a world of thieves, criminals and violence, where the police were your enemy. This was not something to be taken lightly. It was heavy stuff. People died. People went to jail. People would kick your fucking head in. I suppose I kind of wanted that life in a way, having little respect for the prevailing ambitions and dreams of our time, and seeing no other way of getting out of it – than getting out of it. I guess I also wanted to be dead, a little bit, but I couldn't quite bring myself to outright suicide. My advice to you is to try to identify the prevailing idiocies of your age and avoid them whenever possible. If idiocy is prevailing hard, some sort of anaesthetic might be in order. At least then you will have the satisfaction of knowing that you *chose* your idiocy and that there *might* be a way back. I am in no way recommending you make the choices we made. You will not become a creative powerhouse by consuming vast quantities of drink and drugs, and if you doubt that wisdom take a little trip down to the park bench where the alcoholics gather and ask them about their latest creative projects.

Back then, the drug underworld seemed more honest to me, and at least the people weren't as boring. At least they didn't talk about how much their house was worth all the time or what their new sofa cost. Drugs are an honest consumer product. As long as they are good quality you know what you are going to get, and you might even know the price you will be asked to pay, monetarily, physically and perhaps even spiritually. If you survive, that is. I still have survivor's guilt, and sometimes I wonder how I was lucky enough to get through it all when so many people didn't. I felt terrible after Spacemen 3, thinking that maybe we had convinced some lost and easily led soul that heroin was the way forward to a richer life. I got over that when I realised that I didn't blame Lou Reed for some of the choices I had made. His recorded advice had actually helped me negotiate some of the dangers, although, of course, he looked fucking cool as well. For a while. Survival in these situations can be all about accepting responsibility and not falling victim to blaming someone else, which *always* gives your power to change your situation away. Information doesn't hurt either. It's certainly more useful than propaganda.

Drugs it was, and we got some stuff we bargained for and some we didn't. Perhaps it was the least worst scenario for us . . . or the best option we could see. Pat Fish, the man responsible for introducing Spacemen 3 to their first record label, had my favourite quote about it all. He said, 'Spacemen 3: taking drugs so other people don't have to.'

Maybe those drugs gave us a peek into the divine and a little glimpse of what peace actually felt like. Maybe it gave us a good whiff of the demon's breath. These things might well have been an illusion in themselves, but the feelings, however fleeting and unstable, were real.

Rugby is not a great cultural hub. It is a small market town in the Midlands that stands at a confluence of major transport routes. The M1, the M6, major train lines . . . Watford Gap:

Rugby is where the comings and goings of Britain, north to south and east and west, are funnelled into a bottleneck that makes it a great distribution point for the rest of the country. Go there now and you will see monolithic warehouses containing all the food, gadgets and knick-knacks that the hungry people of the country consume as they try to buy their way into a better life. These giant grey boxes stretch out beyond sight on the fields where me and Natty used to pick mushrooms. Rugby is a distribution point and this fact was not lost on some of the major drug dealers at the time. A lot of drugs came through Rugby. We were blessed by geography. Rugby is central. 'In the middle where it matters,' as the signs welcoming you to the town said. Apart from this, Rugby really does not have much to distinguish it. It has a very expensive private school, and the remains of an industrial boom that brought people to the town from all over the country and from some of the countries of the crumbling British Empire. Back then, one half of the town comprised of manicured lawns, old buildings, concert halls and the children of the great and the good, while the other half was made up of a diverse group of people who had arrived in the fifties and sixties to work in the factories and at the burgeoning GEC turbine plant. Rugby is a wholly improbable town for Spacemen 3 to have sprung from. It was an absurd and inhospitable place for the band to exist in, and perhaps that is why it was ideal. Rugby was also home to a huge set of radio masts transmitting extra-low-frequency radio waves that were used to communicate with Britain's Trident nuclear submarines. We all knew, when we were schoolkids, this made Rugby number three on the list of nuclear targets if the Cold War ever decided to get a little more heated – something it always threatened to do in the eighties. As a child, I dreamt of nuclear annihilation. I dreamt of little mushroom clouds appearing on the horizon. I dreamt of the whole world and everything I loved in it being torn apart in a firestorm of shattering atoms and madness. Not many people were just saying no to that possibility.

We were coming of age in the eighties, when all of the industrial promise that had brought people to the town was being asset-stripped and shipped out of the country to cheaper labour abroad. What was there left to do but 'drugs not jobs'? Britain was being sold off, the unions were being smashed and fat money was king. I used to go and read all of the William Burroughs books at Rugby library when I was a young man. They had a great collection. At some point in the late eighties, those books vanished from the shelves, literary victims of a quiet censorship that ruled in law that any book 'promoting' drug use or homosexuality was to be removed from public libraries. Burning books attracted too much attention it seemed. It was much more efficient to quietly remove them from public view, and if the twenty-five weirdoes in town who actually read those books started to complain, who was going to care?

There wasn't much of an outcry about the removal of the books.

So what did we do in the face of all this puritan psychopathy? We took drugs and made a fucking racket, for us and our friends. It wasn't a rallying cry. We were too far into defeat to even dream of any resistance beyond keeping ourselves entertained. It wasn't ambitious. It was survival. At times it was a very self-destructive form of mental self-defence and, like many survival strategies, it eventually became a problem in itself after it had outlived its usefulness.

Coventry

Much of Coventry had been bombed flat during the Second World War. I had talked to old men in Rugby who remembered watching it burn from fourteen miles away. The city had been rebuilt afterwards, a little too quickly, as some sort of symbol of regeneration, and consequently it was a tangle of flyovers and concrete slabs that fitted together like a cuntish giant's puzzle. I bet it looked pretty special on the architects' drawing boards. Like a vision of the future, or something. Coventry, at ground level, did look like the future, but not a future most people would actually choose to inhabit. During the Second World War the bombing of Dresden was retaliation for the destruction of Coventry, which had supposedly been retaliation for Munich. The only bombing we were interested in was of ourselves, and where better to do it?

Here was a city dropped in by helicopters and cranes, poured and laid into a geometric confusion of frightening shadows and unbroken lines that ate the sunlight and gnawed the soul, with little respect for natural harmony or human scale. It was built for, and by, machines, and a fragile bag of bones and flesh was no match for its gargantuan scale and civic appetite. It would eat you up and shit you out without a wink, a fart or a thank you. The annexe to the main swimming pool in Coventry was supposed to look like an elephant, which it sort of did, for about three seconds, if you were travelling by car at a particular angle over one of the many flyovers. It looked like an elephant drawn by a psychopath. Coventry city centre could make a person feel as though the future had arrived to stamp on the head of everything quaint and pretty in the natural world, and those great slabs of cement and concrete laughed at the wonky past, while staring into you with flat dead eyes. The statue over by the entrance of the cathedral, depicting a winged angel with a spear standing over a defeated Satan, succeeded in somehow making the devil appear to be the sympathetic combatant. The horned devil was prostrate, bound, left gazing up the triumphant angel's skirt in a grotesque tableau of victory and defeat. This, in a city that had been destroyed by combat. Coventry had a skyline that bombs had turned into a full stop, and whoever had rewritten it was obviously angry or insane, because they'd just written 'FUCK OFF' in massive concrete letters and dropped them onto the smoking ruins and piles of rubble.

The signs on the way in to the city said, 'Welcome to historic Coventry.' So maybe someone had a sense of humour about the whole thing.

My first ever job had found me delivering fizzy drinks around the city. The Alpine man and I would drive to Willenhall in the early morning because it was safer. We would sell Alpine lemonade, cherryade and weird chemical limeade, travelling door to door, selling these dayglo beverages to our regular customers. I remember one lady who used to answer the door very slowly. Her house smelled of coriander, cumin, turmeric and fenugreek, and when I brought her the lemonade she would reach into her sari and take her purse out from close to her breast. Her money was always warm. Once, I asked her why there was a big hole in the wall of her garage. She said that the local skinheads had burned her car when it had been parked out on the street. The family had paid for a new car and locked it into the garage behind a big steel door with a heavy padlock. The skinheads knocked a hole in the garage wall and burnt the car inside. She had a steel cage on the inside of her letterbox, so that when people put burning things through her front door the house wouldn't burn down.

In the light of this, maybe it is easier to see what an absolute godsend a band like the Specials were to the town. Two-Tone, peace and harmony. Too much too young and the old skinhead moonstomp instead of the National Front and Paki-bashing. Lord knows that town *needed* a band to bring a little peace and harmony and give people a reason to get together that didn't involve violence.

Pete and I would take trips to Coventry. Sometimes we would go to Willenhall, sometimes we went to the other estates. I vividly remember listening to the Suicide bootleg *23 Minutes Over Brussels* while we drove around the city trying to score. Sometimes it took fucking ages, even longer than twenty-three minutes, and then we would listen to the tape over and over again. Marty Rev's panic-attack rhythms and Alan Vega's heartfelt screams were the perfect soundtrack to our search for oblivion in the concrete jungle of flyovers and high-rises. What could any of it have meant to me? Twenty-year-old Frankie? Working in a sheet metal factory in Birmingham? Stamping out washers. Thud, thud, thud, thud, thud, thud, thud. Putting the same bend in five thousand identical strips of metal.

One dealer lived in Hillfields in the big tower blocks. Pete would park the car and we would enter the block and take the lift up to the higher floors. He would knock on the door and call out, 'It's Pete, with the big feet,' because he does have big feet. The guy would let us in to his small flat where a massive tower of speakers completely filled one wall. The heroin dealer liked to play floor-shaking reggae music. I guess the neighbours didn't complain, or if they did, he couldn't hear them. Sometimes we would cook up a hit there because the dealer always had a needle. One needle. We would use that – it was hard to get clean needles at the time. Everyone else who went there to buy heroin in a hurry might have used that needle too. This was common practice at the time, due to a government policy which was supposed to discourage us from doing what we were doing. It didn't stop us, of course, but it was certainly a big bonus for the hepatitis C virus that was silently spreading like wildfire amongst people desperate enough to be using illegal intravenous drugs. Maybe the government wanted us to die.

That little insulin syringe would sting as it went in and slid out, but soon afterwards the warm flush would take away the care and we wouldn't think about the broken veins and the cops and whoever's blood might have been left on the syringe. We might even forget everything else that had lead us up to that flat in a tower block in Hillfields to try to find a little peace in all the wrong ways. After we had finished, we would smoke a cigarette, make a bit of woozy small talk with the dealer, and then we would both walk out of the tower block in a pleasant haze and drive back to Rugby. I was twenty-one years old – old enough to know better but young enough not to care.

We didn't always take the heroin in the flat. Sometimes we would use the public toilets in the city centre. This was worse, because we would have to carry the syringe and the smack and we would both have to try to get into the toilet cubicle without anyone becoming suspicious. We never took water from the tap, because that looked suspicious too. Back with my speed-freak friends it wasn't unusual for us to take the top off the cistern, suck up the water from there, and then cook it up and shoot it. Me and Pete didn't do that. We used bottled water. Once, we did some smack in the toilets and then went record shopping. Pete was pretty wasted and he fell asleep on some records he was looking through. The woman behind the counter was not very happy with this type of shopping. 'Oi!' she said. 'Wake up. What's wrong with you?'

Pete kind of half-woke up, lifted his head from the records, and mumbled something about narcolepsy. The woman was not convinced.

'What's wrong with him?' she said to me.

I walked over, smiled and tried to calm the situation.

She looked into my eyes and said, 'And you're the same?'

I thought that was a bit unfair because I had managed to look through the records without falling asleep on them.

'Fuck off you bitch,' said Pete, undiplomatically, and that was the end of that.

We left the shop and wobbled off to somewhere more friendly.

If we didn't do the drugs in Coventry we'd drive back to Rugby with them. I think we once did that fourteen-mile journey in under ten minutes. Maybe the drive back was more dangerous than the drugs themselves. Maybe the way we were forced to take the drugs (because of the laws that were put in place to stop us taking them) was worse than the drugs themselves. Nobody forced us to take the drugs, of course. We just wanted to.

We really weren't such happy young people, for various reasons, and maybe sometimes we couldn't see what we had to lose. We had problems. We had problems with drugs, we had problems with the police, and we had problems with all of the people who thought we shouldn't take drugs. None of it was fucking helping.

If you think any of this sounds like a good idea you might have problems too. Please believe me when I tell you that heroin is probably not the cure for your problems.

Spacemen 3 on Spectrum

After a brief lunchtime walk around the charming walled town of Chester, we had been expecting a fairly well behaved show, even though we were deep in the godless north of England. Spacemen 3 were often most well received in the north. Maybe they understood drugs and desperation more completely up there.

The promoter met us at the B&B. He was young, enthusiastic, wide-eyed, and very new to the game. He looked like a college kid; he was a fan who obviously thought he was going to have some fun putting on some of his favourite bands in his spare time. 'I've had to change the venue at short notice,' he said, a little warily. 'It's a bit weird but I reckon it will work out all right. It is in a health spa, but we should get a good crowd out.'

We shrugged. At this point, we were able to play in health spas, abandoned nuclear reactors or sweaty shoeboxes with equanimity.

'Do you want any drugs?' he asked.

This brought considerably more interest than the previous statement.

'What you got, man?'

'Ecstasy,' our young friend said, with a serious look on his face.

At this point in time, despite the distant rumblings of acid house and the heartening appearance of the unmistakeable signs of psychedelia in some members of the general population, we had never taken ecstasy and had no personal experience of its spiritual home, the acid-house rave. Dancing was not way up on our to-do list, and the idea of dancing to house music in a room full of happy people smelling of Vicks VapoRub wasn't really our thing. We mocked what little we knew of it – like most things that weren't Spacemen 3 or the music or drugs that we liked.

We were, however, interested in trying ecstasy, and this was the first time that anybody had actually offered us any.

'Hmmm,' Pete said. 'How much?'

'Twenty quid a pill,' our new friend said. 'If you want it, I'll have to give my friends a ring.'

Pete turned to me. 'Whaddya reckon? Shall we get a couple?'

I nodded affirmatively. I'd tried just about everything else by this point, so why not?

The promoter made the connection and within an hour his two friends were standing in our room at the B&B telling us what was on offer. 'We've got doves and we've got this new stuff called Spectrum,' one of the two very young and certainly glint kids told us with a smile. They went into detail about the subtle differences and relative merits of the two tablets, as though they were wine connoisseurs talking about their favourite vintages. They were obviously enthusiastic users of their own products.

We bought one pill each of 'Spectrum', whatever the fuck that was. We were probably hoping that it was going to be better than ecstasy and that we wouldn't end up hugging a room full of strangers while dancing to music we didn't really like. We were, perhaps, not the most touchy-feely, happy-clappy individuals you might encounter in your life. Except for Jonny, of course. He was from Northampton.

With the two tablets in hand, we made our way to the venue for the soundcheck.

It really was a health centre. There was no getting away from

it. There was a sauna and a jacuzzi, and a vividly carpeted conference room containing a hurriedly set-up PA in the corner. It
wasn't all pecs, abs, squat thrusts and muscle quotas because
there was an excessively mirrored bar in another corner of the
room. The whole place was perfectly in keeping with the rapidly
fading eighties obsession with being a panther in the gym and a
tiger in the boardroom, or the estate agent's or wherever. It was
worryingly clean and shiny. This was a place where people came
to do press-ups, to preen and to indulge in competitive vanity
while admiring how externally beautiful they were becoming
in the process. It was filled with jogging machines and tense
people in Lycra. It was a place of worship for healthy-looking
humans who cared about personal fitness. Unsurprisingly, we
didn't really fit in very well. It was as alien to us as acid house
and pretty much everything else we encountered beyond our
fairly insular world. We weren't very well adjusted to the prevailing reality of our times. Considering the crap we had been
bombarded with for most of our young lives, it was probably for
the best that we had adopted a certain siege mentality.

We set up our equipment in the corner of the mirrored and
carpeted conference room. While we were running through the
soundcheck the support band arrived. It was Northampton's
second finest goth superstars, Venus Fly Trap, who were old
acquaintances of ours. We left our equipment on the stage and
they set their stuff up in front of it while we retired to the dressing room to indulge in our usual pre-gig rituals. The dressing
room was a little bigger than most of the pre-show grotholes
we were used to. This being a health centre and everything, we
were shown into a huge mirrored room full of bench presses
and exercise bikes and other contraptions that were used to
torment the body into physical perfection. We lolled on the
various contraptions and made use of the machines to the best
of our ability. Jason struggled to lift a weight while Jonny, who

was probably the only one of us with any degree of physical fitness, actually started expending energy on something that looked like a boat on dry land with oars, which didn't take you anywhere no matter how hard you rowed. As somebody rolled a joint on one of the bench presses, I watched the whole strange scene in the mirrored walls, briefly imagining a keep-fit video featuring the band failing to keep fit. It was not an easy mental image to sustain.

'Shall we take this pill?' Pete said, which was surprising, as we had never taken stimulants, psychedelics or uppers prior to a show before. I suppose it was looking like it was going to be a weird night anyway and he was just entering into the spirit of it.

'Yeah, man, why not? I reckon I'll just do a half though and see how I go,' I replied. Safety first, right?

We each split our little yellow tablets in two, swallowed half, and went back to playing on the exercise machines while laughing at our own pathetic reflections. After about three minutes we took a break and went back to rolling joints. We didn't want to exhaust ourselves before the show, or anything.

The night rolled on and the health freaks cleared out and the music freaks began to arrive. Maybe a few of the healthy people stayed on to watch, but I doubt it. I was beginning to feel the first soft roll and waves of the ecstasy. There were tracers, streamers and a few faint visual distortions but it was all very easy to handle. It didn't feel like it could swing horribly out of control and take you off your axis in a blink, as was sometimes the case with the heavier psychedelics. I felt kind of warm and fuzzy and just a little bit trippy.

'Shall we do the other half?' I said to Pete, who was laughing and clowning around like he sometimes did when he was in a good mood.

'Yeah. I think so. This feels fairly mild doesn't it?' he said, with a little glitter in his eyes.

I nodded and we both swallowed the other half.

We were professionals. We could probably deal with it.

Just then there was a commotion outside the dressing room, and a loud shout heralded the entrance of a gang of extremely wasted young men. 'WOAAAAAHHHHHHHHHHH,' they shouted, as they piled into the multi-gym unannounced, staggering and laughing amongst themselves. One of them went over to the weights machine and started bench-pressing weights. Jason, Pete and I exchanged knowing and worried glances, while casting fast eyes over the new arrivals in the inner sanctum of our dressing room. They seemed pretty oblivious to our concerns, and a couple of them started skinning up joints on the expensive gym equipment. It was a worrying situation and not just because we were on drugs – there was nothing unusual in that. What was unusual about this was that the people who were now making themselves comfortable in our dressing room were not the kind of people we normally saw at gigs. These were full-on football casuals and, up to this point in the eighties, it was very rare to see a gang of casuals at a gig looking for anything but trouble. These were the same people who would normally be up for giving us a kicking if they caught us in the right situation. These were the gangs we avoided on Saturdays when the home game was on in Coventry; the same people who would stop off in coaches in Rugby on the way back from a game down south and wreck the town with glee before moving on again. This gang of casuals from Ellesmere Port were extremely wasted, but not in the usual way, because rather than taking their sport in terrorising us and smashing things up, they were just laughing and lolling around, rolling joints and playing on the gym equipment. One of them walked over to where we sitting. 'All right, lads. You don't mind if we skin up in here, do ya?'

Pete just laughed, because I guess his pill was kicking in and what the fuck else were we going to say? There were seven of them, and there was no security around. We were just happy that they didn't want to give us a beating and that they seemed friendly. We rolled some joints, while they rolled around on the floor. They were actually *really* friendly, or maybe we were, it was hard to tell. We were all getting on well, even if their eyes were going in different directions now and again, and some of them were gurning and pulling weird faces. It never occurred to us that they might have actually come to the gig because, as I mentioned, the football crowd didn't really do gigs at that time.

Pete decided it might be time for a bit of peace and quiet. 'Hey, thanks for coming in and rolling joints and stuff, but we could do with getting our heads together a bit because we are going to play a gig pretty soon,' he said.

'I know,' said the head casual, 'we've come to see you.'

With that, he turned round, let out a loud battle cry and lead the way out of the dressing room. All of his mates mustered themselves to the best of their ability and followed him out hooting and roaring.

We looked at each other in disbelief.

The entire floor of the previously spotless multi-gym was now covered in ripped-up Rizla packets, bits of cigarettes and joint ends. We looked around the thoroughly besmirched room and then looked at each other and laughed. We were becoming increasingly fangled by this newfangled drug. The little pill was now in full effect and after the excitement of the pre-match pep talk from our new-found partners in crime, I thought it might be the right time to take a little stroll around the venue and see what other surprises the seemingly sleepy town of Chester might have in store.

The lights were pulsing gently and my reflection was look-ing more peculiar than usual as I did the soft walk above the vibrant carpet past the floor-to-ceiling mirrors. I wondered why the mirrors went all the way up to the top of the room. Surely nobody was that tall? Even with steroids. I felt a little spongy, but the dark light and the music that was oozing from the distant doorway seemed as friendly and inviting as a warm cushion. I made my way towards it like a happy cat. I heard the dreamy sounds of ketchup leather and a Formica ringtone as what was left of me entered the incipient bacchanal with a glowing sense of anticipation.

Of course, what I was hearing was not the sound of ketchup leather – that would have been absurd – but after a couple of years of hard reality training, I had reached the point where I didn't always take my own brain too seriously. What I was actually hearing was the sound of Venus Fly Trap getting ready for the evening's performance. I entered the smoky churn of beer and fags and found a slouching semicircle of offbeat hooligans and random alternative types who were struggling to pay attention to the band as they took the stage. The black-clad singer was preparing to take the loosely assembled crowd of indie kids, drug specimens and casual casualties on a tour of Northampton's gothic culture. Alex Novak stood perched at the microphone like a pale-faced graveyard raven in sunglasses. The guitarist, an affable hobgoblin profoundly drunk beyond the capacity to tune his guitar, seemed to be finding his own inability to function in any useful way absolutely hilarious. He would tune his guitar for five minutes, crack a joke, ask us how we were all doing, and then play some horrendous chord from another dimension. 'How you doing, CHESTER?!' he screamed down the microphone in his Northamptonian–Scottish bastard brogue.

'CLOOOONG,' his supposedly tuned guitar replied, in no way corresponding musically with any of the other instruments onstage. He was chatting away merrily to the increasingly confused crowd as he made another failed attempt to tune up, while the rest of his band tried to remain cool and oblivious to the fact that their guitarist was making a royal cunt-up of the show and was thoroughly enjoying himself in the process.

The singer glanced over at him nervously and said, 'Sorry about this, folks.'

This spectacle of marvellously inept entertainment went on for a full fifteen minutes. We were totally absorbed in his epic struggle to tune his guitar. The entire audience were willing him to succeed. There were shouts of encouragement and laughter from the dark. Eventually somebody took pity on him (and us), and lent the guitarist a guitar tuner, which he accepted with a loud laugh and a, 'I'll be right with you, folks!' He looked like he was having difficulty being right with himself never mind anybody else. We were so wasted that the lack of a performance was actually becoming a performance in itself.

It was almost disappointing when he finally sprang to his feet and triumphantly played a chord that was in tune. This excited him so much that he whinnied, leapt backwards and crashed into the band's precariously balanced keyboards, sequencers and drum machines. He landed in a hopelessly confused pile of expensive equipment, the crowd gave him a heartfelt cheer and a round of applause, and that was that. The show was over. It was only left for the rest of band to help the guitarist up and out of the tangle, take a bow and leave the stage.

Shaking my head, I looked around the slowly filling room. It had been an interesting evening so far and we hadn't even played yet.

When we arrived onstage the room was full of hash smoke and loud voices. A well-packed and more than comfortably numb crowd had gathered around the front of the stage area in loose abandon. We climbed over and through the sprawled audience carrying our carefully pre-tuned guitars and took our places. We plugged in while the floating drone world of 'Ecstasy Symphony' faded into nothing. The audience let out a cheer of appreciation as the first teasing notes and peals of feedback announced the approaching onslaught. The crowd hushed as Pete leaned in and said his customary, 'Good evening. Thanks for coming. This is a song from Texas,' and the s's of the last word fluttered and echoed through the speakers across the minds of those of us who were feeling the same.

He pealed out the familiar and menacing start to 'Roller-coaster'. The band came in behind it with the force and the fury of an immovable object meeting an unstoppable force as the noise of the crowd was consumed by electricity and intent.

I met someone some time ago and his eyes were cleeeeear to seeee . . .

Jason was howling out the words, the music was making shapes around them and the band moved up a gear, causing the one-note monster to change shape, grow and charge through the room on a rampage. I glanced up from the note I was currently fixated on playing to see fifty faces lost in the moment and surrendering to a higher power. It was a sound so beyond the usual, so fit and trim and devoid of extraneous fat that it could have worked out on every machine in that health spa and left them a twisted pile of wreckage. It was lean, supple and rippling with spare power. Maybe I was imagining it. I was on drugs, after all. The song ended after a quick eternity and the feedback trailed off into a silence ripe with explosive possibilities. The crowd gave out a great release of pleasure and the first joint was passed onto the stage from the people sitting pinned and transfixed at the front of the stage. We passed the joint between us and got ready for the next workout. The two-chord juggernaut grunge of

'Mary Anne' stomped across the boards of the ceiling with a grand sense of purpose. Pretty babe I understand a bit about the way that unappreciative crowds can fuck with one's sense of reality BUT it doesn't matter because you and me, we can just hold each other's hands and go for a walk on the beach and fuck 'em . . . what do they know anyway?

It offered the possibility of consolation in the face of alienation and it was like God was talking to you in a way that was actually possible to understand for a change. Like a beautiful sunset and a wide spread of sky. Like the waves chewing at the cliff and the birds singing overtones in a winging chorus above you. It rippled and it slid and it shimmered as it glid and everything that was anything else didn't really matter for a while, which certainly made a change. I wasn't even worried about screwing it up this time because how could it be possible to screw up something so awesome and beyond and downwrong right. It was a force of nature and all we'd done was put the wires in, get ourselves in the right trance, mutter the invocations and BANG!

There it was, hanging in the sky, waiting to spread its jewelled wings and soar.

'Things'll never be the same' howled out proclamations of certain doom from lost souls, stretching a minute to an hour, saying the same thing about irrevocable change and about how somewhere in our hearts things wouldn't be the same once we'd put love in our veins. That shifted into the desire and the striving for transcendence of 'Take me to the other side'. I took myself, sliding, up to that top octave on the bass and held it for a perilously long time, until that high thin note hid itself in the drone, and when I ran back down the neck, the bass came surging up like a shark out of the deep blue sea.

I have a passion sweet Lord . . .

It was like I wasn't playing it at all. I was just there, holding the bass and letting it do what it had to. Something was in the saddle and it wasn't us, or at least that is the way it felt to me.

Despite the fact that I was on drugs, the entire experience cannot be put down solely to the drugs. If I had been sat in a car park in Kidderminster considering my carbuncles, I would not have been having the same experience at all.

I knew exactly where I was and I was thoroughly enjoying it. Sorry about that.

We dragged the crowd through the mire and maelstrom and they kept us well supplied with marijuana during the journey. After every song a joint would appear at both sides of the stage and then cross over between us, to exit at the opposite side of the stage before the next song began. I have never been passed so many joints during a performance, and the air was thick, onstage and off, with heavy smoke. The two security men watching the show were also smoking joints, having presumably realised early on that they were on the wrong side of a losing battle and that we were having more fun anyway.

We slipped into 'Starship' and the riff growled and crunched into a low orbit and then, exactly as planned, the spaceship faltered, stalled and fell into chaos and confusion, breaking up in the far curve of sky and showering down sparks and smoking curls of broken metal that briefly rested and reshaped, before sucking themselves back together again. They reformed like a puddle of clever metal, finding its original shape and form again, so that the crash seemed like the dream of a dream falling and not the end instead.

More joints. More cheers, and then the final push to the end while the lights wound up and round the stage and the air throbbed and sweated inside us and out. 'Revolution' started, and it was actually possible to believe it might grow from the tiny anarchy and the heresy we had wrought in this puritan palace to the greed for physical beauty. It growled and it slunk and the drums fired a salvo of rolls as Pete drawled ire and myrrh over his discontent, and the whole thing exploded in flames and fury as cannons fired and the end was revealed as a lightshow of stars and not the apocalypse it was never meant to be.

The drone began for 'Suicide' and, as tired as we were, we got ready for the marathon at the end. This two-note hymn to a death that never died and to a life that wouldn't give up on its own death wish pulled itself up from the earth and down from the sky. It drew the walls around us into a dizzying hurricane as it span and twirled, over and over, bringing us back to attention and one last gasp, by the skin of its teeth and the beckoning organ, until it finally, inevitably, died of old age and exhaustion and the crowd went wild. We fought our way offstage through the sweating joy and the feedback and the light.

It was a good gig.

We sat in the dressing room under the too bright lights, sweating off our preferred exercise. The first gang of well-wishers burst in and as the conversations grew and the drug-fuelled friendships flourished, I took myself off for a little walk and a peaceful moment.

Walking back into the now empty performance room was as much of a shock as it had been earlier. The place was fucking wrecked. There were broken glasses everywhere. Cigarettes and joints had been left to extinguish themselves in fresh pools of vomit and beer on the carpet. A couple of stubborn souls were still holding onto the far reaches of consciousness, propped against walls, fitfully dreaming in chairs or snoozing on the floor amongst the detritus of our transportation. I walked up onstage, collected my effects, wound my cables and packed my Gibson Thunderbird safely into its case.

I walked back out into the corridor and bumped into Pete.

'Have you seen the state of this place, man?' he said. 'It's fucking trashed. Come and have a look at this.'

I followed him into the jacuzzi and sauna area. All of the hairdryers and beauty thingamajigs had been ripped from the walls. They were lying in piles in the sinks. The water in the previously pristine jacuzzi had turned a yellowy-brown colour and there were cigarette ends and empty bottles of Newcastle Brown Ale floating on the surface.

'Oh dear,' I said.

We wandered further in, past the piles of trash and broken equipment, until we reached the sauna. When we got close, the door opened and one of our friends from earlier looked out at us from the billowing clouds of steam. 'It's fucking impossible to get Rizlas to stick together in here,' he said, and then he showed us the two cigarette papers that he had in his hands. The papers were obviously not sticking together at all. The sauna was pumping out steam and he was sitting in there, alone and fully clothed in expensive sportswear.

We were all back in the main room, packing up the gear, when the promoter approached us, looking a bit less relaxed than he had earlier in the day.

'Oh, man,' he said, looking worried. 'The management are *really* not happy about the state of this place.'

We nodded sympathetically. It was pretty easy to see why they might not be over the moon about the situation.

'Do you reckon I'll get my deposit back?' he asked us, seriously.

Gerald and the Two-Handed Shuffle

Gerald Palmer was a bullet-headed man with an easy smile. He knew his business, and his business was business. Nothing else really seemed to interest him beyond that, except that which might serve his interests, which were business. He talked about his family sometimes, but his eyes only lit up for business.

When *Playing with Fire* had been recorded and mixed and we were all sitting down at VHF listening to the playbacks and patting ourselves on the back, Gerald turned up to do some business. He smiled, as he usually did, and then produced two pieces of paper and held them out like a stage magician. In one hand was a contract, and in the other hand were two cheques.

One for Pete and one for Jason. I can't remember how much the cheques were actually for, but they weren't enough to buy anyone a house. It was a simple deal. Sign the contract, get the cheque.

Pete and Jason had a cursory read through the agreement. There was a short discussion between them while Gerald just kept on smiling.

After a little more discussion, the contracts were signed and the cheques were handed over. Gerald kept on smiling the same old smile.

A few years ago, I was talking to Gerald about his new business venture, which involved cleaning up old recordings that had fallen out of copyright. He would digitally clean up the songs and make them into stereo, register the songs in his name, and then sell them, digitally, on the internet. He told me he had thousands of other people's songs registered in his name and he was making money from them. It was all perfectly legal.

After he had told me that, he said, 'I much prefer working with dead musicians, Willie.'

I told him I felt the same way about managers, and we both laughed.

Elvis Plays 'Revolution'

Sometime towards the final demise of Spacemen 3, we were playing a show in the south-west of England and had somehow managed to secure free passes to Glastonbury festival. 'I'm not going!' Pete Kember said. 'I hate those people and I hate camping.' Kate was the only one of us who could drive, and she had a car, so she agreed to give me and Jonny a lift down to the festival after the show. She and Jason were then going to drive back to her parents' house and join us the next day at the festival. We played the show, packed all the stuff up, and the four of us got in the car and headed down to Glastonbury. It was the first time at the festival for all of us.

As we got close to the site peculiar stragglers appeared on the roadside, briefly illuminated by the car headlights. Up ahead, blue flashing lights and hi-vis jackets indicated we were involved in some sort of police stop-and-search operation. This was bad news in many ways. I was carrying an eighth of hash in my hand and was ready for the situation. I put it in my mouth and held it between my teeth and my cheek and tried not to panic as the two policemen waved our car over into a side road that led up to the back of a frighteningly well-lit truck and more police cars. Standing in the back of the truck were two policemen, backlit and silhouetted like a scene from a horror film. They were theatrically snapping on rubber gloves. Everybody wants a nice cavity search on the way to a festival after a show at two in the morning, right? I swallowed the hash. 'Has anybody got anything?' said Jason, looking a little nervous. 'Not any more,' I said, and we all got ready for the inevitable questions. Kate did the talking. Her old man had been a fairly high-ranking copper and she knew the routine. She was pretty and well spoken and after a few initially probing questions she charmed the copper on duty enough for him to let us pass without looking up anyone's arse. This was a big bonus for everyone, including, one might hope, the policemen on duty. The whole thing had been a 'scare the hippies for a laugh' kind of operation – and it had worked on me.

'Bollocks,' I said. 'I've swallowed my hash. It was everything I had for the whole festival.' It was also more than enough to fuck me well and truly up.

Kate and Jason dropped Jonny and me off at the gate to the festival and said goodbye. It was dark and late and I was getting ready for the unbearable levels of intoxication that were about to become my lot for the next twenty hours or so. Jonny had a tent and some things that campers sometimes take camping, but I think the only thing I had brought with me was twenty quid and the hash I had already swallowed.

We didn't have any wristbands or tickets, but we had been told to pretend to be Brendan Croker and the 5 O'Clock Shadows who were, presumably, a band. Because it was late, and because security was slack in those days, we were let into the festival grounds without question and told to pick up our wristbands the next day.

Jonny and I walked through the darkened campsites, occasionally twanging our feet on unseen guy ropes and tripping over tent pegs. We were looking for a good place to put the tent in the dark – with no torch, and with a quickly approaching drug casualty. I could feel my body becoming increasingly heavy as peculiar notions began to surface in the unclear waters of my mind. 'Jonny,' I said. 'We really have to get this tent up soon or I am going to zonk out on my feet.'

'Yeah, man, don't worry,' said Jonny in his cheerfully excited and enthusiastic way. 'We'll find somewhere good and then you can sleep it off.'

We walked a bit further and then we walked further still. With every step, each step became a little more difficult to take.

'Jonny . . . I am not fucking kidding, man. Pitch the fucking tent. Now. Here.'

'OK,' he said, and we found the nearest clear spot and started pegging out his cheap two-man tent. When it was up I crawled into the baggy interior and fell asleep instantly without saying goodnight.

When I woke up, I wasn't even sure that I was awake. I could see stuff with my eyes shut. I kept my eyes shut, mainly because I was feeling very worried about what I might find if I opened them. Something was not right. I tried to feel all right about the thing that was not right – I think part of my brain had forgotten that I had recently been made to eat a very big chunk of strong Afghani hash by a policeman wearing rubber gloves and a strange smile.

'Jonny,' I whispered. 'Jonny, are you awake? Man . . . something is wrong.'

I still hadn't opened my eyes but then I remembered that I had swallowed the hash, and I knew that I could not feel my legs. It was freaking me out a bit.

'JONNY!' I shouted quietly, 'I FEEL WEIRD. I THINK I MIGHT BE PARALYSED.' I know all of this sounds stupid, but I was absolutely stoned to the bone in every possible way and the occasional lapse into paranoia and peculiarity was, perhaps, unavoidable. Jonny groaned, moved around a bit, and then started laughing. This did not help my paralysis or my feelings about it at all.

'HAHAHAHAHAHA.'

'What? What?' I said in a frightened little voice.

'Open your eyes, you twat.'

I opened my twat eyes, reluctantly. Jonny was twice my size. He was a giant and I was tiny. Not only was I paralysed but I had shrunk in the night so that I only came halfway up the tent. I was a paralysed dwarf and it was probably permanent, and it was all my fault.

Reality dawned slowly and in a way that was difficult to comprehend. Somehow, we had managed to pitch the tent on a ridiculously steep hill. Because we had failed to zip the front of the tent up, during the course of my night of deep dreams I had gradually made my way out of the tent feet first and been blissfully unaware of the fact. My legs had spent the night sleeping outside of the tent and the rest of me had been . . . well, in some exotic garden in Marrakesh.

It was quite a relief. 'Hehehehe,' I laughed weakly and unconvincingly.

'How you feeling?' said Jonny.

'A bit weird,' I said, as I made the long journey to my feet and stumbled around the steep hill like a newborn deer on my unparalysed but not entirely functional legs.

'Oh dear,' said Jonny.

'Exactly,' I said, walking and falling, falling and walking. 'Why did we pitch the tent on a fucking mountain?'

Jonny merely laughed, the heartless bastard, and then he took me for a walk around the festival ground, as though I was a totally bemused dog. We met Kate and Jason at the sound desk of the Pyramid stage as Van Morrison began his set. 'Hi, Will,' they said. 'How are you feeling?' I just nodded and then we listened to Van Morrison singing 'And It Stoned Me' until it all made a bit more sense, as these things sometimes do.

Later on, when the hash had worn off enough for me to function a little bit, I bought two squares of LSD from a passing dealer.

'Here you go, man. Watch out, they are pretty strong. Black witches,' he said to me as he pocketed the five quid I had given him.

The little squares of paper had pictures of black witches on them, but I was not feeling superstitious . . . yet. I ate one and lay back on the very steep hill just up from the main stage, where we had pitched our tent.

A policeman stepped over my body, which was a bit weird, but he just smiled and carried on walking.

I waited . . . and waited . . . but nothing happened, so I went off to drink cider and meet the rest of the gang. We were sitting underneath some electricity pylons, sipping cider, and I was complaining about the weak LSD. 'This stuff is weak as shit,' I said, taking out the second black witch and eating it. I lay back on the grass amongst the plastic cups and listened to the buzz of electricity and the music, which was phasing in and out on the wind. I became fixated on the buzzing electricity, which seemed to be growing louder. I opened my eyes and the unmistakable first stirrings of the LSD emanated from my stomach up to the edges of my vision, sending ripples across teeming fields that were now somehow vibrating at the exact frequency of the buzz from the overhead cables. It seemed that the first black witch, although slow to get started, was not quite as ineffective as I had initially thought – and I had just eaten another one. I braced myself for the incoming waves. 'Uh oh,' I managed to say, which made a change from nodding. 'I think that first black witch just kicked in.'

Jason looked at me sympathetically and with a little pity. 'Shall we move away from these electricity pylons?' he said, perhaps sensing I would be better off some distance from the thousands of volts of electricity surging above our heads. I nodded and we wobbled off into the festival, as everything around me caught fire and was lit in increasingly vivid colour. It was really going to be a long night, maybe every thirty seconds or so.

As day passed to night and the second witch almost completely tipped me over the edge, Jonny and I decided to go and watch Elvis Costello headline the main stage. He was playing solo and came out in a suit that seemed to light up, but it was impossible for me to say for sure. At one point he played a section of a Beatles song. The lyrics were 'So you say you want a revolution,' and then, unmistakably and blown up to the size of the universe, he played two sarcastic bars of 'Revolution'. 'Did you hear that?' I said to Jonny, who was deep in the arms of cider.

'Yeah,' he said, encouragingly but obviously unconvinced as to what it was he was supposed to have heard.

'He just played fucking "Revolution".'

'Yeah,' said Jonny, but I could tell by his eyes he thought I was bananas.

The set finished and Jonny carefully shepherded me back through the chaotic crowds and campgrounds making sure I did not become irretrievably lost or buy any more drugs on the way. Eventually we found our tent amongst the surrounding sea of very similar-looking tents. Jason and Kate were already trying to make themselves comfortable despite the lack of any kind of anything that would actually make a tent comfortable for anyone to sleep in. Jonny was pissed and I was still tripping my face off. 'I'm going to sleep, man,' Jonny said, peering into my face with half-cut concern. 'Will you be all right?'

I assured him I would be, and so he crawled into the tent with Jason and Kate while I sat out on the hill and looked out across the heaving lights of the festival. A police helicopter was sweeping low over the crowds and I heard a man with a megaphone shout up to it from the seething masses below: 'Will you lot please fuck off and give us a break. We're tripping our nuts off down here.'

Eventually, I crawled into the tent around dawn and the four of us slept squashed into Jonny's little tent on the hill that was a bit too steep.

'Are You Just Peripheral Shit or are You in the Band?'

The band played the biggest show of its career down at the Town and Country club in Kentish Town. Before that show, feeling the expectant and intimidating energy of a large crowd for the first time, Pete and I crouched down behind the curtain at the back of the stage and smoked a last cigarette. Pete turned to me and, for the first time ever, I saw fear in him. It put the fear in me too. 'I can't do it,' he said. 'I can't go on.' His eyes were wide and white and shifting in the dark.

'You can do it, man,' I said, acting brave. 'Come on, we know this set inside out. We'll blow their minds. We've got to do it.'

He looked at me but he didn't look at all sure. We both finished our cigarettes and then walked out into all those bright lights in front of a thousand people, pretending that we didn't give a fuck.

The show went well, despite the nerves, and a couple of weeks later we had another three shows approaching. There was a gig booked for Rugby and one at Subterranea in west London. They were both warm-up shows for the final date of the three, which was to be at the Reading Festival.

We rehearsed in the back room of the pub where we were going to play the gig. I had never played in my hometown with Spacemen 3; in fact, I had only played the one show in Rugby, with the Cogs of Tyme in the back room of the Blitz two short years previously. I felt a million years older than that now and a whole lot more ready to play, but I was still unsure about this show. I don't think any of us were relishing the idea. In

some ways it was more of a 'fuck you' than anything else. A
big 'fuck you' to everyone who had talked behind our backs
and snarked and been jealous, or offered us out, or hated us for
trying . . . or whatever, really. Our answer was to put on a free
show and just let the music speak for itself, because the music
was speaking pretty loudly at that point and we were confident
enough in its voice, if not always in our own.

We were sure enough of that music to put it in front of anything, or anyone, on a good night. We had played shows and
been watched by various luminaries and pop stars and it never
fazed us. Bryan Ferry, Keith Richards, Lemmy . . . if God and
the devil themselves had said, 'Show us what you've got to
save your mortal souls,' we would have played it, looked them
both in the eye and said, 'Fuck you if you don't like it.' It was
all we had, really. It was certainly all I believed in at the time,
except for getting wasted. The sure power of redemption in
music. It might have been optimism, but it had got us somewhere. We knew we were good.

The band rehearsed in that old-timey back room, where
Spacemen 3 had played to a bikers' party years before and
been told after a couple of songs that their services would no
longer be required. That room, with its fading Victorian façade
and its dated decorations, had seen a thousand discos, dances
and wedding receptions. That shabby back room, in a shabby
corner of Rugby town, would see the last-ever Spacemen 3
show in Rugby . . . but none of us knew that then.

It seemed a good place to play a free show for all of those
people had seen us on the telly and who wanted to come
and see exactly who we thought we were. It was for all of
those people who had never been in the back room of the Blitz,
who had never come to a Spacemen 3 show and loved it. It was
for the haters as much as the lovers, and that was perhaps as it
should have been. Spacemen 3 had never made an appearance

149

in the local papers all the time we'd been making records and making waves, internationally and within Britain. The locals couldn't be proud of us. We were fucking junkies and pariahs and everyone knew it, or at least they thought they did. We were biggish fish in a very small pond, and we were fairly strange fish at that. The local press and most of the wider population of the town ignored us, and we ignored them in turn. That was that.

Playing for free was kind of masochistic, really, because it was only going to attract the very people who would have hated putting any money in our pockets. Not that there was much money in our pockets in the first place. We were getting paid ten quid a show.

We were going to play the same set we had been playing for the last year – it worked, and the idea of rehearsing a fresh set and working on new live material had become increasingly remote as the relationship between Pete and Jason grew strained. The quiet stuff was difficult too. People wouldn't shut up and listen when we tried it, and it always sounded weak after the full-on assault that we used to get people's attention. In a way, the band had become a little conservative. Perhaps, in the glare of publicity, Spacemen 3 had become a little timid. The pressure was on and maybe we stuck with what worked because of it. The rock crowd were not going to sit around and be satisfied with gentle ballads about Jesus and love, so we just did what we knew best: turned it up, ripped it out, and left no room for protest. People loved it and, even though there was frustration on Jason's part (perhaps more so than on Pete's) that the quieter stuff wasn't getting a chance, I think it was understood that limitations in equipment and in the band's ability to communicate made a new set impossible. Put simply: Pete and Jason weren't getting on well enough to even want to work on any new songs together. There was no room for the gentler sides of *Playing with Fire* or *The Perfect Prescription*. We were playing songs that we knew inside out, and it was strictly *Sturm und Drang*. It didn't take long to rehearse.

On the evening of the show we set up our equipment and got ready to do what we did. The crowd came in and by the time we picked up the instruments the small back room was fairly well filled with the curious, the killjoys, and the genuinely interested. We plugged in and played, and we sounded pretty good by our own standards, given this wasn't a proper venue. There was no stage or lightshow – unlike the ones in the back of the Blitz, and numerous other shows that Spacemen 3 had played, which hardly anybody in town had bothered to turn up to. After the first song we received a reception that was weirdly muted. We didn't give a fuck. Next song. Bang. Same weirdly quiet reaction from a full crowd. We were looking out at a room full of extremely visible people, most of whom we recognised, and not many of them looked particularly happy to see us. It was the strangest set I ever played with the band. It felt like people actually didn't *want* to like us – that feeling was palpable on stage. We played it out.

No fanfare. No party. No glorious homecoming show. It felt like a grim gig in a grim little town, played with grim determination. And that was that for Rugby and Spacemen 3.

The second show went as planned. Generally, I don't think we ever really enjoyed the London shows. Somehow, there was press pressure down there, trendsetter pressure, capital city pressure, and, really, the crowds didn't seem to go quite as mad as they did north of Watford Gap. People with less to lose seem to get more out of music sometimes. The shows in London were good, but I doubt any of them would be the ones that individual band members would mention as being the greatest. Subterranea was a mid-size venue – maybe three hundred people – and by the time we were due onstage it was a packed house.

We played the set we knew too well. 'Revolution' was played twice, once during the set and once as an encore, and then we came offstage and all sat together in the small window-less dressing room by the side of the stage. It was too brightly lit, covered in crude graffiti – it was nobody's idea of a great place to relax. The depressing room, scene of many a misery. Despite the problems between Pete and Jason, the atmosphere was OK. We had played well, the crowd had loved it and we all still cared about the music no matter what we thought of each other. The music was always the strongest thing. It was stronger than any of us and it wanted to be heard. It was a thing beyond us that was made by us. None of us could make the sound alone.

We sat in the dressing room drinking our drinks and smoking our joints while we waited for the first people to come back-stage and say hi. Dean Wareham from the band Galaxie 500 popped his head in and immediately went over to talk to Pete. The crowd started bustling through the dressing-room door, all excited, ready for a party and buzzing from the show. Gibby Haynes burst in, looking wide-eyed and excited, walked up to me, jabbed a finger in my chest and said, 'Are you in the band or are you just peripheral shit?'

'Er, both actually, I think,' I said, with a smile. 'My mum fucking hates you,' I added, because she had mentioned her dislike for the man after seeing him on a TV show.

'Here, man. You wanna smoke with me?' said Gibby's friend, who seemed quite amused by our little exchange. So I smoked some weed with Paul Leary, while Gibby wandered off to entertain someone else. It was a fair old celeb fest in there, if indeed any of us could have been considered celebrities. We didn't even know who we were half the time.

We drank a bit, we smoked a bit, we chatted a bit, and then we packed up and went back to Rugby and the van dropped me off at my mum's house. I went up to my old bedroom and fell asleep.

Two days later, we loaded ourselves into the van and made our way down to Reading to play the festival. It was an unpromising day weather-wise – the spots of drizzle that flecked the windscreen of the rented minibus did not promise a fine day in the British countryside. Reading is nobody's idea of paradise anyway, and when we arrived the festival site looked like a grim prison camp for indie kids. We were due to play as the second band on the main stage on the opening day of the festival, just after Gaye Bykers on Acid. It was the first time playing at a big festival for any of us, and we had no idea what to expect. Reading was a big deal back then, and we had been advised how important the show might be for our career. Nobody knew at the time quite how important. The festival had been trying to shed its hard rock image by putting more alternative bands on the bill. It was us, Swans, The Sugarcubes, My Bloody Valentine, That Petrol Emotion, the House of Love and New Order. I can't even remember if we were excited or not. I don't think we were. We were beyond excitement somehow. We turned up in the drizzle, and were herded through the festival site to the caravan that was going to serve as our dressing room. We went up onstage, set the equipment up on the movable risers, and had a little line check because we were on so early. With everything ready to go, we were told that there was no room for our usual long tune-ups or gaps between songs. Having only forty minutes to perform, we had arranged a 'medley' of our songs in the back room of the Imperial, chopping up the songs, dropping some chunks here and there and condensing the set down to the required time. It lacked a forty-minute 'Suicide' and the two versions of 'Revolution', but it was fast paced and accessible, I suppose. At least for us anyway.

The time came to go onstage. Standing up there, looking out at a muddy field sparsely filled with visibly bedraggled people, was a most unedifying experience. We played the first song and the second song, and then somebody threw a muddy shoe at us. The music sounded different – thin and blown about – but we could have probably played it blindfolded and upside down at that point. Jonny thwacked it out with the usual precision and we hit all of our cues and our crescendos. Jason and Pete sang everything in key and on time, and it all sounded fairly professional – as long as you weren't onstage. That is how festival sound is sometimes. You just grit your teeth and bear it. You don't expect to enjoy it. Somebody threw another mud-caked shoe up onstage. I don't think it was really aimed at anyone. It was just the crowd's idea of fun.

Eventually, we played 'Revolution' and the crowd went as nuts as they thought they could manage, given the fact that it was daylight and nobody was drunk enough to pretend to want a revolution yet. That was that. We were finished and being rushed offstage to make way for the next band. Before we knew it, we were sitting back in our caravan smoking and drinking the seven cans of lager that had been provided for our refreshment. It was a relief not to have to worry about getting it wrong any more.

We sat in the caravan, looking out at the rain, then tried to summon the energy to go for a trudge through the mud to watch My Bloody Valentine. Pete and I stood and watched them as the light rain fell from the unrelenting grey skies above. When the band shifted from the blank racket and free-form noise into the gliding melody of 'You Made Me Realise' it was as if the sun came out for a moment. That was probably the high point of the day. We never thought to be bothered about the fact they were further up the bill than us. We weren't competitive like that. The Valentines finished their set and we walked through the mud towards the backstage area and the relative comfort of the caravan. On the way through the festival ground we were laughing about the fact that people were taking shelter from the rain underneath the toilet blocks. We got back to the caravan and had just started to roll a joint when an official from the festival popped their head in and said, 'Can you be out of here in twenty minutes, please, lads. We've got another band coming in.'

We thought we were going to have the caravan for the whole night, or something.

We cleared the guitars out and stacked them in the van.

It was raining quite a lot, so we took refuge in the backstage bar where it was dry. The beer tent had been done out in ribbons and bows – it looked like it was going to be the scene for a bad wedding reception. Given that this was the height of acid house there wasn't much of a party going on. The place was filled with all sorts of people we wouldn't usually hang out with. They were sipping drinks and talking. There was no music. We found a dry spot and sat on the floor away from the crowd. Mary Mary from Gaye Bykers on Acid walked into the tent looking like everyone's idea of a good trip. 'SKIN UP, YOU BORING BASTARDS,' he screamed, laughing through his psychedelic megaphone. 'This is supposed to be a fucking party. What's wrong with you?'

He spotted us, and came striding over laughing and pointing. 'THANK GOD!' he shouted through his megaphone, even though he was quite close to us. 'SOMEBODY HAS GOT SOME DRUGS.'

'All right, man,' he said to Pete, without the benefit of his megaphone. 'How's it going? You want some acid?'

'Err, no thanks, Mary,' said Pete. 'I'm good, thanks.'

I briefly considered taking some of Mary's acid, but one look around the frankly depressing tent and out into the drizzle beyond it was enough to dissuade me.

'This is fucking boring, isn't it?' our megaphoned friend said, emphasising his point by taking up the megaphone and shouting, 'BORING!' at the assembled drinkers. He smoked the joint we'd rolled and surveyed the crowd. 'BORING BORING, BORING,' he megaphoned. 'Right. Thanks for the joint,' he said. 'I'm off.' And then he pranced off in his pink docs and his tutu with his psychedelic megaphone.

We sat there and smoked hash and didn't say very much.

It was boring.

After a while we got so bored of sitting on the floor that we had to go and find a seat. We settled in the food tent and commandeered a table, where we continued to roll joints of hash and smoke them while watching the different bands come in and eat their dinner.

We watched Michael Gira eat his dinner. He didn't look very happy.

The Sugarcubes came in and ate their dinner. They didn't look very happy either. Maybe they were unhappy because we were smoking hash. Sometimes that made other people unhappy, for some reason.

We weren't very happy either, so maybe it wasn't our fault.

After a while we just got sick of sitting in the food tent.

We went and watched New Order and, in a way, we were happy because when it was over we could go home. I don't know why we stayed, really.

That was the last show Spacemen 3 ever played.

The Monkey Grinder's Organ

The queen doesn't carry any cash either. That's why they call them royalties.
Ancient musician wisdom

The final straw had come, as final straws must, towards the end of things.

I received the royalty statement that I hoped would pay off my debts. Having already spent the cheque I was yet to open, I tore the envelope, removed the contents and quickly scanned to the bottom line. I was left quite confused by the figure I found. It said, in fairly plain figures: £0.00.

Which seemed a little on the light side to me.

There was no royalty cheque.

I looked through the accounts again.

It was a reality I did not want to accept, and so I continued turning the sheets of paper looking for the real payment figure, which I had fondly imagined might amount to slightly more than nothing.

It was a grim truth that dawned on me and, in many ways, I wished it had still been dark so that I could have pretended that what was looming out of the light was not what it appeared to be.

Perhaps, in a way, I had been doing that for quite a while. That optimism will get you every time.

There were accounts attached to the statement and, in desperation, I started going through them. They seemed a bit wonky. I'd seen accounts before, and these didn't seem to be like other accounts. I grabbed a calculator and started doing some sums. The more sums I did, the more things started

THE KEY TO THE DOOR

moving around. Apart from the fact that my royalty statement was for £0.00 which, with the benefit of experience, I
now realise is not that strange at all, it seemed that some of
the (admittedly rather sparse) lines of figures didn't add up,
even when I had totalled them up three times. I finally came
to realise that whoever drew them up must have been horribly
overworked, or something, because there were a few glaring
and obvious errors that even a half-sharp Saturday boy with a
glue habit and a hard-on should have noticed.

I made a phone call to a friend who had more experience
with this kind of thing, and arranged to show the wonky and
possibly deranged accounts to her.

'Umm,' she said, thoughtfully, after looking through the
papers for a while. 'These figures don't really add up, and they
are quite confusing.'

'I know,' I said. 'Whoever drew them up must have been up
all night doing them and maybe they accidentally forgot to pay
me. It's a simple oversight and I am only a bass player. These
things happen, you know. It's tough at the top and we have all
been working quite hard.'

'Yes,' she said. 'That is probably what happened. Have you
shown these to the rest of the band?'

'No,' I said. 'But I intend to, because it seems obvious to me
that whoever drew these up is probably in need of some help,
and I want to help them get it.'

She nodded and so did I. There had to be a simple explanation for it all, and I wanted to hear somebody make one up as
soon as possible, so that I could get back to playing the bass
and pretending that all of this wasn't even happening.

We arranged a meeting and I showed the accidental mistakes in the accounts to Pete and Jason.

'Hmmmm,' they both said, thoughtfully.

'There do seem to be quite a lot of accidental mistakes in

these hurriedly put together accounts, and there do seem to be quite a few accidental financial mistakes here and there . . . and there, as well. We should do something about it. What shall we do?'

We decided it would probably be best if we all had a meeting about it, like gentlemen, so that we could get to the bottom of the financial discrepancies immediately, and then we could all pretend it was all right and get back to doing the things we'd rather have been doing. It was agreed that we would wait for Gerald at VHF, set up a mic and a tape recorder and record the whole thing for posterity, and possible inclusion on a future album.

Pete had an urgent appointment in Coventry, so he could not attend the meeting. It was just going to be me and Jason at the showdown with the lowdown. I had all of the points fairly well covered, so it was just a matter of clearing it up and moving on.

Gerald arrived in his white Mercedes. Jason let me do most of the talking.

By the time our meeting had been adjourned, the last words on the tape were, 'Jason, I can't work with Willie, he's a troublemaker,' which seemed a bit unfair because I had only been trying to help.

Gerald had left the studio in a bit of huff and we were left with the tape.

'Hmmm,' we all said after we had listened to it. Pete and Jason went off to have a conversation about it all and then at some point it was decided that maybe Gerald was in need of a rest. He was given leave and Spacemen 3 didn't have a manager, except for the bits of business that were still to be taken care of, which were nothing to do with me, so I could just relax again.

During the conversation with Gerald down at VHF, after I had mentioned the accounting oversights and my own lack of any remuneration whatsoever, Gerald had used the phrase, 'If you pay peanuts, Willie, you get monkeys.'

I am sure, in retrospect, that this was probably an insult. Whatever. One of us got the sack and one of us left, so at least I was a monkey with some degree of self-determination, even if I didn't have any bananas.

Better Off Alone

Pete and Jason had come to a point where they were barely communicating beyond matters of essential business. The gap between them that had started to grow even before I had joined the band was becoming a chasm that neither of them were prepared to cross. Kate and Jason were spending a lot of time together, understandably, and maybe Pete resented that intrusion into the band. Pete and Jason had been thick as thieves for the last four or five years. When Jason got together with Kate, he had something else to care about that wasn't the band. Things were changing and, as they changed, the changes increased, because that is the way that change works. It wasn't all about Kate. She had simply been an inevitable catalyst in the band's demise. If it hadn't been her maybe it would have been somebody else.

Anybody who knows anything about the music business, knows that if there is any money to be made in a band, then that money comes from songwriting. That was the way it had been set up, way back when those appliance salesmen were looking for a product to use with their brand new phonograph machines that just weren't selling at all. It was as though they had invented the toaster before anyone had invented bread. It was a gun with no bullets. Welcome to the world of recorded music. Really, the people who wrote the first contracts for music recording were not immediately concerned with the wellbeing of musicians. They were concerned with money. Money was much more expensive than musicians. Musicians were always lying around in the streets – you could just pick them up and give them some gin, or something, and they would probably play. Nobody left money lying around in the street. The musicians would turn up, play the songs they were told to play, a recording would be made, and then the musicians would get their gin for the night. Those drunk musicians probably thought that the recording contract was a joke, or that recorded music was some newfangled flash in the pan that wouldn't last. Maybe they were right.

Writers and publishers, of course, got paid. In the olden days, musicians did not write songs, and if they did they had any mysterious rights stolen from under their unsuspecting noses before they even knew what they were. By the time they had sobered up and figured it out, it was too late. It was broadly accepted business practice. It was the same with the advent of radio. Musicians initially were never paid for the broadcasts of their work. They might receive a one-off flat fee and then they were given some gin and told to fuck off.

This leads to situations where, for instance, the Funk Brothers, who played on all of the Motown hits, were left almost penniless when the operation packed up and shipped out of Detroit. They weren't songwriters. Despite the fact that nobody was charting out the parts for them, and that they were coming up with unique and timeless music, their contribution wasn't considered to be songwriting. Unless someone sampled it, of course. Songwriting is the thing. If your name isn't in the brackets you are gonna get chump changed, even if you play on a recording that sells a million, or play on a song that has fourteen billion plays on some internet jukebox.

Jason and Pete understood this and they began to argue over songwriting credits. They had begun to argue over a slice of pie that was not big enough for everyone in the band to get fat on. Of course, the real nutrition was in the music, but nobody gets fat eating music. They had shared songwriting credits between themselves without question, up to the recording of *Playing with Fire*. That is where the problems started. Cracks were appearing, mistrust was growing, and into a situation that was already stressed through hard work and the pressures of increasing public success were thrown those old demons of fragile egos, fame and money. Some things are much more destructive than drugs, it seems.

These difficulties had grown, as they do when people cease to communicate and lose sight of their ultimate goals behind initially petty differences and ongoing recriminations. It can be difficult to remember what is really important sometimes. Especially in a fight.

When we went into the record company to finalise the artwork for *Playing with Fire*, Pete had swung a punch at Jason during an argument over the songwriting credits on 'Suicide'. 'Suicide' became the last Spacemen 3 song on which the two of them eventually shared writing credits. It has no words, no distinct melody, and the main riff was borrowed from The Stooges, who had probably borrowed it from somewhere else. It wasn't funny to watch the two main songwriters coming to blows, but it was kind of funny to watch the reactions of the people in the office. They had just signed a boxing match, and it was unlikely that there were going to be any obvious victors in the end.

If the band hadn't been on the brink of success they would have walked away from each other long before it got nasty, but it was getting close to payday, so they stayed together like a husband and wife team who couldn't stand the sight of each other but knew it would have cost them too much to get a divorce. Perhaps if they had gone their separate ways after *Playing with Fire* they would not have become enemies. Perhaps if nobody had ever cared about the band they would still be friends.

Bear in mind, that the little fight in the Fire Records office (and it was a little fight) happened before *Playing with Fire* had even been released. Sometime after it had been released Pete was offered a deal by Silvertone Records for a solo album. He took the deal and began work on the *Spectrum* album in VHF studios. We began spending all of our time down at VHF recording his solo album. I think he wanted to be free of Jason at this point, and maybe Jason started wanting to be free of him, but it wasn't financially practical just yet. I tried to convince Pete round this time that it might be in his best interests to try to look after the working relationship that he and Jason had. I thought they worked well together and I could see no reason why that couldn't continue, but by then it had begun to turn into a personal feud and, by God, could that band feud when it put its mind to it. Grudges. Resentment. Revenge. That full scorpion treat bag of nastiness could burst out and leave everyone in the vicinity as sticky as shit and twice as smelly in a second.

I certainly had no desire to see the band break up. That made me a hopeful idiot in some ways, because maybe the band was staying together for all the wrong reasons.

Pete and I spent more and more time down at VHF. Behind its unspectacular façade was a small reception room that led to a building inside a building; a windowless, breeze-block box, divided into two rooms, with a glass pane between them. One was a small control room, containing a sixteen-channel desk, outboard effects and a tape machine, and the other was a live recording room, big enough for a five- or six-piece band at most. It was a good basic studio but it was nothing spectacular for the time. Paul Adkins, who ran the place, was a good-natured, sober family man who also worked another full-time job beside his extracurricular activities down at the studio. He would work late into the night as the place filled up with hash smoke while some new drone monster was being worked into life and we sweated and strived for perfection – all this was long before the advent of digital editing. It was not unusual for a guitar track to take four hours to lay down, or a bassline to take an afternoon. We took our time and tried to get it right, and Paul would engineer like a trooper. I'd often look over from my beanbag and see him falling asleep at the desk as the hypnotics and the repetition took their toll and lulled him into the dreamworld, while we went for the umpteenth take on another obscure overdub. We worked for hours down there, late into the night, and the poor fucker would be dead in his seat, sometimes waking up only when the music stopped or one of us gave him a little nudge. *The Perfect Prescription* was recorded at that studio; *Playing with Fire* was finished and mixed there. The Sonic Boom *Spectrum* album was recorded and mixed there. The bulk of *Lazer Guided Melodies* was recorded there. A great deal of music came out of that little industrial unit during the course of a few long and productive years. Not bad for a little studio on an inauspicious industrial estate in a little market town in the Midlands. Not bad for a bunch of wasters.

As the *Spectrum* album was getting close to completion, Mark, Jonny and I had all contributed parts. I had a conversation with Jason. He was properly concerned about the way things were unfolding and he was understandably uncomfortable with the fact that Pete was making a solo album. Jason always played his cards pretty close to his chest and he would never give too much away. Pete had asked him to play on the album, but Jason was in two minds about it. 'What would you do?' he said. 'If you were in my position?'

I answered, more out of my own selfish desire to see the band stick together than anything else. 'Jason,' I said, 'I think you should go and play on that track and lay down the best fucking

165

guitar you can and hopefully he'll realise that the two of you still have work to do together.'

Jason, to his credit, went and played a glorious and soaring wah solo over the top of one of the tracks called 'You're the One'. It's still my favourite track on the *Spectrum* album. Sometime later, when we were playing in Spiritualized, Jason said to me, 'I really wish I had never played on that track of Pete's.'

I still believe that they were an excellent team when they were working together, and that is in no way to disparage either of their skills as solo performers. Together they shored up each other's weaknesses and complemented their respective strengths. Sonic's raw and instinctive talent for innovation and his bloody-mindedness (which could be a nightmare to work with sometimes) also made him able to take the risks he took musically and personally. He made his innate lack of traditional musicality work for him. The sheer brass neck required to play one chord for ever, and to take it as seriously as hell while you did it, was an innovation born of necessity in some ways. It was this same brass neck that drove a man who had been mocked for many of his young years for having been to a private school to write a song called 'Revolution'. Pete took a fair amount of crap off people for the school he had been sent to and expelled from. He never hung out with his mates from public school anyway. He was hanging out with us, and with all sorts of other low life too. Pete took a lot of grief from people for doing what very few people who went to Rugby School actually did, which was to mix outside of his circle. Maybe that made him a bit oversensitive sometimes. I lived in that town for years, and Pete was the only friend from Rugby School I ever made. He talked openly and bravely about drugs. People do die from the stupid illegality and the criminalisation of people with problems. Our mates had died and, even now,

I know more people from Rugby who have died of hepatitis C for want of a clean needle than ever died of an overdose. These were unwelcome truths and I still admire him for standing up and pointing them out, even though it made us few friends in our little town. It certainly earned us the suspicion of the people who didn't agree and it was an understandably unpopular viewpoint with some members of our families. It also made us few friends amongst the drug users, some of whom thought we were bringing unnecessary attention to parts of their lives they preferred to keep hidden for legal reasons.

Pete is a peculiar and difficult character in some ways, as are many of the talented people I have had the good fortune to work with over the years.

I never got into this business to make music with accountants.

Jason was a very different character. He said very little and was never an obvious risk-taker in terms of standing out from the crowd. What he did have was a natural musical gift and an unusual flair for melodic invention. Music was in him in a way that music wasn't in Pete – traditional music that is: scales and harmonies, and fluid improvisation. Pete would rarely improvise. Jason had a magpie's ear for tunes and melodies and musical ideas, as every great musician does. They hear a thing and use it and sometimes, maybe they forget where they borrowed it from. Jason could put together strings, he could orchestrate and harmonise, and he could arrange like a motherfucker. He was also a singer and songwriter of rare power and commitment. He could make you believe a song, live a song, and raise you up with the sheer power of his voice. What that voice was saying might have been altogether less interesting if it had hidden behind a desire to not be seen. His musicality, without the courage to be different, without the gall to experiment, without the controversy, and without that good old dumb one chord, might have blossomed into an inauspicious flower indeed.

Pete would be the first to admit that he is no virtuoso. Two chords: good; one chord: better, right? But he made that into a strength through good taste, a highly tuned aesthetic sensibility, and sheer force of will – but then without someone to supply the musicality would he have turned out something as beautiful as 'Walking with Jesus'? Together, they made a great team and when that team fell apart, it fell apart hard, with each member perhaps resenting the gifts in the other that they did not possess. A tragedy then, really, but not one that didn't leave some great music behind. Both of them have done great things afterwards, but sometimes I can hear a little 'if only' in some of their separate achievements.

We all lost, Gerald included, because we couldn't see just a little bit further than our own ambitions and egos. We couldn't see that we would have been stronger together, and that ultimately we might have all got more of what we wanted by compromising and staying together instead of cutting off our own feet and selling them at the market. Then again, Spacemen 3 were not known for their compromising style. People seem very interested in the idea of why that band broke up. Perhaps it is more interesting to ask why it stayed together for so long.

Listen to the lyrics of some of those later songs: 'don't ever change', 'stay with me for ever' . . . there is a longing for something even as it slips away. Perhaps especially as it slips away. That junkie's longing to stay high. A desire for things to remain as they are and to never change. To never come down. Life isn't like that, but some things are constant, and if we can only remember what they are, then maybe we can find some of that security that we feel we lack and search for in all the wrong places. In money, in drugs, in other people's opinions. In our fear.

If we had kept a better focus on the music (which was presumably the thing we all loved most anyway), and trusted each other, maybe even looked after each other a bit better, we might have been strong enough to make it through all of the surrounding bullshit. But then, maybe, the band would still be together, crapping out albums to pay the mortgage, and maybe that would have been a bigger tragedy. Sometimes it is better to fall apart gracefully.

All of the fallouts, the 'you did', 'he said', 'she said' bickering, will hopefully be remembered by very few people. Never mind how much it made such good press at the time, or served people's prurient interests in a good fight, it serves as an unflattering and strangely fitting epitaph for a great band torn apart by some unsavoury vices . . . and I'm not just talking about drugs, either. Hopefully nobody will care about any of that when they are out on some distant star, in a small town in the middle of nowhere, listening to 'Ecstasy Symphony' and it sounds like everything which nobody ever told you was true and beautiful in life. Nobody will care about who got paid and who didn't and whether or not it matters. Nobody will care about who played the bass.

Maybe nobody will care at all about anything, including the music, and that's all right too. They don't call it 'playing' for nothing, even if it is the game that might save your life and give you something worth living for.

Dependence

The recordings for the final Spacemen 3 album began almost immediately after Pete had finished his solo album. The band were still contracted to Fire Records but negotiations were beginning with a brand new record company called Dedicated. At this point, in the late eighties, the major labels had realised that the independent music scene was flourishing and they wanted a piece of it. In fact, they wanted the whole damn thing. Like they always do.

Long before 'indie' became a genre of music and a high street brand, it actually meant something. It was short for independent. Independent of the major labels, that was. The independent charts were a heady and intoxicating mixture of many different genres and styles. There was goth, industrial, grunge, metal, our floppy-haired brand of effects-heavy psychedelia, Kylie fucking Minogue, new wave, avant garde, acid house. In the light of that, it is kind of ironic that 'indie' came to represent tepid guitar bands on major labels trying to sell out stadiums. But anyway.

BMG is a corporation. It stands for Bertelsmann Music Group, which was a huge German publishing house. They could, in no way, shape, or form, legally or otherwise, be considered to be independent of what they actually were, which was a major label.

Of course, they came up with a cunning plan.

That plan involved setting up new 'cool' indie labels, using all of their major-label money and influence to increase sales and grab back the section of the market that was out of their control.

These new indie labels sprang up all over the place.

Dedicated was one of them.

The head of the label was a man called Doug D'Arcy. Doug features briefly in a film called *The Great Rock 'n' Roll Swindle*. He is shown in a clip where he appears hurt and baffled at the treatment he has received at the hands of the dastardly 'Sex Pistols', a Neolithic, post-opera rock trio who were briefly famous for shitting in trumpets. In the film, Doug says, 'I stuck my head around the studio door to say hello and they told me to fuck off.'

That's it. Doug had been in the industry for years and he was very well mannered, expensively dressed and carefully groomed. Perhaps worryingly so.

Spacemen 3 were getting bigger even as they were falling apart. 'Hypnotized' had reached number one in the indie charts and, in another of those weird flip-flops of genre-hopping that Spacemen 3 managed so adeptly, it was getting played at raves.

One of the music journalists who had come up to Rugby, and who was a fan of both acid house and Spacemen 3, had been absolutely baffled when Pete had poured scorn on the whole acid house scene. After a few good-natured questions about his previous comments in the press, Pete eventually admitted, 'I don't know much about it, really.' That old siege mentality which had sustained us against all of the crap surrounding us proved to be a problem sometimes.

Recordings for the final album began down at good old VHF, but by this point all semblance of a working relationship between Pete and Jason was over. Jason was going to work on his songs and Pete was going to work on his, and they were going to work separately. Things were getting ugly, but we still had to flog the almost dead horse of Spacemen 3 while pretending we weren't.

'Hypnotized' had come out as a single while we had been

on tour, and Pete had been livid that his song had only made the B-side. Jason had recorded the whole of 'Hypnotized' by himself, with Jonny playing drums. 'Hypnotized' was a great single, but what was good for the band didn't seem to matter any more. It had partly become a self-destructive competition.

At VHF, Pete started tracking songs and Jason started tracking songs, and I would get rough mixtapes of the work in progress and take them back to my mum's, where I would sit at the stereo with my headphones on and work out parts that might fit. I'd take those parts to Pete and Jason and they would tell me what they did and didn't like, and then they would arrange them into the songs and we would lay down the tracks. I didn't play on all the tracks on *Recurring*. The music sounded as good as ever. Although Pete and Jason were now pursuing separate visions, those visions were still somewhat coherent due to the proximity of the mutual experience that had informed them both.

I was growing frustrated with the pressures of the band and the constant arguments, and it started to weigh on me. I was growing tired of the bad feeling, and was tired of living at my mum's and having no money. I was just plain old tired. We had done a lot of work in a short time. This was the third studio album in a year and we had recently completed a big European tour. Pete and I were beginning to experience tensions in our relationship too. One time, we were sat in his room at his parents' house and he cooked up a shot and took it.

'I don't want a hit,' I said.

He looked at me in disbelief. 'Why not?'

'I just don't feel like it, man,' I replied. 'I don't want it.'

He looked annoyed. 'Why don't you want some?' he said.

'I just don't. I don't know why.'

I had never had a habit all of the time I was in the band. I couldn't afford one for a start, but, more than that, I didn't *want* a habit. It didn't look like much fun, and the drug itself was kind of boring after a while. I wasn't looking down at him for doing it. I just didn't want to do it myself. I know heroin is supposed to be instantly addictive. I know you are supposed to have no power against the all-consuming hunger of the drug, but it didn't work like that for me at the time. I suppose I was lucky. I didn't feel like I needed it.

However, I had taken a taste, and that was a taste that would prove difficult to forget. Wherever you go, the past is never far behind, whether you care to remember it or not.

Play the Fucking Hit

Being in a band is absurd at the best of times. Maybe when you are sixteen it is a great idea. Everybody wants to be in a gang then – except for the weird loners, outcasts and misfits who have spent their formative years locked away in bedrooms learning to play instruments. Their grand reward is being in a band. If they are lucky.

So get in the van, eat your crisps, and shut up.

We are going for a drive around the world.

You will see things from a distance and meet people you could love who you will never see again. You might be forced to fake the joy and the feeling that you had when you first made that hit song fifteen years ago. The memory of the dead feeling will haunt you for ever if you are lucky enough to have had something resembling a hit. A 'hit'. There is a word to conjure with. There is no time like the first time, and if you are forced to carry the memory of that first hit down the road with you like a dead love as it sustains you and sucks the life from you, then, well, what did you expect? Fucking glamour? Say hello to the pact you made with yourself and all of your stupid dreams.

The hit. Play the hit. Play the fucking hit. Nobody cares about what you are up to now. Nobody cares that you wrote it a million lives ago. Play the hit.

Play the fucking hit.

There are many reasons to stay together and there are many reasons to fall apart.

Here comes your Chinese rug.

Play the fucking hit.

Going Solo

There's something vile (and all the more vile because ridiculous) in the tendency of feeble men to make universal tragedies out of the sad comedies of their private woes.
Fernando Pessoa

The *Recurring* sessions had been continuing down at VHF and the recording for the album was almost complete. Pete and Jason had not worked together at all: their separate songs were recorded during entirely separate sessions, and the two singers were now doing everything in their power to make sure that they didn't meet. I was working with Pete on his tracks, and I was also working with Jason. Jonny and the newly drafted Mark Refoy were working with both Pete and Jason. It was obvious by this point that there was to be no reconciliation between the two songwriters. Of the two of them, perhaps Pete was the happier with the arrangement. He was perceived, by the people who were interested in those things, to be the leader and main man of Spacemen 3. Jason barely got a look-in as far as publicity was concerned, and Pete certainly wasn't doing anything to push Jason's interests, or talents, at that point.

The two sides of *Recurring* perhaps reflect where they were at regarding the oncoming split. Pete's side is joyous in many ways, filled with possibilities and hope. There were lyrical references to big cities, where everyone could be found, and to letting the good times roll. The subsequent video for 'Big City' even saw him dancing. The sight of Pete dancing was a fairly unusual one at the time. The song itself was loosely based on an old Roxy Music B-side and it is a glorious mixture of electronics and sequencers that foreshadows some of Pete's later interest in pop and obscure electronica. The closing song on his side of the album 'Set Me Free/I Got the Key' is practically a declaration of intent regarding the way he feels about the imminent demise of the band he had devoted the previous six or seven years of his life to. The song fades out with a spoken aside that declares, 'I think it's gonna end pretty soon,' followed by what appears to be a burp and a laugh. This, coming after a song in which he declares that he has the key and then sings about a desire to be set free, is not the sound of a man wracked with concern about what is to come. He sounds hugely confident. At that point he had every reason to feel that way. Between him and Jason he was, by far, in the more obviously strong position in terms of a springboard to the future. His songs on *Recurring* also deal with love. 'I Love You' is a positively rambunctious declaration of intent, but not without a trace of bitter understanding that there was nothing to be done about the inevitable end. It again returns to the idea of being set free, and after the idea of freedom is brought into the song, Pete sounds positively happy about it. The song ends with a jaunty flute solo, courtesy of Pat Fish. There are traces of bitterness and of love going wrong but the general mood is optimistic, forward-looking and even a little scornful in places.

The two halves of the album meet in the middle on 'When Tomorrow Hits', which is a cover of a song by Mudhoney, who had covered 'Revolution' in turn for a planned double A-side single. Mudhoney had changed the lyrics in 'Revolution' into a junkie's lament about the 'long uphill walk to the methadone clinic' and shoving morphine suppositories up your arse, which had gone down like a shit sandwich with Pete.

'When Tomorrow Hits' is the last Spacemen 3 track to feature both Pete and Jason and it is somehow appropriate that it never made it onto the original album. It never featured on the planned double A-side with Mudhoney either. There were fallouts and recriminations there too. At this point there were recriminations almost everywhere. This was a band, after all, that spoke beyond itself and that was ripe with synchronicities, occult meanings and hidden depths that were sometimes lost on the members themselves. The significance of some of the timings of key events in the band was completely lost on us sometimes. It had to be. If we had known, we would never have been able to play the parts.

Jason's side of *Recurring* is a much more subdued and introspective affair. It starts with the lament and eulogy of 'Feel So Sad', in which he sings about wishing for his bitterness to be taken away, as he prays to a God he maybe doesn't believe in. He sings about how sad he feels. His side of the album then progresses into a gently woozy psychedelia suffused with the idea of true love as a feeling sometimes difficult to distinguish from the effects of drugs. 'Hypnotized' is a joyful horn-driven lackadaisical boogie concerning itself with being so in love with someone that they have you under the power of hypnosis.

'Feelin' Just Fine (Head Full of Shit)' meanders beautifully through spiralling effects and countless overdubs into a submerged, warm and fuzzy wonderland of feeling all right. The lyrics, though seemingly 'druggy', are noticeably about a person rather than about any drug in particular. Jason seems to be losing himself in love on his side of the album. To the point that he sometimes sounds like he is hardly there at all, as he escapes the realities of the imminent split and the internal warfare, seeking refuge in the bliss of music. The only overtly 'drug song' on *Playing with Fire* or *Recurring* is 'Billy Whizz/Blue 1', which is the final track on Jason's side of the album and the last song on any official Spacemen 3 studio album. It is practically incoherent in its mumbled references to 'Billy Whizz' and 'Mary Anne' and it plays with imagery in ways that are hard to understand.

For a band sometimes remembered as a 'drug band' there are actually very few overt references to drugs on the last two Spacemen 3 studio albums. People never mention that. From the *Sound of Confusion* to *The Perfect Prescription* many of the songs were obvious hymns to various drug experiences, but that changed on *Playing with Fire* and it continued into *Recurring*. Love almost replaced the drugs somehow. Almost.

The two sides of *Recurring* couldn't be more different, and those differences partially clarify what were the strengths and the weaknesses of the two estranged partners. It is an album that illustrates how far they had drifted apart, musically and socially. There are echoes of the past albums in the record but *Recurring* seems like an album that openly and implicitly acknowledges the different paths which lay ahead for Pete and Jason.

I didn't enjoy the making of the album at all. The discord and the disunity were agonising. The constant bickering and the inability to come to terms for the good of the music were a source of constant frustration and disquiet. It seemed like a waste. Maybe the album would have been better if Pete and Jason had found a way to work together. Maybe music was all that mattered to me at that point, and maybe I was stupid because of it. Whatever. Who cares anyway? That's a good fucking point. Maybe, if anyone at Dedicated had listened to the album, and believed it, they might have had an inkling of what they were getting into before they signed the deal that would see them wrong-footed and out of pocket within a year.

Shortly after I had received the royalty cheque for zero pounds and zero pence from Gerald Palmer, Pete had booked himself to play his first ever solo show. It was in Rugby in the back room of the good old Imperial pub, supporting The Telescopes. Leading up to the show the situation between me and Pete had become increasingly fractious and I had reached the point where I could not see a future for myself within the band.

It wasn't that I didn't want to continue making music, I just couldn't see a way through. I suppose I was fairly well mangled, for various reasons, and in my wisdom I decided that the best way to broach the delicate subject was to first consume a delightful chemical cocktail of Sudafed and Special Brew.

Sudafed is a cold remedy that is a bit like speed; Special Brew is a brain-loosening beer of frightening strength that tastes like fermented soup dribbled out of a forgotten vending machine and strained through an unwashed sock. Street drinkers used to drink it before the government started allowing people to manufacture that shit-awful cider that costs two quid a bottle and which kills people quicker than euthanasia.

I was three cans and four pills into the evening when I appeared at the Imperial, unsuitably refreshed in preparation for the night's entertainment. I was also, if it needs to be said, thoroughly miserable. In my perilous mental state I continued to drink myself into an alternately incoherently enraged and completely morose state. I guess I don't deal with break-ups very well. Bands, people, places . . . whatever, it turns me over in ways I still don't understand nor fully have control over. By the end of Pete's set it felt like my world was coming off its axis. I was ready to break the news about leaving the band.

After that, it seemed to me, in my fit of self-loathing, that perhaps the easiest way to spare myself any further torment through music was to actually break my own hands in some irreversible way. That night, I punched many, many, things that were too hard to punch. I punched walls, doors, random bits of wood – I probably punched myself. Thankfully, I didn't punch anybody else. I didn't feel a damn thing. Eventually, I put my head through the ladies' toilet door in an effort to quieten my considerable mental confusion. Finding me with my head stuck in his toilet door, the landlord (an ex-police officer) quite rightly decided that I was not much of a good customer. He put me in a half-nelson and marched me off the premises. 'Don't fucking come back until you've sobered up!' he said, quite reasonably, as he pushed me outside and slammed the door in my face.

I continued to punch things outside until I realised that my hands were hurting quite a lot. I jumped over a wall in the garden and fell a bit further than I would have liked. I picked myself up and found the breath I had knocked out of my body, then began walking down the street blindly raging at cats, street lights and parked cars. Pete pulled up alongside me in his car. 'Do you want a lift, man?' he asked.

'Fuck off!' I unreasonably replied.

'Look. Just get in the car, man. You are gonna get arrested if you carry on like this.'

I told him to fuck off again.

After a while of his asking, I finally relented and let him do me a favour. I was too pissed to walk home, and all of the wall-punching and falling over walls had worn me out, despite the un-medicinal doses of cold remedy. I got in the car and didn't say very much at all. What was there left to say? 'Wrote for Luck' by the Happy Mondays was playing in the car. When we got closer to my mum's house, Pete said, 'You're fucking mad. Beating yourself up like that. You need help. I'm gonna tell your mum that you need to get some medical help.'

I turned to Pete, and with a vehemence he understood, said, 'If you say one word to her about any of this I will kill you. Do you fucking understand me?'

He didn't say anything. I got out of the car and walked the last fifty metres up the road under the street lights.

When I woke up in the morning I could hardly move. My hands were cut and bruised and swollen and I couldn't bend some of my fingers. I had a raging hangover and there wasn't an inch of me that didn't hurt.

I had also left the band.

Part Three

Look Ma . . .
Three Hands!

In the Trenches

*The reason why the grave-digger made music must have
been because there was none in his spade.*
Herman Melville, *Moby Dick*

It was really quite annoying. Every time the spade full of soil
got close to the top of the narrow trench, one edge of the blade
would catch on the side of the torn earth and upturn the precious cargo. I'd hack away at the clagging mud, get a good
load, lift it up, and . . . splat . . . it would fall back into the hole
I was standing in, leaving me no deeper down and just a little
more tired. I had been digging for about five hours and the
hard physical nature of the work was in no way being helped
by the workings of my own mind. I felt like fucking Sisyphus
but with less of a sense of purpose and no mountain view.

I was wondering what had gone wrong. The various scenes
and situations that had lead to my current predicament played
over and over in my mind with a maddening intensity and
with no obviously happy ending.

I'd spent a solid year recording and touring with Spacemen 3.
We'd made *Playing with Fire*, *Recurring*, *Dreamweapon*, *Live
in Europe 1989*, and the Sonic Boom *Spectrum* album. We had
completed a thirty-six date jaunt around Europe, a couple of
full tours of the UK, and we had played a few singular pres-
tigious shows. We had been on the covers of the music press,
we had been on TV. The records had received glowing reviews
from the critics and they had sold well.

I was experiencing a fair degree of cognitive dissonance as
I struggled to come to terms with the reality of my current
predicament. I had a quick look round to make sure nobody

was watching and then I started yelling into the bottom of the soggy trench: 'FUUUUUUUUUUUUUUUUUUUUUUUCK! FUCK, CUNT, FUCK, WANKER, CUNT, FUCK, CUFK-CUCFUCK . . .' It wasn't aimed at anyone in particular.

'WHAT THE FUCKING FUCK HAPPENED?' I asked my shovel.

The shovel was mute.

I stabbed it into the ground at the base of the trench and stamped a little bit too hard on the protruding edge. The pain was both satisfying and utterly futile. 'OWWWWWW-WWW,' I screamed, while hopping briefly in the mud and sending a couple of small birds into flight from a small tree. 'FUUUUUUUUUUUUCKK YOU, BIRDS!' I shouted after them as they twittered off to somewhere more peaceful. I was in the grip of a fairly incoherent rage and it was not helping the trench get any deeper. It was too much effort to be so tired and so angry at the same time, so I climbed out of the trench, stuck my narrow trenching shovel into the earth with a spiteful jab, and then sat down on a pile of earth, quite enjoying the fact that I was wet and cold. I got my cigarettes out. 'Fuck this,' I said, knowing full well that I actually couldn't fuck it at all, because it was the only job I had, and my bank manager was quite keen to get his money back.

Not only was I obviously not having sex with fabulous groupies, taking cocaine, or helping to thrill great crowds of people with powerful and innovative music, I was handing over the money I was making to the bank and couldn't even look forward to the forgetful waste of spending it all on drink and drugs at the weekend. I was in debt and I was going to have to dig my way out of it. Literally. The only problem was that as soon as that heavy and preciously loaded shovelful of soil made it to the top of the trench, and my aching muscles went for the final push over the top, a little fucking root or random protuberance would twang the edge of the spade and everything would fall back into the hole again. I briefly considered digging myself a grave and then lying in it, but I realised that I wouldn't be able to shovel the soil over myself once I was comfortably pretending to be dead. 'Fuck it,' I said, 'and fuck it again.' I flicked the butt of the cigarette into the trench with as much venom as my cold and spiteful hands could muster. I watched it burst into a pleasing shower of orange sparks and fizzle out quietly in the damp earth. Rather like my recent pop career.

It wasn't that I had expected to get rich, I just hadn't expected to get quite so poor, quite so quickly. In retrospect, I now recognise this as the ultimately self-destructive optimism that has taken me almost twenty-seven years to get rid of. That optimism was still there in the trench with me, lurking underneath my misery like a poisonous snake, but at the time I thought it was dead, and I was quite unhappy about it.

I had read all of the rock star manuals. I had read the Rolling Stones books. I had read *No One Here Gets Out Alive*. I had studied them quite carefully, and at no point had any of them offered any useful advice about working on a building site or friendly tips on how to shovel the painful shards of your own broken illusions from the bottom of a soggy trench in the Midlands. In the rain. With wet feet.

'Fuck it,' I repeated, and not for the last time in my career, as I climbed back down into the trench, retrieved the spade, and stabbed it into the earth at my feet. I'd done shitty jobs plenty of times, but I had never done a shitty job while carrying the full weight of disappointment before.

I concentrated my thoughts and heaved a good shovel of earth over the lip of the sewage trench. In the circumstances, actually getting a shovel full of earth out of the trench seemed to be a minor triumph, so I kept on doing it, and doing it, and doing it. While I did it, I learned to take pleasure in the small victories of the task at hand until, little by little, I had dug myself further out of the hole I'd found myself in, both mentally and financially. Then it was time to go home.

Six months previously I had taken a bundle of our recent press to a meeting with my bank manager. He was an affable fellow and he obviously found me a bit more entertaining than most of his clients. 'I used to read the *NME* when I was at university,' he told me, with some pride and a wink, as I handed over the three major music papers containing the recent reviews for *Playing with Fire*.

My bank manager had previously received a letter from Gerald Palmer assuring him that I would indeed be getting some monies for my musical endeavours, and that it would be a very safe assumption indeed on the part of Midland Bank, Rugby plc, that I would, at some time in the nearish future, be able to pay back the overdraft that I was trying to arrange so that I could eat and buy guitar strings while I was in Spacemen 3 – the ten quid a day I was getting for the shows being barely enough to keep me in cigarettes and ice cream. It was clear, even to these men of business and commerce, that I was a safe financial bet. Things were looking up and it was only a matter of time until these trivial financial teething problems were a thing of the past. Big things were on the horizon, but we had no idea at the time quite how big, or just how much manual labour it would involve. At least on my part.

We were renovating an old vicarage in a village outside Rugby, where a group of hippies had lived in the sixties. Rumour had it that somewhere in the grounds somebody had stashed a big bag of LSD and forgotten where it was. We knocked down walls and pulled down ceilings in that place, and I was always keeping half an eye out for that lost bag of acid. After a while of digging trenches on-site and demolishing things I was promoted to hod-carrying. My first eight hours on the hod left me concerned that I might die of exhaustion and aches and pains. The second day left me certain I was going to die. On the third day I wished I was dead. After that, the nerve endings started to die off and it all got a bit easier to deal with. Nobody wanted to hear me moaning about it, so I shut up and saved the energy for carrying bricks. Hod-carrying really focuses the mind. A three-sided box full of bricks on a stick supported on your shoulder while you run up and down ladders all day is certainly a matter for concentration. I was still smoking a bit of hash, sometimes at lunchtime, and afterwards my concentration was not always as concentrated on the matter at hand as it might have been. On one particularly nice day, after a lunchtime of buckets and bowls, I had loaded the bricks into the hod, heaved it onto my shoulder and started the climb with my one free hand gripping the ladder and the other holding onto the pole of the hod. As I reached the top I took an ill-timed moment to look out across the rich green fields to enjoy the glorious English countryside. Lost in my blissful reverie of cows and distant fields of rape, I reached for the top rung of the ladder without looking and missed it. For one heart-stopping second I was standing with both feet on the top rung of the ladder with a load of bricks on my shoulder and no supporting hand. It was one of those moments where time slows down and stretches just long enough for you to react and save your own life if you are fast enough. And lucky. I snatched out a hand and grabbed the top rung, while the adrenaline in my pumping heart told me just how close I'd come to lying at the bottom of the ladder in a pile of broken bricks and bones. I laid off the hash at lunchtimes after that.

My anguish at having completely failed as a musician was diminishing a little as I realised that life actually would go on, and that maybe I had some sort of a future beyond Spacemen 3.

It wasn't easy, but it was necessary for survival, and in many ways the absolutely exhausting physical work was helping me deal with the situation. I was so tired at the end of the day that I had no energy left for worry, regret and recrimination. I also had no money for drug-induced self-destruction, which was probably a good thing. Sometimes when I was working I used to sing Leadbelly songs to myself to get through the day. There is a song of his called 'The Gallis Pole'. I guess this refers to the gallows. The song itself is sung from the point of view of someone who is looking out from their prison cell seeing various members of their family coming to visit them. The protagonist is pleading from behind bars, asking if anyone has brought enough silver and gold to prevent his imminent execution because, in the olden days, if you were rich you were innocent enough to walk free.

I was not about to hang, but I could relate to the song in some ways. On the plus side, I was getting stronger, physically speaking, and it certainly worked as a paying gym and detox after my first proper year of rock and roll. It was not to be the only time.

You Say You Want a Revolution?

The Blitz had closed for business. There was no more Reverberation Club and no more fighting with the psychotic hicks from the surrounding villages. We drank in the charmingly named Saracens Head, which was probably a reference to the decapitation of Muslims during the Crusades, or something fucking charming from our glorious colonial history. I had learned social and economic history at school and consequently my knowledge of historical events was limited to the broad and neatly ploughed field of the Industrial Revolution. I knew who made the seed drill, I knew who had invented the water-powered conger eel defenestrater in 1849, and I knew very little about revolution. There had been footnotes during our history lessons concerning the Diggers, the Levellers and the Luddites, but . . . the end always seemed to be the same. You lose, they cut your balls off in front of a cheering crowd in the marketplace, and then someone digs you up after you are dead and sticks your head on a big spike while the peasants piss on your body. What's cool about that?

When we used to walk into the Saracens Head some local wag would always play 'Revolution' by the Beatles on the jukebox. John Lennon's sarcastic voice would mock us as we stood at the bar trying to hold on to whatever dignity there was left in being a small-town rock star with no money. 'You *say* you want a revolution,' John Lennon's voice would snark from the stereo, and people would laugh behind my back.

We had played the song 'Revolution' a lot of times but had perhaps never tried to imagine what a *real* revolution might entail. Death? A party? I really didn't know, and these being pre-internet times it was difficult to find out. I went to the library to try to do a little research, but most of the books relating to the subject had been silently removed by Margaret Thatcher's silent librarian storm troopers. I drank my lager and tried to imagine where this situation actually left me in terms of being cool.

We didn't really want a revolution, we just wanted to live our largely self-harming lives in peace and not get arrested. I sipped my lager. The absurdity of my own situation was not lost on me. We had been defeated and to pretend otherwise was to indulge in the posturing of the ponce. Maybe that was better than nothing. We had absorbed all of the counterculture sixties rebellion stuff as a reference point. Very little of that had been concerned with overthrowing the state in any meaningful way. Those people just wanted to live a different life, and they were subsequently beaten with sticks and imprisoned on ridiculous marijuana charges. Check out the story of the Thirteenth Floor Elevators. Hounded, maligned, imprisoned and fried for daring to dabble in Eastern mysticism and for entertaining the idea that maybe there were ways of looking at the world that didn't involve burning in eternal hellfire for masturbating or smoking a joint.

I liked the MC5, but even they had fallen short of *actual* revolution, and it was piss-easy to get guns in America, where shooting people was considered to be a socially acceptable way of settling your differences. Britain was different. We just destroyed ourselves with pollution, cultural atavism and hopelessly outdated hierarchies. Sometimes we just glassed each other when we were drunk. Sure, during the eighties Handsworth and Brixton had burned, there had been riots, there had been the miners' strike. A political war had been waged in Britain and it had been won before most of the losers had realised it was even being fought. We were now at the beginning of a new decade. People were getting mashed in fields on ecstasy, but even that was in the process of being made illegal. We had lost and we weren't even allowed to drown our sorrows in any way we saw fit.

Perhaps stupidity was the only way out, and all of our talk of revolution had merely been an intellectual conceit and a teenage pipe dream. Jesus and revolution had both been used as convenient vehicles for emotion rather than actual concepts in themselves. But then, to even float the ideas of rebellion and an honest religion with conviction in our time required a suspension of belief that came at the price of a little absurdity.

We weren't alone in playing with ideas and wearing the costumes of rebellion.

There had never been street fighting men in the Rolling Stones – they had all been quick to live the life of the landed gentry and be absorbed into the upper echelons of the class system. Nobody could blame them, unless perhaps that person was accidentally exposed to one of the lacklustre albums the band had made after it irretrievably lost parts of its soul. It seemed that the devil didn't actually come down to the crossroads at midnight and buy your soul with one convenient blood-signed document. Losing it was actually an incremental process of attrition through luxury, decadence and things that were nicer than getting shot. The road to hell was paved not with good intentions but with resigned sighs and a pleasant buffet. Let's look at Mick Jagger and David Bowie singing 'Dancing in the Street' at Live Aid. When those two flew in from Mustique on a private jet to sing about having a boogie with the great unwashed it looked like a charity photo opportunity or an invitation to shake a leg at the Conservative Party conference after a couple of Pimm's. Fuck that. Everyone was scared of revolution, but perhaps tepid capitulation was worse. Have you ever heard 'Let's Work'?

What's in a Name?

'We need a name for the band,' Jason had announced. Kate was sitting beside him smiling. Jonny, Mark and I were sitting in their flat. We were all a few drinks into the evening. 'What we are going to do is, everyone is going to write their ideas on a piece of paper, we'll put them in box and then I will look through them later and decide which one to choose. If any of them are any good, of course,' he said and then he laughed.

It seemed like fun and we did need a name.

The initial Spiritualized rehearsals had taken place in an old school building in Rugby and they had gone well. We had played long and rambling versions of some of the Spacemen 3 songs that had never gotten an airing live, and we were working up a completely new set. Some of the songs that would eventually become *Lazer Guided Melodies* had been written live in the back room of the Imperial. The music was sounding good, and it was time to take it out on the road. The public perception back in the days of Spacemen 3 had been that Sonic Boom was the leader of the band and that the rest of us were just along for the ride; Jason had never been great at pushing himself forward in interviews and, despite being the singer, he had been content to rest in Sonic's shadow in some ways. Subsequently, when Spiritualized started, we were viewed as Sonic's backing band who were having a little go at being in a band by themselves. We had fallen back in the popularity stakes as far as the public was concerned and we were now in the unenviable position of having to prove ourselves again.

We were a new band, with a new sound and we were very

different to the live blitzkrieg of Spacemen 3. Here were songs about love, wrapped in gentle, meandering psychedelia; gone was the revolution and the steamroller of yore. We had yet to release an album and, well, we weren't Spacemen 3. Brands mean a lot to people and we had effectively put ourselves in a position where we were playing to less than half of the crowd we would have been playing to six months previously. We had work to do.

Spiritualized was fun at the start. It was a much looser entity musically and we had free reign to express ourselves within that. Having been out touring and making records constantly for the last year and half, we knew how we worked. Certainly myself and Jonny had developed an almost telepathic ability to communicate rhythmically; all of us had developed that subconscious instinct common to all good bands, wherein we could predict each other's musical intentions and react as one to subtle cues within the sound, even as we were making it.

There was no more of the bad atmosphere that had come to dominate Spacemen 3. Pete's rigid and strict laws of simplicity and his insistence on extremely tight arrangements had given way to something more relaxed, and in that freedom there was a certain joy. Having said that, I hear many bands that attempt to recreate the sound of Spacemen 3, and it seems to me that the element many of them lack is the discipline and the accuracy that made it so direct. We inevitably carried much of Pete's aesthetic over into Spiritualized but, at the same time, we found the space to improvise around it and attempt more of the quieter and nuanced songs from the later albums in a live setting. Without the elements of destructive competition and control between Pete and himself, Jason was freed into a new live creativity. It was a completely new thing and although it was good to be playing different songs, initially it won us few friends. The first Spiritualized show was in Glasgow. We travelled up the M6 towards Scotland and stopped at my dad's village on the way. He lived in Gosforth, a small place close to the nuclear reprocessing facility at Sellafield in Cumbria.

We had woken up hungover at the old man's place and then gone for a quick look around the Sellafield visitors' centre, leaving the gift shop with badges and t-shirts proclaiming the legend, 'I've been to Sellafield.'

From there we had driven up to Glasgow and arrived at the cheap bed and breakfast mid-afternoon on the day of the show. We checked in and got ready to play the first ever Spiritualized show.

We weren't very rock and roll – or at least we didn't sound obviously rock and roll. We didn't really care. We played a mixture of Jason's songs from the old Spacemen 3 albums and some new Spiritualized songs that nobody had ever heard before. The audience was unconvinced. We were quiet and delicate and the amateur efforts of our new soundman hadn't helped us to get the dynamics of the music over at all. A friend of ours called Neal Bradshaw was working as soundman and tour manager. Neal had never done sound for a band in his life but had somehow managed to talk his way into the job. At one point during the set, somebody in the crowd called out, 'I should have brought my granny.' Flying feedback and screaming guitars this wasn't.

After the show a young Glaswegian woman came up to me and introduced herself. 'My mate really wants to fuck you,' she said smiling and pointing over her shoulder at her friend who was waiting by the bar.

'Ah, that's, ah, very nice of you to say so . . . for her, and everything, but I'm a bit busy at the moment and, ah . . . maybe I'll be out tomorrow night,' I said.

I had never been approached so boldly by someone who

wanted to have sex with me because I was in a band. Lorna was not to be so easily deterred. She directed her attentions to Jonny and dragged him off for a night of passion somewhere.

We had a day off the next day and I decided to go out and drink with Jonny. We went to the same place we had played the night before. Lorna and her mate were standing by the bar. We went and had a few drinks with them and after another couple we were all sat in a darkened corner. Lorna had one hand on my crotch and one foot in Jonny's, who was sitting beside her as well. I guess she had a thing for the rhythm section. She went off to get another pint of heavy, and I turned to Jonny and said, 'Jonny, man, do me a favour and leave us alone, will you?'

'Fair enough,' he said, and made his excuses when Lorna got back from the bar. Eventually, Lorna and I staggered back to the hotel and crept into the room that I was sharing with Mark Refoy, who was asleep on one of the single beds. After a while of fumbling and drunken groping, Lorna whispered something in my ear about condoms. I had no condoms.

'Hold on a second,' I whispered, and left the room.

I knocked as quietly as I could on Jonny's door and he answered the door with a smile on his face. 'How you getting on, man?' he said with a leer and a laugh.

'Jonny, I need a condom . . . have you got any?'

He laughed. 'Yeah,' he said. 'But I've only got banana ones.'

'OK. Give it to me, man,' I said.

I took the suspiciously yellow-looking condom back to the room, snuck past the sleeping figure of Mark, and returned to the warm arms of Lorna.

'Did you get one?' she whispered.

'Yep,' I said, and started to peel the packet off.

As the bright yellow latex was revealed the room began to smell strongly of chemical bananas.

'Fucking hell,' she said. 'Whit's wrong wie ye? Fucking bananas . . . the pair o' ye.'

And then we fucked on the bed as quietly as we could because we didn't want to wake Mark up.

Twice-Dead Pork (in Treacle Sauce)

The piece of pig had been cooked beyond the limits of endurance and lay in the puddle of congealing treacle sauce as though it was undergoing some advanced form of culinary rigor mortis. It is said that we should not speak ill of the dead, so how then should we speak of the ill-cooked dead? This was a pig that had died twice, the first time at the hands of a slaughterman, and the second time of embarrassment at the indignities it had been forced to endure on the plate. The curled edges of the cutlets stood proud of their unctuous brown shroud as though the ghost of the pig was urging its insulted earthly remains to sprout wings and fly away. I was in agreement with the imaginary voice of the ghost pig, in that I too was hoping it would fly out of the window of its own accord, thus saving me the unavoidable task of eating it. I had been invited round to Kate and Jason's to have dinner and had been promised a special dish. Kate was going to prepare pork in treacle sauce. I had put my initial gag reflex down to my own unsophisticated taste buds, existing as I was on Chinese takeaways, chips and packets of toxic dust baked by robots on industrial estates and fobbed off on the poor as a viable source of nutrition. I had looked forward to the dinner until I was actually faced with it, and now I was feeling like someone stuck on a blind date with an ugly psychopath who smelled of BO and treacle. Even to write this makes me feel as ungrateful as that poor piece of pig looked.

'Yummy,' I lied, 'that smells good.'

Jason was also making encouraging noises about the food.

'Thanks, Kate,' we both said. 'Treacle sauce, eh? Wow.'

He was wearing a t-shirt that said 'drugs not jobs' and I briefly imagined it with the last word replaced by 'dinner'.

Kate was aware that perhaps we were not being completely honest in our enthusiasm and was watching us both for any noticeable signs of displeasure at her brave attempts to broaden our cultural horizons. An air of suspicion and fake enthusiasm mingled with the smell of cooked pig and treacle. None of it was helping any of us to begin chewing the strange meal. It was a dinner that cried out for an immediate end to experimentation on animals and not just while they were alive.

It would be fair of me to say, at this point, that Kate was an ambitious cook. I had known her since I had been a callow youth riding my BMX around the suburban streets of Rugby, trying to learn tricks to impress myself and my friends. She had been going out with my best mate's older brother, and we had lusted after her in that desperate and hopeless way that teenage virgin boys know so well. The idea of sex was obviously high on our agenda, but the actual chance of getting any, with anybody, was as likely as a package holiday to Narnia. Kate and I were friends, and I no longer lusted after her. She was way out of my league anyway, and I had accepted it. I was a bass player, after all.

Kate had replaced Steve Evans as the keyboard player in the band. I was fine with that, despite the fact that she couldn't really play and had never been in a band before. It didn't really matter. The keyboards were simple and Jason told her what notes to play. Why not, right? We were one big happy family.

I lived in the flat next door to Kate and Jason, above the plumber's on the corner of Hunter Street and Cambridge Street in Rugby. Their flat looked fairly unassuming from the outside, except for the psychedelic dummy in the window and the black and white blobs on the wallpaper, which were like a toned-down version of Oxford Street weirdness and which were nowhere near visible enough to scare any timid souls who might look up from the shop window display of pipes, toilets and strangely coloured baths.

Jason and Kate had helped me organise the move, partly because it suited all of us to have someone we knew living next door, complaining neighbours being a perennial problem for all musicians. It was the first place I ever rented by myself and I set about the decoration with peculiar zeal. I contacted my friend Rowley Ford, knowing he had experience with painting and decorating. I had once seen him walking amongst the well behaved shoppers in the town centre, wearing a jacket that had some crude words painted on the back in white decorator's emulsion. The words said 'I AM A CUNT' in bold and primitive letters. I don't think he had painted it himself but it was certainly a brave fashion statement. Rowley wasn't a cunt, of course, Rowley was a sharp-witted fool who laughed at himself, you, that guy who had just got out of prison for stabbing someone, and pretty much every figure of authority our small town had. He was a good dancer too, which is pretty useful for dodging punches and stuff that people throw at you when you won't shut the fuck up. A moving target is always harder to hit, and Rowley rarely stood still: 'Every day I get up and I take my medication and I spend the rest of the day waiting for it to wear off.' That was how he had described his life under the influence of enough Dexedrine to keep a roomful of narcoleptics bright-eyed and bushy-tailed for a week. In the morning he would look like a grey deflated balloon as he waited for his prescription to begin its work, and then, as the chemicals took hold, he would become very lively and inflated indeed, often to the point where somebody would punch him – because Rowley associated with some people who would quite happily punch you in the face rather than ask you to be quiet.

I decided that Rowley's medication would suit me just fine

for the purposes of painting and decorating. It wasn't like I was doing drugs for fun. I wanted to get the work done. I asked him for a single dose of his magical green 'jollop'.

After completely ignoring all of his warnings about the strength of his medicine, I consumed the peculiar-tasting liquid with my morning coffee before heading out to the paint shop to choose my colours. I suppose that I was in the grip of a fully fledged Dexedrine typhoon by the time I got to the shop. 'I'll take that one, that one, that one, and that one,' I said, with unnatural enthusiasm, indecent haste, and with little actual concern for the long-term aesthetic implications of my choices.

I picked the colours that looked most exciting.

Waking up in the morning, feeling slightly less enthusiastic about everything, I walked into my newly decorated front room. There was a bright green wall. There was a weird orangey-salmon wall. There was a big blue stripe and there was a huge purple wall. It had seemed like a very good idea at the time, and the work had certainly been done quickly. I was renting out a room from Natty at the time. He came downstairs, took one look at my hasty paint job and burst out laughing. 'It's pretty bright,' he said, and then he laughed again.

I lay on the couch groaning.

Natty had also set his considerable talents to work in the house. He had drawn a huge picture of Mickey Mouse on the woodchip wallpaper in the brutally unheated bathroom of our flat. Our bathroom was a fairly hostile environment in many ways – even Mickey Mouse looked like he could feel the non-relaxing chill. Mickey looked distraught. Eyeballs on stalks were growing out of the ground and they had wrapped themselves around his spindly limbs. Mickey was struggling to get free and escape the confines of the eyeball stalks and the bathroom wall, which was understandable because the bathroom was horrible, especially in winter when long icicles would form at the dripping taps, making bathing a springtime possibility rather than a day-to-day necessity. Over the course of a couple of years, black patches of mould broke through the wallpaper into Mickey's eyeball, and the paper began to peel away in sheets. Mickey's disturbing world disintegrated around his big round ears.

That piece of work was never recorded for posterity. Much of Natty's art went the same way. Many a psychedelic scene was painted on friends' rented walls to be eventually stripped away in horror by new inhabitants eager to replace it with something more soothing and pastel-hued. Probably something with fewer spaceships and eyeballs. There wasn't much of an audience for Natty's work in our hometown. There had been an exhibition of local painters at the town library where Natty had displayed some of his work. Incongruously sandwiched between oil paintings of foxes and pretty watercolour canal-side scenes was a terrifying canvas that had been burnt, cut and generally abused in all sorts of socially unacceptable ways. It featured a ghostly skull face and was titled *Syphilis*.

It was pretty funny, if you had the right sense of humour. I don't know what happened to *Syphilis*. Natty probably gave it to someone. He gave most of his art away.

He also painted a picture using some of the leftover paint from my ill-advised Dexedrine shopping expedition. Painted on a scavenged hairdressers' sign was the face of some psychedelic *Mona Lisa* bursting out of a salmon pink and lime green blob world. In our flat it looked as though it was manifesting through the weirdly coloured wall it had been hung on. It's all about context sometimes, and the picture did tie the room together a bit. Natty was playing occasional percussion in Spiritualized and he had also designed and drawn the devil and the angel that became the trademark for the band on its early releases.

The band were rehearsing in Jason's spare room, which was right next to our kitchen. Jonny Mattock and Mark Refoy were frequent visitors, and we were all hanging out together like the fucking Monkees, or something. We were also drinking together. In the early days of Spiritualized we would get forty-eight cans of Red Stripe on the rider for every show. There were five of us in the band, and Kate didn't really drink. That is twelve large cans each. During one show at the Pink Toothbrush in Rayleigh, Essex, I had been mystified by a low and irregular knocking sound that was audible as we played. I had checked my own equipment and the monitors until, looking around the stage, I realised it was the sound of Jason's head gently striking the microphone as he was lulled into a pissed mid-song nod by the throbbing tremolos and the beer.

There were very few illegal drugs around during the making of the first Spiritualized album. I was taking LSD fairly frequently, sometimes even onstage, and smoking a bit of hash, but Spiritualized, in the beginning, were not really a druggy band at all, unless you included alcohol. We drank a lot. Perhaps in the light of this it should come as no surprise that some wit at the record company had suggested that the album be called *Lager Guided Melodies*.

Those Lights are Cold and Pretty and Nothing Like My Love

Spiritualized had a show to play in Blackpool. The guy who was driving was called Steve. He was Gerald's right-hand man. Despite the fact that I had been instrumental in getting Gerald the break he so dearly needed with regards to Spacemen 3, Jason had taken him on as a manager for Spiritualized without telling me. I was kind of shocked, but he assured me it was only in the interim and that Gerald was the man to help the band get into a good position. There was nobody else to do the job. That news worried me a bit. I just kept playing. What else could I do? It had already been arranged. Jason had assured me that things were going to be different in Spiritualized. We were going to be a democratic band and everybody would get a say. We were all going to get an equal cut of the money we were getting for *Lazer Guided Melodies* and it was OK that I was going into a little debt again (to pay for my time making the record and touring) because the inevitable pay cheque was just around the corner. We even got a pay rise for the live performances. We were getting paid fifteen pounds per show now, so things were really looking up.

The band were all sitting in Jason and Kate's flat waiting for the van, and it was getting later and later. It is a good drive up to Blackpool from Rugby, and Gerald's apprentice was late. Steve was around our age, but even though he hung around with us sometimes and even did some of the things we did, he was never our friend. He was Gerald's right-hand man. He probably knew that even when we forgot.

When he arrived, he was an hour late and it made me kind

of angry. One hour late meant we might miss our soundcheck, and sounding good was fairly important to the band. He walked into the flat smiling and said he was sorry he was late.

'Why are you late?'I said.

'I'm just a bit late,' he answered, not looking particularly sorry.

'It's not fucking good enough, Steve. We've been waiting an hour for you, it's a long drive, and we'll probably miss sound-check now,' I said, which were all fair points. If your driver's late without a solid-gold excuse, sack your driver. There are enough random variables and flaky personalities involved in any band, at any given time, without bringing yourself the unnecessary stress of a flaky driver.

'What's it got to do with you?' said Steve, instantly on guard and defensive.

'I'm in the fucking band, Steve, and I want us to get there on time. That's what it's got to do with me. It's not fucking good enough, mate.'

'You're a fool, Willie,' he said. 'I don't take orders from you. You're a fool.'

'Steve, you are late and you don't have a good reason for it. Fuck you.'

He laughed and said again, 'You are a fool, Willie.'

He was probably right.

We loaded the equipment into the van and set off up the M6 towards Blackpool. It was a bone-cold day and we were soon shivering in the weirdly small van. The vans we rented were never big, there was never much room to stretch out and get comfortable – but this one was a step in miniaturisation too far for people of our size. I was sitting in my usual position by the large sliding door, which gave me a chance to stretch out a little and rest my head on the endlessly vibrating window. I always slept in the van. The ability to do so was my greatest gift as a working musician. Sleeping is cheap and it is not boring.

In this particular van sleeping was not proving to be a viable option. The ceiling was low and started curving into the walls very early, which meant it was impossible for anyone fairly tall to sit next to the windows and remain comfortably upright. We laughed about that for a while, until it became apparent that the heating system didn't actually heat the back of the van very well, and that the door didn't shut properly. This meant that the back of the van was quite cold and the sub-zero motorway air was making its way into the vehicle and doing a little dance around our extremities in ways that were not entirely pleasing. Sitting on your arse in a van for three hours is not the best way to keep warm. We laughed about it, until it became too uncomfortable to laugh about it any more, and then we just shut up and gritted our chattering teeth as the long hours crawled by and we made our way towards the Riviera of the North.

By the time we saw the gaudy lights of Blackpool, we weren't even thinking about alcohol. We wanted cocoa and a fire.

Blackpool, a popular holiday destination in the north of England, is famous for its 'pleasure beach', illuminations, kiss-me-quick hats, and for selling rock and candyfloss. Seaside rock, that scourge of dentistry and nice smiles, is sugar in stick form, sold in a million colours and flavours. Sometimes it is shaped like a massive red dummy or a walking stick. Children are taken there to watch the sub-psychedelic lightshows and to be filled with sugar until they reach the point of delirium. As a ten-year-old, the Blackpool illuminations looked pretty fucking trippy after five or six sticks of pure sucrose mind-warp and a chemist's arsenal of additives and dayglow E-numbers. We had basically been introduced to drugs as children. Sugar works on the same receptors in the brain as cocaine. I didn't make that up. Science did.

As we drove along the main promenade underneath the neon Rudolphs and the leering Santas, it seemed that the very lights themselves held the promise of the warmth we lacked. There was a shooting star flashing a rainbow trail and a train of cows gurning and flickering at epileptic frequencies. It all looked fairly jolly and joyous. Perhaps everything was going to be all right as soon as we ate some rock and raised our core temperatures above imminent hypothermia. We huddled around a lit cigarette in the back of the van and oohed and aahed the last of our bodily warmth out and the cold clouds of our breath were illuminated by the colours shining through the van window.

We found the venue, parked up and gratefully opened the partially shut door to step out into the wintry Blackpool night. It was only slightly colder outside than it had been in the van. A large man was standing outside of the venue. He was wearing a black suit and white shirt that marked him out as member of security. 'Are you the band?' he said.

'Ye-ye-ye yeah,' we managed to say through chattering teeth.

'Follow me,' he said, as he turned and entered the brightly lit doorway behind him and began walking down the stairs beyond it. We practically ran after him, eager for warmth, delirious at the prospect of not being cold any more. As we followed the appropriately penguin-suited bouncer down into the bowels of the club, we were quite happy. We had been happy for about twenty seconds when we arrived in the large basement area that was the venue for the night's performance. It was as cold as the van. It was the coldest venue I have ever had the misfortune to be cold in. We looked at each other in disbelief. There may have been some nervous laughter.

'Err, it's cold, isn't it?' somebody said, with a hopeful smile.

'Yeah, sorry about that,' the bouncer replied. 'It warms up when it's full.'

He didn't seem very worried about the fact that we thought we were freezing to death.

'There's some tea-making stuff through here if you want a hot drink.'

He kept walking and we followed him with a hope that was increasingly born of desperation. We arrived in a dirty half-kitchen containing four chipped cups and a bowl full of hard damp sugar.

'There is no kettle, I'm afraid, but you can use that tap for hot water. It's quite hot.' He pointed at the hot water tap. He was not smiling. 'All right, I'll leave you to it, then,' he said, with a smile. 'The dressing room is over there behind the stage and your lager is inside.'

With that, he turned around and walked off, leaving us exchanging worried and disappointed glances.

'What the fuck? I'm not drinking tea made with tepid water from the attic of this shithole. I'll get Legionnaires' disease,' someone said.

'. . . And it could be fatal combined with pneumonia,' cracked another half-chilled wag. 'Let's get the gear in.'

We were there to perform, after all.

We dragged all of the stuff out of the van, set it all up on the stage and did the soundcheck. Soundchecks are always boring. Nobody ever said, 'Wow, what a *fun* soundcheck.' A good soundcheck is one that is not completely agonising and that leaves you half-hoping you might be able to hear something approaching music when you're onstage later in front of an adoring crowd. If it sounds good at soundcheck it normally sounds shit later so, after a while, even the good soundchecks only seem like horribly optimistic precursors for later despair.

At least moving around and carrying things had warmed us up for a few precious moments. We went into the dressing room and tried to remember why we bothered. We tried to drink lager. The lager was freezing cold even though there wasn't a fridge. Sitting in the dressing room was like sitting in a fridge, except there was nothing to eat. It was like sitting in a fridge with forty-eight cans of lager and five people moaning about how cold it was. It was like sitting in the van had been earlier, but now we had cold lager.

After a while, we gave up, and went off to sit in a pub until it was time to play. It didn't matter that some of us were spending money we didn't have. It was warm, and that warmth felt like the breath of heaven. We sat around the table eating crisps and rubbing the feeling back into our hands as we all cracked jokes about how cold we had been. Sadly, we still had to go back to the polar dungeon and play the show. We grumbled out into the street again, hoping that there might be enough paying customers to warm the venue.

About forty people showed up, and by the time we took the stage our hands and feet were freezing again. It is quite hard to play the guitar when your hands are cold. We shivered through the first few songs, and the audience clapped and danced around a bit, probably in an effort to keep warm themselves. They looked cold. I felt sorry for them but maybe not quite as sorry as I felt for myself.

The next song started. It was a gentle song from *Playing with Fire*. 'It's so hot and I ain't got a lot,' Jason sang in a tremulous and plaintive voice. We arrived at the chorus.

'LOOORD ittt's SOOOOOOOOOO hot.'

I was laughing so hard by this point that I could hardly play the bass. I caught Kate's eye as she was playing the keyboard and she started laughing too. By the end of the song I had tears in my eyes and they were not there because I was sad.

We finished the set, packed up the gear, loaded it and fucked off as quickly as we could. We sat in the van and steeled ourselves for the crick-necked, draughty hours of motorway

winter wonderland that lay ahead of us. I had heard that a
sense of warmth can sometimes be a sign of impending death
by hypothermia, and I awaited the first signs with increasing
hope. We hadn't even been able to drink enough of the free
cold lager to get drunk. It was like God hated us. When we got
back to Rugby we all went into my flat for a cup of tea. I went
upstairs and got duvets and blankets and everybody wrapped
themselves in whatever was clean enough to bear, while we
fought for proximity at the measly bars of the gas fire. People
began to speak for the first time in about two hours.

'That was fucking horrible,' someone said.

We were all shivering and our teeth were still chattering. I
put on a record and we stared into space as the feeling gradually returned to our extremities.

Playing the Bass with Three Left Hands

On one occasion we were due to play at Leeds Warehouse, a rave club that on a good night at full capacity would have held around three hundred sweaty ravers. We were not expecting to play to an audience of three hundred.

At the time I was quite partial to LSD, and sometimes I was even partial to taking it before a performance. On this particular night, I had eaten a small yellow microdot shortly after soundcheck. By recounting this tale to you, I am in no way recommending that you take LSD before a show . . . or even at all. I am simply telling you what happened, and due to my unusual research in this largely uncharted field I can confirm that should you ever find yourself onstage playing the bass guitar with three left hands, it is usually the one in the middle that is the real one. The other two are probably phantoms. Also, should you encounter any fireballs emanating from the lightshow during the concert, it is probably best to try to avoid them, even though they may not be real in the traditional sense of the word. Nobody wants to be hit by real or imaginary fireballs while trying to negotiate a tricky descent through the octaves.

The acid had just begun to warm itself through my glittering receptors when I was approached by Jason. The club was pretty empty and everything was in place for the imminent performance.

'Did you give Dave some acid?' Jason asked me, with a searching look.

'Why would I give Dave acid?' I replied.

Dave was our guitar tech. It would have been foolhardy to give him LSD before a show, especially as he didn't usually take the stuff at all. He was from the Scottish Highlands and was built like a man who could pull a caber up by the roots and toss it a good distance without too much effort. He was also a thoroughly kind and good-hearted fellow, which was just as well, because if he had been a complete cunt there wasn't much that fewer than three people could have done about it.

'He's acting very strangely,' said Jason. 'Come and have a look.'

At this point, the irony may not be lost on you that Jason was asking me, a person increasingly under the influence of LSD, to judge the behaviour of someone who was acting strangely, to see if they might have taken LSD. Funny old world, isn't it?

I never told the rest of the band when I was tripping onstage because I didn't want to worry them, and they never seemed any the wiser. They knew I took it sometimes, they just never knew when, or maybe I just thought they didn't.

Anyhow, we walked across the largely empty club and looked out onto the dance floor. Usually at this point in the evening Dave would have been up onstage, carefully attending to business and making sure that nobody interfered with our equipment. He would have been checking the intonation on the guitars, changing strings that weren't broken, even polishing our beloved instruments in an effort to help us look professional. We had played more than a few shows with Dave and the man had, so far, proved himself to be a miracle of efficiency and unusual diligence.

On this particular evening, Dave was not up onstage making sure everything was in order, protecting the sacred space of the stage. Dave was not even having a cup of coffee and a sandwich. Dave was performing a weird and fairly intimidating war dance around three terrified indie kids who had, perhaps unwisely, decided to sit in a twee campsite they had made in the middle of an otherwise unoccupied dance floor. They were sitting cross-legged on a little rug they had brought with them, eating some homemade sandwiches.

I felt the acid come into sharper focus. The lights bulged and a strange tendril of fear crept into my heart. 'That is weird,' I said. Obviously, I was not referring to the people eating sandwiches.

'Shall we go and talk to him?' said Jason.

'Yes,' I said, and then we both stood there for quite a bit longer as we wondered how to best approach Dave, who was grimacing and twirling in the depths of his strange and frightening Highland haka. He prowled around the three huddled audience members like a stripe-less tiger, sweating and glaring and occasionally cracking a huge and deranged smile at them, presumably to let them know they were not in any imminent danger. It was pretty impressive.

Jason and I made our way across the dance floor towards Dave, who turned and acknowledged our presence with a deep and frightening stare that contained no flicker of recognition or familiarity.

'All right, Dave?' I ventured hopefully, gazing into the deep abyss of his peculiar eyes. 'Everything OK, is it?'

'Aye!' he said emphatically, as he returned to the dance, stamping, grunting, and shouting at things only he could see.

'Do you think anyone else gave him any acid?' Jason said.

'Maybe he's drunk?' I said.

'That's not the only thing that's weird. Come and have a look at this,' Jason said.

I followed him across the dance floor and we both climbed the stairs to the stage. Half of my third eye was still warily observing Dave on the dance floor.

Jason looked down at the floor of the stage. He was not gazing at his shoes. 'Look at that,' he said.

I looked at that.

There was a lot of that to look at.

Normally, Dave would have put several neat crosses of gaffer tape on the stage, indicating the places that we were to stand so that the stage lights would hit us in a pleasing way.

For some inexplicable reason Dave, in the grip of his fever, had been inspired to get a bit artistic. Instead of his usual boring but useful crosses, he had gaffer-taped weird hieroglyphs and magical symbols of unknown and indecipherable origin and meaning across every blank space on the stage. They looked alien . . . or Pictish . . . or demonic, or like the gaffer-taped scribblings of a particularly determined and demented child. It was hard for me to tell at this point because the adrenaline had kicked the acid in to such a degree that I felt the need to have a little sit down somewhere less weird and quite a bit further away from Dave and his gaffer-taped art from another dimension.

'Hmm,' we both said.

'What the fuck is up with him?' asked Jason.

'I have no idea, man,' I replied. 'I haven't given him anything, and I am pretty sure nobody else has. Maybe we should just wait and see if it wears off? Whatever it is. He seems harmless enough.'

'Yeah,' said Jason, looking down at the peculiar symbols on the stage. 'What else can we do, I suppose?'

I knew what I was gonna do. I was going to go and sit outside under a tree, or a big tractor, or something.

'All right man, see you in a bit,' I said, exiting stage left and warily passing our dervish on the dance floor, who was showing signs of neither normality nor fatigue despite his ongoing discophonic exertions.

I needed to find a tractor fast. There were no tractors outside – no trees either. Sadly, this was Leeds, so all of the posh people had stolen the trees and taken them to York. I was going to have to settle for a beer and a soothing sit down in the street instead. I would imagine my own damn tree.

'Aum,' I said, settling in to the great breath of the universe. 'Aum,' I said, centring my being and bringing my energy down from my overactive crown chakra. 'Aum,' I said, with placid determination, as someone poked me and a voice from the universe said, 'Why did Spacemen 3 split up, then?'

I tried to focus on the real reasons, and the reasons I was prepared to offer as an explanation. 'Do you want to know the real reason?' I said, seriously, earnestly, and with peculiar intensity. 'You can never, ever, tell anybody else.'

'OK,' my new friend said.

'I am trying to imagine a tree, our guitar tech has gone bananas, and I am on LSD. Please fuck off,' I said, kindly.

He seemed to accept this as a perfectly believable reason for the demise of our previous band.

'OK,' he said, and fucked off.

Gradually, I managed to rein in the skittish horses of my mind and settle into some sort of vaguely stable equilibrium. I was not new to this, and even though the peculiar events from earlier had unsettled me at lift-off, I was now cruising at a reasonable altitude with serenity. Some turbulence was to be expected. So what if Dave had decided to have a dance? Why not? Let it all hang out? Peace and love? I was in a good band and everything was groovy? The audience was friendly, though sparse, and nothing was going to stop the show? I did not pay too much attention to the question marks at the ends of my own self-assurances. Sometimes you just have to kid yourself, though, right?

It was nearly showtime, so I made my way into the club. Passing the bar, various faces loomed in and out at me through the tracers and twinkling lights, like strange underwater creatures peering through the windows of a deep-sea exploration vehicle. The crowd was decent, the lights were pleasing, and I was feeling ready to make some music, so I mounted the stage and made sure everything was in order with my equipment. Everything was as I had left it after the soundcheck. The only thing missing was my bass. My trusty Gibson Thunderbird was nowhere to be found.

'Has anyone seen my bass?' I called out to the rest of the band, who were also getting ready to play.

'Nope,' said everyone.

I began to experience a little confusion.

I looked around for Dave. Dave was not onstage. Dave was still giving it the large and weird with his dance floor boogaloo. I approached him warily and tapped him on the shoulder. He snapped around and gave me a peculiar grin. Sweat was pouring off him, and light, and other stuff that doesn't have a name yet.

'Err, hi, Dave. Sorry to bother you, man, but, err, have you, err, maybe, by any chance, seen my bass anywhere . . . please?'

He grinned again, and a weird gleam appeared in his eyes that I could not blame entirely on my own perceptions. Keeping me fully in the headlights of whatever the hell it was that had gotten into his eyes, he pointed a finger at me. Then, very slowly, deliberately, and with a most unreassuring smile, he gave me the 'follow me' signal with his outstretched, hooking and crooked finger. Was he leading me into his eyes? Was he taking me down the rabbit hole? Was he about to chop me into pieces? I had neither earthly nor extraterrestrial idea at this point, but being bass-less and with the show rapidly approaching I was left with little choice but to follow him. We walked onstage and began to cross his wasteland of incomprehensible squiggles. The gaffer-taped runes began to make sense to me. He had spelled out my doom in silver symbols that I had been too naïve to understand earlier, and now I was being led to the scaffold to pay the price for my ignorance. It was my fault for taking the acid in the first place. I kept walking. It was my fate. He led me down into the dungeons in the bowels of the club, where doors creaked and lost souls wailed, as I grimly trudged behind him towards the end.

He led me into a cupboard and there, like the holy grail itself, was my bass, lying on a bit of cloth on a table. Dave walked over to it, took it gently in his hands, turned solemnly to me, and offered it to me with a tear in his eye.

I looked at it. I looked at it again. I looked at it a third time just to make sure that it looked as horrible as I thought it had looked the first time I looked at it. Wires were hanging from it. It had been largely discombobulated, dismantled and disassembled and, unfortunately, this was no hallucination. Bits of it were missing. Bits of me were missing.

I took the bass from him. A bit of it fell on the floor. The echoes of its impact echoed along the ruins of time. I wanted to cry.

Dave was smiling a beatific smile and I was due onstage in five minutes.

'Uhhhhhhh,' I said. I put my gutted and previously beloved bass back onto Dave's operating table. 'Uhhhhh,' I said again, in an effort to verbalise my feelings and come to grips with the situation. 'Fuck it, Dave. Nice job and everything, man, but maybe I will just use another one tonight. Don't worry about it.' I said this in an effort to placate him. Dave smiled and he seemed to understand even though he had clearly lost his reason. Even I could see that. I ran back over the stage because the trip down into the dungeons had, in fact, been a frightening and purely mental journey brought on by my quite justified intimations of impending wrongness.

I found the bassist from the support band. 'Sean, mate, lend us your bass. Dave has taken mine to fucking pieces.'

Sean laughed, 'What? What did he do that for?'

'Because he is clearly deranged,' I said. 'We can work out the details later.'

He handed over his bass and I took my place on the stage.

I tuned the bass and tried to deal with the rip tides of adrenaline.

The first song started and my fingers did their thing. Muscle memory is a beautiful thing in these situations. I could play these songs through strobes, smoke, flying glasses, drugs and other minor complications. Or could I? 'Just settle down, listen to the drums, and focus,' I told myself. 'Everything beyond music is unimportant at this point.'

The first note brought its customary relief and the music began to make sense of the situation where I could not. I had found my tree. The great branches spread over me and I was curled in the trunk with the trills and ululations of songbirds drifting down to me from its leafy heights as the pulse of the sap fired nourishment to the tips of the furthest twigs. I was the tree. I was the pulse.

We made it through the first song. The audience cheered.

The first fireball came ripping in from the glare of the stage lights. It was a big orange and yellow miniature sun and it was heading directly at me, at high speed, crackling as it came.

'Holy FUCK!' I swerved out of the way and heard it fizzing as it passed my left ear and continued directly through Jonny who, despite my horrified expression, smiled at me and carried on drumming. It seemed that the man was impervious to fireballs. I dared not take that chance.

We started the next song and with its increased tempo and ferocity came more of the completely believable fireballs. It seemed the music was encouraging them somehow, so I swayed and dodged and ducked them but, naturally, I kept playing, because to do otherwise would have been unprofessional. I

offered a prayer to God, or the fireballs, or the acid, or something. 'Look,' I murmured, perhaps to myself, 'I'm sorry, OK?
I will never do it again. Just let me get through this set and I
will never, *ever*, take LSD onstage again!'

WHOOOOOOSH . . . another big fireball ripped out of the
lights trailing stars and smoke and smelling faintly of lavender.

I took this as a divine answer. I had invited the fireballs to
the party and now they were going to dance for a while. Perhaps, if I danced well enough with them, the Gods would be
merciful.

I glanced over to make sure my hands were still there. Somehow, by virtue of the strobes, the passing fireballs, the smoke
and the general peculiarity, I found I had been blessed with
two extra left hands. This made perfect sense to me at the time.
Three hands are better than none, right? The only problem
was, the more I became aware of the three hands the more I
began to wonder which of them was actually mine. I became
conscious of my general lack of unity, and with this I began to
falter. Whenever I started to look at my hands and consciously
try to make them do what I wanted, the less they became willing to do so.

I looked away and everything started to flow again. I looked
back, and everything became mechanical as I wondered how
the fuck to play the guitar with three hands.

The less I thought about it, the better it got, and I even
started ignoring the fireballs – though, to be honest, they were
a welcome distraction from the three-handed conundrum that
was somehow better off playing the bass without me, or at
least without the part of me that couldn't stop thinking about
how to play the bass with three hands.

This continued for some unspecified time, until finally the
last song of the set ended and the audience cheered. The air
was thick with violet and green smoke and it was impossible

to see more than three feet in any direction. Even for normal people. The strobes were flickering and the fireballs were flying when I sensed a disturbance at my feet. It was Mark Refoy, the guitarist. He was crawling offstage.

'Mark, what are you doing, man?' I shouted.

'I can't see a fucking thing,' he said, as he continued to crawl through the smoke to the dressing room. I switched the amp off and followed him in a dignified and mostly vertical silence. We all sat in the brightly lit dressing room enjoying the relief and the mixture of adrenaline and endorphins that we were all happily pouring alcohol into. Perhaps I was more relieved than my bandmates that everything had gone well.

I was massaging a little Tiger balm into my overactive third eye when the first members of the audience came backstage. Two extremely wide-eyed young gentlemen bundled in through the dressing-room door and began shaking hands and congratulating us on the show.

'Nice one, mate,' one of them said to me.

'Is that Tiger balm? Can I have a bit?'

He dug his finger into the tin I offered him, took a large blob, and stuck it directly onto his eyeball.

I looked at him disbelievingly.

'Erm . . .' I said, 'You aren't supposed to put it in your eye, you know?'

'Oh, really?' he said, laughing. 'What should I do?'

'Don't panic. It'll wear off eventually,' I replied.

'I saw you dancing onstage tonight, Willie,' he said, excitedly. 'You were getting right into it. Sounded fucking brilliant!'

'I wasn't dancing, I was dodging fireballs. How is the Tiger balm?' I said, as he looked at me and the first tears began streaming down his face towards his unstoppable grin.

'FUCKING INTENSE,' he said, and we all laughed.

I got paid fifteen quid for that show.

That's Not Normal Behaviour

Our particular brand of gentle and relaxing pastoral psychedelia had always found a natural home amongst people sitting
in chemical baths of unnaturally fizzy water so, in many ways,
Middlesbrough was a spiritual home for the band, there being
not just one, or two, but three large chemical factories gracing
the skyline of this peculiar seaside town.

It seemed not only right but fitting to change my own
chemical composition while visiting a place that was so obviously dedicated to the moving around of molecules and the
alchemist's art. Although both myself and the town were
experimenting with better living through chemistry, some of us
were less obviously scientific about the procedure.

Two members of the touring entourage at the time were also
milkmen in Rugby. As well as being milkmen, these multi-task-
ing gentlemen were also distributors of the fairly ubiquitous
psychedelics that were becoming so fashionable amongst the
brave and foolhardy proponents of all things acid house and
rave-related that were working like a scourge against the prevailing religions of normality and boredom.

These abnormal entrepreneurs would pop a couple of squares
of cardboard, or a yellow microdot, under your morning pint
of milk and then you would be fairly well set for a weekend in
which you might feel that your own head was crowned with
silver and that your brains were also pure cream being gently
pecked by small, feathered, tits. Of course it might always go
the other way. Nobody ever said that exploration and adventure was a guaranteed bowl of cherries in a bed of roses. On

one particularly harrowing occasion I had been travelling on a milk float with one of these milk-plus milkmen when we had become involved in a particularly nasty speed wobble on Bilton Hill. It was dangerous, and a little bit of milk was spilled, but we were both spared the indignity of sudden death by milk-float speed wobble, which might, at least, have made for an entertaining epitaph.

Our two unconventional Ernies were keeping me fairly well supplied with non-dairy related products while we were on tour and consequently, by the time the show began, I was once more in the realm of the gold top.

Flying fireballs, deranged roadies and extra hands being noticeable by their absence during the performance, the evening had progressed as smoothly as well-churned butter, and the fifty or so residents of Middlesbrough who had crowded into the spacious hall for the night were well and truly entertained. I presumed so anyway. Perhaps they had not been as well entertained as me, but I can't really be expected to take the blame for that. I had done my bit.

The after-show and load-out passed colourfully and uneventfully, and by the time we had all arrived at the bed and breakfast, everyone was in a good mood and ready for bed(ish). The support band, Electrahead, were touring with us and, because they were not getting paid very much, they had been sleeping in their van when it was too far to drive home to Rugby. In the grips of psychedelic philanthropy and filled with the acid milkmen's milk of human kindness, I had offered the floor and the spare bed of the room I was sleeping in to the paupers, despite the fact that none of us was feeling very sleepy.

Laughing and giggling, while trying our very best not to disturb the sleeping landlady with our high spirits, we tiptoed through her terrifyingly floral hallway. There were weird ornaments everywhere and, in the grip of my fever, I became entranced by their strangeness. Normally, a large statue of a Greek nymph pouring imaginary water into an empty plaster pond would not have given cause for closer inspection but, under the spell of the fumes from the three combined chemical factories, I could not bear to leave the lonely nymph to pour dry water into the darkened corridor alone. I was in the mood for company, so I tucked her, very carefully, under my arm and proceeded up through the psychedelic thicket of the spongily carpeted stairwell. On the way through the undergrowth of decoration I may have also accumulated a few more knick-knacks and fripperies to decorate the comparatively spartan room that we had rented for the night.

Mark and Jonny and Jason and Kate retired sensibly early to their respective rooms, while myself, the driver and assorted members of our extended touring party stumbled into my room, where we proceeded to make ourselves as comfortable as possible in a small, brightly lit bedroom in a bed and breakfast in Middlesbrough with a potential dragon asleep downstairs.

Undeterred by the unpromising surroundings I began to arrange the gathered ornaments in a way that was pleasing to my delirious senses. I made an altar, with the previously lonely nymph as the centrepiece. Around her, I carefully laid a small basket of vibrant yellow chickens, an unnerving picture of a dog (I think it was a Jack Russell) and several doilies, totems, geegaws and mementoes of bygone holidays in presumably sunnier places. There was a donkey from Spain, a couple of snow globes and a weird glass bird full of red liquid which pecked at a glass full of water for no obvious reason. I served no disrespect to these precious items; rather, I treated them with a reverence reserved for religious artefacts and relics of a better time. Who knew which spirits they served or what they had once been used for? I genuinely loved them even though I didn't understand them. When the room was dimmed and the atmosphere complete, the previously unremarkable room resembled a sylvan glade, or a venereal Roman grotto in a suburban back garden. At least it did to me.

With the stage set for our little after-show comedown, it was time for the music. I had become overly fond of one cassette in particular on the tour, a tape I had played so constantly that I had been asked to not play it quite so constantly, more than once. I continued to enjoy it in secret, regardless of the philistine protestations of my bandmates.

It was time for Dr John, also known as 'the Night Tripper', aka 'the *Gris-Gris* man'. We were all set for a relaxing re-entry (via the bayou) into normal earth atmosphere, if indeed the atmosphere in Middlesbrough could ever have been considered to be normal. We sat and smoked fags and had a bit of a laugh about stuff. After a period of small talk I felt the need for something more in keeping with the tone of the evening and the surroundings. I felt the need for something biblical. I fancied the *Book of Revelations*, because it was quite easy to imagine strange and terrifying creatures rising from the chimneys of those factories we had passed on the way into town and I was already beset by weird visions.

Luckily, as is the case in most godforsaken hotel rooms, there was a bible at hand. I retrieved it from the chipboard drawer, blew the dust off it and, using the ancient scrying technique of bibliomancy, opened the book at random, and began to speak in somebody else's tongue. At some point in the sermon, to which my colleagues were paying a sort of weary and bemused attention, I decided I would be better served to preach the word of God from a pulpit of some kind.

This being a bed and breakfast, pulpits were in short supply, although there was a wardrobe made of wood that looked like it might hold my weight. With a supernatural agility, I mounted it and continued my slightly confused sermon from the wardrobe top. It was going pretty well, I thought. We were somewhere in the New Testament and it was all peace and love and forgiveness, until I got a bit bored and flipped back to the front of the book where things weren't quite so fluffy. I was probably deep into some passage about smiting and dismembering the enemies of God when I started to get the horror. I could see those poor sinners, all dismembered and tormented, and it was wrecking my vibe with some force. I ploughed on through the blood and the guts and the thunderbolts until, eventually, I dropped the book from the lofty chipboard pulpit with disgust. It landed on the floor with a blasphemous and reverberating thud. Now that I was no longer plagued by visions of slaughter, I felt considerably better, so I let out a loud laugh and pulled a little book of John Clare poems from the coat of my Russian admiral's jacket.

Sparrows and rivers and little hedgehogs would soon dispel that Old Testament gloom. I could revel in the joys of creation as seen through the eyes of a lover of creation, and there would be no more of the Old Testament destruction and misery (at least not until we got to 'The Lament of Swordy Well' anyway).

Alas, our collective journey to the pleasant pre-enclosure fields of Northamptonshire was to be short lived, for lo, the terrible judgement of the landlady was upon us, and she said, 'Let there be light,' and there was a lot of it, and it came as a bit of a shock, for she was standing there in righteous and vengeful fury in her dressing gown, and lo, we the assembled sinners did sore tremble in our fear and were verily chastised. She had appeared, in full Old Testament mode, in her anger and curlers, and she had entered the room without knocking. She was ready for some smiting. 'WHAT ARE YOU DOING ON THE WARDROBE?' she asked reasonably but in an unreasonable tone.

I didn't really have a reasonable answer, so I just shrugged and smiled a wonky smile.

'THAT IS NOT NORMAL BEHAVIOUR!' she said, which was also a fair point.

Then she turned her eyes away from me, which was probably difficult, because I was sitting on top of her wardrobe in my rather fetching jacket, which had a fair amount of gold piping and inscrutable Russian military finery festooned across the arms and shoulders. It had been a gift from Dave, the big roadie who went bananas in Leeds . . . but, anyway . . . somehow she stopped looking at me, which made me feel better for a moment, even though I was obviously seeking attention.

She cast her disgusted eyes across the room until they came to rest upon the final indignity. The ultimate insult. She saw the half-naked lady with the vase surrounded by many items from her treasured collection of stuff that had been arranged in a weird and unnatural way.

'GET OUT!' she screamed with the force of a banshee. 'YOU MUST ALL LEAVE. GET OUT OF THIS HOUSE.'

At this point it seemed wise to actually leave the relative safety of the wardrobe, purely as a diplomatic move and a conciliatory gesture. I hoped that might serve to calm her after the shock of finding her knick-knacks in my boudoir. With the speed and agility of a seal I slipped down onto the carpet and started making apologetic noises. 'Look. I'm sorry,' I said, actually, genuinely feeling sorry, and also realising that it might be a bit cold outside. 'I didn't mean to bring those things of yours up here. I just liked them and I haven't damaged them. I was very careful and we will just go to bed and not make any more noise and—'

'NO,' she said, to everything. 'You must all leave. Pack your things and get out!'

'But . . . but,' I stammered. 'It was all my fault. Don't throw them out. I'll go and then there won't be any more trouble.'

'I DON'T CARE', she said, while gathering her belongings from the decidedly unmystical-looking altar. 'I won't have this kind of funny business in my house. You must all LEAVE.'

And with that final and terrible proclamation she left the room and started banging on Jonny and Mark's door while screaming, 'C'MON, GET UP. You have to leave. NOW!'

Jason and Kate appeared on the landing looking confused and sleepy.

'What's going on?' said Kate, half to me and half to the obviously inconsolable landlady.

'You must all leave,' the landlady repeated. 'He was on the wardrobe, and he has people in his room who shouldn't be here. And he woke me up. God knows what all of that banging and crashing was.'

I thought that this wasn't the best time to mention my struggle with the visceral stories of the Old Testament, so I just kept saying sorry.

There was the sound of weary, slippered footsteps from the stairs and her husband appeared, looking tired and as though he wished he wasn't there. He was sporting a finely checked and tasselled dressing gown. Ten minutes previously he had been tucked up in a nice warm bed dreaming about kinder things, and now he was standing at the top of the stairs surrounded by confused and sleepy people, a battleaxe wife on a mission to destroy, and a strange-eyed creature in a Russian admiral's jacket. He looked at me with a mixture of weariness and annoyance.

'What's all the bloody noise about?' he said.

'Sorry,' I replied, for the fiftieth fucking time, 'we have just played an exciting concert in your lovely town and we were having a couple of drinks with our friends here and then we were going to bed and somebody knocked something over. It was an accident and we all just want to go to sleep now. Everyone wants to go home and nothing is broken. Please don't throw us all out. It wasn't their fault.' I kept a low and reasonable tone despite the fact that my eyes were probably singing a much higher song.

He looked at me and I looked back at him.

As I looked at him, I was thinking, 'It's all OK. Go back to bed. Go back to bed. We are reasonable people. Go back to bed.' Like a Jedi mind trick.

He looked at me for a bit longer, then he made a kind of satisfied and pissed-off humphing noise, turned round, and went back down the stairs. 'Keep the bloody noise down!' he said over his shoulder as he left. 'Some of us have got work in the morning.'

'WHERE ARE YOU GOING?' his wife screeched after him.

'Bed,' he said with firm resignation, and then he vanished into the darkened hallway at the foot of the stairs.

The landlady looked at me with something approaching hate.

'Look, I'm sorry,' I said. 'Our friends are leaving now and we all just want to go to bed. We are very tired.'

She looked at me again in a way that I could physically feel. There was no way any mind tricks were going to work on her; she was too far gone. I wished I had never touched her precious water-bearer, even in a respectful way.

'All right,' she said. 'You can stay. BUT NO MORE BLOODY FUNNY BUSINESS.'

'OK,' I lied.

My bandmates returned to their rooms with a palpable sense of relief and the members of Electrahead, who had lost their chance of a warm room for the night, were ungraciously sent packing courtesy of my stupidity and the landlady's hostility. 'See you tomorrow, boys,' I said, under the baleful stare of the landlady, while silently mouthing the word 'sorry' to them as they left.

She looked at me again. 'GO TO BED.'

I knew when I was beaten.

'OK,' I said, and turned back to enter the room.

'We had those Happy Mondays in here the other week, and you lot are worse,' she squawked, as a parting shot.

I was secretly pleased about that, to be honest.

In the morning, we snuck out of the undestroyed rooms and left the B&B under the chilly wind of the landlady's sullen and reproachful stare. All of her valuables were back in one piece, in the exact places I had disturbed them from the night before. I could barely look the water-bearing nymph in the eye as I passed her in the hallway and we said our goodbyes.

We got in the van, leaving the chemical factories of Middlesbrough behind us, and made our way down the dreary motorway to the next show.

At the venue, we met up with Electrahead and I apologised once again for the night before.

'Ah, it doesn't matter,' said Steve. 'It was pretty funny in the end. We drove down to the beach, parked up and slept in the van for the night. The weird thing was, in the morning we were woken up by all of these blokes outside in full-on moonsuits, and they were taking samples of the water. We didn't bother going for a swim!'

Despite our own occasionally stupid chemical indulgences we'd never had to face a hangover wearing fully protective chemical bodysuits and helmets, and we never polluted anything beyond our own bloodstreams, so I suppose that was something to be said in our favour.

Little Thief

When a large part of your job involves travelling, and the unsociable hours you work force you to rely on the muck-hole eateries that pepper the motorways you are forced to travel on in order to get home because you can't afford a hotel, then motorway service stations are your friend, no matter how much they secretly despise you.

I have no idea what makes people so placid in the face of service-station food in Britain. We all take it for granted that ten quid is a perfectly acceptable price to pay for a tepid cup of Nescafé, a damp and pale lasagne, and a cake as big as your head filled with chemicals that will cause your body to remain fresh in the grave like a crap vampire from a seventies horror film.

That's if you can afford to be buried.

Welcome to the glamorous world of being in a touring band.

Now, imagine you are lucky.

Imagine you are getting paid.

Imagine you are getting paid fifteen quid a day.

Ten quid is quite a lot to pay for anything when fifteen quid is all you have in the world.

Now let's add some airports into this delightful mix, because you are now so successful that you have to travel the world to play for people. You still aren't getting paid very much but let's not dwell on that. Let's imagine that this airport is in Scandinavia. Oslo, for instance. The band is hungry. They have travelled very far and they are tired. They have only eaten a tiny bag of pretzels in six hours. They forgot to bring a packed lunch again. Shall we just get something cheap to tide us over until dinner time, which will probably be at four o'clock in the fucking morning at some poison buffet in a field somewhere? Shall we have a pizza? It's only cheese on toast, after all, and how expensive can dough and cheese be?

Even with tomatoes.

Even in Oslo.

'That will be fifty-eight euros, please.'

If I were paying to eat pizza out of the gilded crack of a supermodel while her friend was blowing cocaine up my arse with a straw I would still consider fifty-eight euros to be a little expensive for cheese on toast. Even if it was circular and it had some sort of sauce on top.

When we toured Europe with Spacemen 3 in 1989 we were getting paid ten quid a day. Ten quid in Budapest paid for a three-course meal at a nice restaurant, with fizzy wine, polite waiters and clean white tablecloths. Of course, the restaurant was empty because most of the people were lined up in the freezing fog to eat a Happy Meal for the same price at the first McDonald's to open in the Eastern bloc. Our visit to Budapest had coincided with the first appearance of everyone's favourite clown. The circus was in town and so were we.

Budapest was one thing, and Stockholm was another thing entirely. In Stockholm, ten quid bought us a loaf of bread, four squares of cheese, and a can of lager which we consumed in a park surrounded by gaunt speedfreaks whacking up bags of shonky sulphate. No wonder we had such a tenuous grip on reality.

Look, I know other people have bigger problems. As I type this I can see the faces of drowned children swimming up through the fog of my dreams to scream at me while their parents sob endlessly on a blow-up boat in the Aegean as they try to escape the bombs that have been dropping on their villages.

I know. I know people walk for miles just to get a mouthful of muddy water and camel piss. I understand that some people would just like not to get killed as they go to work. I realise that sea levels are rising and pretty soon the world will be full of desperate people with AK-47s and dirty bombs looking for a mangelwurzel and a dry rock to shit on. I know.

But still, is it more difficult to transport a sausage roll to a service station on a motorway than it is to ship one to the Outer Hebrides? What are the logistical difficulties and additional costs involved in taking a sandwich to an airport that make it twice as expensive as its precious equivalent in a Spar in Hunstanton?

God help you if you want a drink.

God help you if you *need* a drink.

'That'll be eight pound fifty, please! SECURITY! SECURITY! Security to the imaginary lager section, please. Customer is showing signs of sarcasm and discontent.'

It was around three in the morning when the van pulled off the M1 and took the slip road leading to that most fabled of British motorway service stations.

Watford Gap has traditionally been a place of transport since Roman times. On a gibbous moon, it is sometimes possible to hear the ghosts of Roman centurions complaining bitterly in the car park about the quality and the price of the food on offer. Watford Gap is a name to conjure with, rich with history and a stopping place for every self-respecting band and traveller on their way up and down the country since the golden age of motorway travel began. Situated between two hills in the county of Northamptonshire and traditionally known as the official point at which the gentle civilisation of the south of England gives way to the wildlings and whippets of the north, it sits in the middle of the country like some festering belly button full of fluff, bits of crisps and stale spunk.

The van parked up and we fell out of our varying degrees of uncomfortable sleep with a mixture of relief and disappointment.

'Where are we?'

'What time is it?'

'Why are we?'

This was no time for philosophy. It was late, we were hungry and the Little Chef was the only game in town. We had all earned our fifteen pounds and it would have been churlish not to spend it on something quite disappointing.

'We are going to the Little Chef.'

'Little fucking thief more like.'

The little chef on the glowing red sign looked like a fat and hungry ghost carrying a plate of shit, or maybe like some off-duty Klansman who has rolled his hood up in preparation to stuff his face with doughnuts.

'Have a fucking burger if you don't like it.'

'Why do we always have to eat here?'

'Why don't you ask the Romans?'

Anyway, a little lively and half-drunk conversation does wonders for the appetite at four in the morning.

We walked past a large group of ravers who were dancing to their car stereos in the car park. They looked like itching phantom limbs enjoying the memory of a party they had once attended pre-amputation.

'What are they doing?' someone asked.

'Taking drugs,' came the fairly obvious answer.

We passed the gurning ravers, casually swatting away their happy questions about where we were from and what we were on. We didn't understand happy people when we weren't on drugs.

We made our way into the disturbing light and frightening aesthetics of the service station and were instantly attacked by massive and garish art that demanded we lose all reason and eat everything in sight. It was fucking horrible. The building was empty of everyone but the insane, the addled and the working. We fitted into all three categories.

'What'll it be? Burgers . . . burgers . . . burgers . . . chocolate and crisps? Or a proper meal?'

'Let's have some real food, shall we? I think I'll die if I eat any more crisps.'

So we entered the glum hall of the best restaurant at Watford Gap. It looked like a scene from a zombie film, after the zombies have eaten everybody and won and then died of starvation and turned to dust. Congealing puddles of nameless slop and glowering eggs sweated under the merciless heat lamps, and the air was wobbly with grease and desperation. It was like being in a sauna that smelled of meat and piss, where everything was too bright and expensive and none of it was particularly appetising.

'Eight quid for that?' someone said, ungratefully, pointing a scornful finger at a waterlogged shepherd's pie made out of horse gristle and entrails. 'I'm not paying that. I'm just having chips.'

The chips were as hard as misery, as sharp as spite and cost as much as Christmas. An indestructible bun and margarine to grease it down was extra.

'Watford Gap, Watford Gap . . . a plate of grease and a load of crap,' somebody sang, mournfully, as the whirr of sinister motors signalled the attention of electronic surveillance.

I couldn't face anything.

I couldn't face my hunger, my wallet, or any of the food.

Perhaps it was a combination of all three.

A battle-damaged soldier was shouting post-combat death orders at the trifle. I made my way to the checkout, where a grim and pustuled youth was trying not to commit suicide. 'All right, mate?' I said, in a cheery fashion. 'How you doing?'

'All right,' he said, but his eyes told a different story.

'Bit depressing in here, isn't it?' I said. 'I hope they are paying you all right?'

'Huh,' he grunted, with a face somewhere between derision and hatred. 'Not fucking likely.'

'What?' I said. 'When they are selling toast at a quid a slice? That's criminal.'

'I know,' he said. 'I fucking hate it here.'

'Look,' I whispered, conspiratorially. 'Can you help me out? I'm skint and I'm starving. Where are the security cameras?'

He looked at me, winked, and said they were mainly watching him to make sure that he didn't steal any money from the till.

'Any cameras by the breakfast?' I said.

He shook his head.

'Nice one, boss,' I said. 'I'll leave three quid on my table when I'm done.' And with that I walked off, got myself a nice big breakfast, ate the whole thing, and then drank the grease off the plate with a slurp. Three quid was a fair price, and he looked like he needed a pay rise.

Working on a Building

One year after leaving the building site and paying off the Spacemen 3 debts, I was back on site and getting into debt again. The only difference was that this time I was still playing in the band.

We had finished the recordings for *Lazer Guided Melodies* and it had yet to be released, but we had toured fairly extensively in Britain to try to kick-start the band and to promote the singles from the upcoming album. The band had received a fairly hefty advance for the record as part of the contract with Dedicated that Gerald had set up. This was a deal for five albums with an ever increasing advance on each one. All of the recording costs were to be paid for out of the initial advance, and the rest was to be split between the band. It all seemed pretty good to me, although I hadn't been involved with the intricacies of the deal, nor signed a contract, nor talked to a lawyer about it all. I was still a trusting soul.

Lazer Guided Melodies, on the whole, had been a joy to make. There were no bad feelings within the band; our main focus had been on making music. We had recorded 'Anyway That You Want Me' and from there we just carried on writing songs, gathering the ideas live in the back room of the Imperial and on the road, and working out the main parts in Jason's rehearsal room later. Jason would often turn up with a couple of chords, or three, and a full song to sing. Sometimes the words would come later. Sometimes he would play one chord and we would play round it. This was not music of great complexity in terms of chords and key changes. The beauty of the creation lay in what was wound around the simple structures and in the melodies and lyrical sentiments. Nobody told me what basslines to play in that band. Often I would take home rough demo recordings and work out the parts on headphones with my bass plugged into the stereo. I would spend hours coming up with the various possibilities and then I would present them to Jason in the studio or the rehearsal room, where he would arrange them. Some of the songs we had worked up at rehearsals were played live at shows long before anybody had heard a recorded version of them. We were playing some of them before we had even recorded them. This brought the songs into tighter focus and we knew what would work before we took them to the studio. Jason was becoming a wizard with the desk, and with a full working band behind him he was inspired and inspirational in turn.

There is a narrative that the public seems very fond of, and maybe it fits with the times somehow. The individual genius, with all of the parts mapped out in technicolour in a grand 3D map they carry around in their illuminated heads. None of the bands I have ever been in work totally like that. Genius steals and borrows, as does plagiarism, and there can be a fine line between the two if the genius in question lacks the self-confidence and the strength of character to admit their debts, however small or large they may be, monetarily or musically. It doesn't matter anyway, I suppose. The music itself is what matters when all the bullshit is forgotten. In the meantime it's all about getting paid and who's in charge, right? It's all about too many dogs fighting over too small a bone, and when nobody knows when the next pay cheque is rolling in, well, maybe it's tempting to just grab what you can and hole up in the hills. Every man for himself. YODELAYHEEHOO. But, who are the winners when eventually that costs you some of the essential value of the thing you are selling? When it isn't actually good for music? What does business serve when it actually kills the thing that gives it life? Who is the boss in that situation?

Hard-luck stories are cheaper than musicians in the music industry, and most people just shrug and look at you with a kind of 'what did you expect?' expression when they hear another tale of woe. No one wants to hear about the bum deals and the bitterness. It takes the shine off the music and the dreams that we, as listeners, spin around the creation and its creators. If music is escapist in nature, who the hell wants to hear about the hard realities behind it? Nobody wants to hear about how good love turned sour, how your dog died and your woman done gone and left you with nothing but a bottle full of pills for company. Not me, that's for sure. Not unless it has a good tune.

I think I got about five grand from *Lazer Guided Melodies*. For a year's work. That is all I was ever paid and probably ever will be. I never understood about cross-recouping deals, or what had been signed and decided. Maybe dear old Gerald had never really had my best interests at heart when he made that deal.

Maybe he was just tired.

Me too.

Fifty Tons of Blood

John was a brickie and I was labouring for him. It was getting close to Christmas. He picked me up at seven in the morning in his battered car full of builder's crap, cement and tools, which had a big ragged hole in the bonnet where he had used a claw hammer to get it open when the bonnet-release had stopped working. He said he loved his car. I mentioned that I hoped he treated his wife a bit better than the car. He just cackled.

He had told me that the job was in Crick, a small village on the outskirts of Rugby, right next to the M1. As we were driving along the road that led into the village, John made a left turn that took us along an innocent-looking lane past some raised grassy mounds that barely concealed a large, dark factory. A big old smoky chimney and the roofs of some serious-looking, metal-clad buildings were visible over the pretty green embankments.

I started to get worried. 'Fucking hell, John, this is Midland Meat Packers. Are we working here?'

'Um, yeah,' he replied innocently. 'Didn't I tell you?'

'No, you fucking didn't,' I shot back, getting increasingly agitated as we drew closer to the security gate that lay at the end of the little tree-lined lane. 'You know I'm a vegetarian. I can't work here, man.'

John was ready for this. He had deliberately not told me that we were going to be working at the biggest slaughterhouse and meat processing factory in Europe because he didn't want to upset me. 'It'll be good for you to have a look,' he said, as if he were some sort of tour guide offering me a pleasant holiday.

'Y'know, you can get an inside view on the place, like.'

I failed to thank him for giving me this once in a lifetime opportunity.

'We're only doing the building anyway. We aren't going to be working in the slaughterhouse,' he said, continuing with the pep talk as we pulled up to the security gate.

Midland Meat Packers had fairly high security, as it was sometimes targeted by animal rights protestors.

'C'mon,' he said. 'It'll be all right.'

'You cunt, John,' I muttered, as I got out of the car. 'They probably won't even let me in anyway. I look like a member of the ALF.'

He laughed, and we both walked towards the security guards, who were eating biscuits in their little guardhouse. We went inside and the two security guards looked us up and down. John did the talking, while the security guards eyed me with a mixture of amusement and suspicion. 'Who's the hippy?' they said, laughing.

'He's my labourer,' John replied, which prompted more laughter from them. I laughed too.

We got back in the car and the guards pressed the button that lifted the barrier, allowing us to drive into the car park beside the factory. John parked the car as I whined and moaned and tried to deal with my terrible feelings of impending doom.

He laughed. 'Stop fucking moaning,' he laughed again. 'You're here now. You might as well have a look.'

He was right. I was there and I wasn't about to walk home. I thought I needed the money. We got out of the car and grabbed the tools out of the boot. We walked into the main courtyard and I cursed every rebellious sense I had as I took the first breath of death and shit. John made some reassuring noises as I struggled to make sense of my new environment. There was a lot to take in and I did not want to get any of it inside me.

We walked into the main courtyard, which was surrounded by looming buildings. Over to our left there was a pen full of cows, wedged tightly together. Their eyes were wide. The beasts were skittish as they awaited their turn on the efficient line of production that would see their various body parts neatly wrapped in plastic within the hour. They knew they were fucked. I almost knew how they felt.

The concrete floor was stained with blood. Bloody plastic curtains were hanging over the various entrances to the surrounding buildings concealing what was happening inside. We passed a big metal container and I dared a glance inside. It was full of ears. Hundreds of them. It was a skip full of ears. Next to that one was another one full of hooves. I didn't look in any of the others. We kept walking.

'Fucking hell,' I said.

The grey buildings loomed over us through the noise of invisible machines and the final bellows of the doomed animals in their pens. The stench thickened into a taste that clawed at the back of our throats. We passed a huge steel drum up on a little hill, and the stench deepened to a physical sensation.

'Fucking hell,' said John finally. 'That stinks.'

I could see him holding back retches. I was doing the same.

'Yeah,' I said, 'Fucking hell.'

We kept walking, until the processing factory and the slaughterhouse were about a hundred metres behind us. The air had less of the taste in it as we passed through a farm gate and crossed a little stream. I looked at the stream and noticed it was a sickly yellow colour. 'Do you think that's piss?' I said to John as we crossed over it.

'Yeah,' he said grimly. 'Pure piss.'

Even John's usually undentable cheerfulness seemed to be failing him.

'Fucking hell,' I said.

We arrived at our building site, three torn and treeless fields that held a few half-finished silos and the first courses of a small brick building surrounded by thick drifts of mud and puddles of dirty water. John looked over towards a little shed and a dirty cement mixer in the corner of the field. 'That's our place,' he said. 'We can dump our stuff there.' He pointed at the half-finished brick building that was standing just proud of the earth a hundred metres away across the potholes and churned-up ground. 'That's the building we're gonna be working on. It's going to be the control room for these storage containers,' he said, pointing off to the big metal silos. 'That's where they are going to store all of the blood, piss and shit. It is all going to be controlled by computer from the place we're building.'

It all sounded very sanitary and reasonable, as long as you were totally unaware of the reality of the place.

We looked back at the factory we had just walked through. The tall chimney rose up out of it like an unholy church spire, puffing dirty smoke into the grey December sky.

'They kill a thousand cows a day up there,' John said. 'It's the biggest slaughterhouse in Europe. That's a lot of piss and shit. Get a mix on and we'll get started. We'll do a couple of hours and then go for a cup of tea up at the café in the plant.'

A cup of tea and a sandwich had never sounded like such a daunting prospect. I started the cement mixer and shovelled in the sand and cement as John slithered his way through the mud to the jagged fledgling walls of the little control room we were building. I stared into the mixer and allowed myself to be hypnotised out of my immediate surroundings. When I looked away from the mixer the whole world was turning at the edges of my vision at the same speed as the turning mixer had been. The things you see have an effect on the things you see afterwards sometimes.

I snapped out of it, squirted a dash of fairy liquid into the mixer, and then poured the whole lot into the wheelbarrow. It looked like dark grey chocolate mousse. The first bricklayer I ever laboured for told me that good bricklayer's muck should always look a bit like chocolate mousse.

I grabbed the barrow by the two plastic handles and set off across the mud towards John. I must have looked pretty funny as I stumbled and slid through the mud and the maze of trenches, pushing the reluctant wheelbarrow in front of me. I hoped somebody, somewhere, was having a laugh at my expense. Some cruel ancient goddess on some windswept corner of eternity had to be getting some laughs out of this. It couldn't be for nothing, or, even worse, for the sixty quid a day I was getting paid so I could cover my rent and keep myself in lentils.

I finally reached John with most of my delightfully mixed chocolate mousse still in the barrow. I grabbed the shovel and dropped some on his spots.

'Get us some bricks, would ya?' he said. 'They're over by the mixer.' I trudged back through the mire with my feet getting heavier and more mud-caked with each step. I filled the barrow with the freezing bricks and then made my way back to John in a slapstick fashion. I stacked the bricks for him and then went back for more, as he put the corners in and set his lines. That was pretty much the routine for the first two hours: him laying bricks and me flailing about through the mud with a wheelbarrow full of whatever he needed for the job. He was a fast enough brickie to keep me fairly busy, which was good because it meant I wasn't spending too much time standing around getting cold. Eventually he said, 'Fuck it, let's have a cup of tea.'

We both clumped back through the mud towards the bridge that crossed the stream of piss. Both of us looked down at the pretty yellow trickle.

'We should wash the mud off our boots,' he said.

So we washed out boots in the river of piss and headed back to the slaughterhouse for a cup of tea.

Normally on the building site you look forward to a tea break like a prisoner looks forward to release. Ten minutes of comfort, sitting on your backside – a little respite from either the heat of a hot day or the biting cold of winter. It's a chance to rest your bones, have a sit down and a smoke. We plodded back up the path towards the factory and, as we approached the deadly tank of the permanent stench, we both held our breath a bit.

'Fucking hell,' I said again, through gritted teeth and with a rapidly dwindling appetite. 'What the fuck *is* that *smell?*'

Neither of us knew, nor had we smelt its exact like before. We walked past the dog-food factory and entered the main courtyard that held the dirty steel containers full of the carefully sorted bits of cow people didn't like to eat. We headed for a door in the corner of the courtyard. There were random bits of flesh and unidentifiable soft things under our feet, as the cows mooed in their miserable corner and a lorry pulled up with the next load of their unlucky brethren.

We opened the door, stepped inside to the relative warmth, and were met by rows of bloodstained, chainmail aprons hanging on hooks in front of us, which were dripping red over shiny stainless steel. We climbed the stairs into the café. It was filled with workers and it had that hot, happy, chattering atmosphere that workers' cafés sometimes have. The pots and pans from the kitchen were clattering along with the sound of cutlery on plates and the air smelled of fried food and stew. It was steamy and comforting despite the prevailing grot outside. We joined the line of people waiting to be served, obviously not fitting in with the slaughterhouse workers and meat packers around us. I was doing my best to appear inconspicuous when John piped up, loud and clear, 'Fucking hell, I bet they don't do veggie burgers in here, eh, Will!'

I wanted to disappear into a bloodstained crack in the floor. 'Shut the fuck up John,' I hissed in a vehement whisper. 'That's not funny.'

John cackled loudly. He thought it was hilarious.

'I'll have the poached eggs on toast and a cup of tea, love, please,' I said to the woman behind the counter with my nicest, obviously not a vegetarian, smile. We collected our food and I scuttled off to a window seat as far away from everyone else as possible. John sauntered over and sat down, revelling in my obvious discomfort.

'Fucking hell,' I said, staring into my poached eggs and talking under my breath. 'That's not funny, John. You know what they do to vegetarians here? They'll probably throw me in the blood tank.'

Everybody who had grown up in Rugby had heard tales of people being thrown into the blood tank at Meat Packers. It was usually a special treat reserved for your birthday, or so I had heard, but who knew for certain? I was so far out of my comfort zone I had begun to wonder if I even had one. The whole blood tank thing was probably a complete myth, or one of those cruel initiation rites and punishments that brutal institutions sometimes have. I was familiar with the history of one person who'd worked at Meat Packers for quite a while. He sat next to me at school when I had first arrived in Rugby at the age of ten and he had punched me every day for about two weeks until I had finally punched him back. He never punched me again after that but he had gotten a job at Meat Packers when we all left school. He was eventually sent to jail for stabbing a taxi driver while trying to steal money to fuel his fruit-machine addiction. To be fair, I knew a few other people in town who had worked there and hadn't stabbed anyone, so maybe the old British law that stated that no slaughter-man was allowed to serve on a jury due to a diminished sense of reverence for life was completely unreasonable. They had repealed that law anyway.

I was moaning again.

'Oh, calm down,' John said, stifling his obvious merriment. 'Nobody gives a fuck if you are a vegetarian or not.'

I gave a fuck.

I gave a big miserable fuck.

I prodded my eggs and gazed out of the window at all of the ruthlessly efficient slaughter. We were in a slightly raised building, so from my window seat I was looking directly into another skip full of ears, which was nice. We made some small talk, finished our food and headed back to the site. We passed the hanging bloody chainmail and left through the door we had entered. As we crossed the main yard I noticed another big steel container that looked like it held something weird.

I couldn't quite grasp it mentally. There seemed to be a small yellow hoof poking out of the top of the container, and some weird pale alien flesh that didn't quite look like any part of a cow I recognised. My curiosity got the better of me.

'What do you reckon is in there, John?' I said.

'Dunno,' he replied, 'let's go and have a look.'

As we got closer to the container we wished we hadn't. We saw the bright yellow partially formed hooves, the pale almost fur, and the eyes that had never seen anything. This dirty steel industrial container was full of unborn cows. Full. There must have been thirty of them in there, all rudely piled and ready for some weird and occult part of the process. Maybe they had already been through the process.

'Fucking hell,' muttered John. 'This place is enough to turn me vegetarian. That is fucking wrong.' John had grown up on a farm in Ireland and was one of the least squeamish and sentimental people I knew. 'Why would they do that?' he said. 'What's it for?'

I didn't know. If I had to guess now, I would say it had something to do with foetal bovine serum, but we didn't know about all that hi-tech stuff back then, not having computers and everything.

'Let's go, man,' I needlessly said.

We walked away from the skip full of foetuses, away from the chatter of the café, away from the cows that had actually managed to be born. We didn't say anything until we reached the stinkiest tank in the world, which was being tended to by a man dressed in overalls standing on the little hill.

John greeted him and the man greeted us in turn. 'What's in there, then?' asked John cheerily.

The man in charge of the source of the reek invited us up to have a look.

In for a penny in for a pound, right?

We climbed up the stairs to where the man was standing.

'Have a look in there,' he said.

So we did.

It was a huge circular tank of horrible-looking, foul-smelling glop, with an endlessly rotating mechanical paddle that was stirring the stuff up.

'That's mainly blood, piss and shit,' offered our new friend. 'We turn it into fuel and compost eventually. That paddle stops it clotting. Nothing is wasted here!' He looked pretty pleased with himself, and why not, I suppose?

'Fucking stinks, doesn't it?' said John.

'Yeah, it does, but you should try getting some in your mouth. That's really fucking horrible!' Having said this, the man laughed a bit too loudly and weirdly, and for a little bit too long.

'Obviously, we can't process all of the blood,' he went on

jovially. 'That's why we are building the new waste management system down in the field where you're working. At the
moment, we collect a lot of the blood and put it in these big
trucks, which inject it into the ground. Sometimes they inject
fifty tons of blood a day into those fields where you two are
working.'

I tried to process that information. Some giant hypodermic
syringe on a truck, injecting fifty tons of cow blood into the
earth?

We left the shit stirrer's attendant on top of his little hill of
shit and walked past the tidy piles of carefully graded compost
that were ready for sale. They didn't smell of anything at all.

Jumping Ship

To say I left because of money is too simple. It went much deeper than that. They say that craziness is doing the same thing over and over again and expecting the outcome to be different, and I suppose I had hoped it would all turn out OK if I did my best. That stupid optimism that had been lurking at the bottom of the trench while I had been having my little tantrum in the hole I was digging after Spacemen 3 came back to bite me on the arse again – and, you know what? Looking back, I'm glad. I don't give a fuck that I was living in a caravan on twenty quid a week because I couldn't sign on because I was on the run from the debts I had incurred in the band. I gave a bit of a fuck when one of the songs had been leased to an advert for Nestlé for seventy grand and I didn't receive a penny. Now, I don't give a fuck. Because I can look back at that work I did and feel happy with it. I can look myself in the eye and say, 'Well, it wasn't too easy sometimes but maybe it was worthwhile.' And maybe that's worth something too. I didn't leave because I had no money. I left because I did not want to mix my soul with a thing that I believed was not fair. It costs you too much. And I ain't talking about money. I left because I lost faith in the people around me to do the right thing. We were divided and conquered and everybody lost something in the process.

That was the hardest thing to take after two years of hard work. Really. I lived and breathed it and I loved it. But, it wasn't the music that hurt me. It was the business. I made the mistake of confusing the making of music with the making of money, and for short periods of my life that made me hate music itself. That was one of the greatest mistakes I ever made. I can still imagine us making most of the music we made even if we had never been paid. Maybe we would have fought over who got what pittance from the beer-sodden hat at the end of the night, but I reckon we would have still done it. I hope so anyway. I like to think so.

I poured my heart and soul into that music the same way I am doing so into this book.

I have been holed up in an attic room in Zagreb now for over two months. Eating cheese sandwiches, agonising over what to put in and what to leave out. It matters to me. Art is sacred and you should never whore the muse. That music was sacred to me when we made it, and whatever happened afterwards . . . that's just business. I do not believe that the business ever served the music as it should have.

I finally decided that it was time to leave the band on a trip over to Dublin. It was to be my last show with Spiritualized but I didn't know it at the time. We were due to play at a club in the newly opened Temple Bar district. We'd arrived a day early and I had a room to myself in the hotel, so I'd gone out drinking alone and made some new friends easily enough. Dublin is good like that. They'd taken me off to the Trinity College bar and we'd had a few pints and it was all good, but the way things were going in the band was gnawing at me. We played the show and it all went well. Afterwards we got drunk and danced in the club, and it was the first time I ever heard 'Smells Like Teen Spirit'. We didn't know what it was but we danced like idiots to it, and when it was over I pranced over to the DJ booth and demanded to know what the song was called. It was all good spirited and I really had no problems with any-one in the band, even as I was thinking about jumping ship. I jumped ship, metaphorically and damn near physically at one point, on the ferry on the way home. After sitting alone drinking myself into enough courage to actually say what was on my mind, I had called Mark over to a bar away from the other members of the band and I poured my heart out to him. I didn't know what to do. I loved the band but I could see where it was heading and I knew there was no longer a place for me in it. Mark fetched the rest of the band and I spilled a few more tears and told them I couldn't go on any more. I didn't even mention the financial stuff, because I didn't want to cause problems. I wanted the band to be OK and I thought the best way was to keep my mouth shut. On the way out of the ferry Jason came up to me and said, 'Is it because Kate is in the band? It is more important to me to have you in the band than it is to have Kate in the band.' I was kind of touched by that but, in another way, I was surprised he didn't get it. I had tried to talk to him about my worries. Maybe he didn't care. Maybe it doesn't matter.

Despite his earlier promises that the band would be a democracy and that we were all going to get an even split, Jason had approached me a couple of months earlier and mentioned that maybe it wasn't such a good idea to give Jonny and Mark an equal split in case they took the cash and ran. He'd mentioned putting them on a wage. He'd said that I could still have my cut of the advance but that he didn't trust them.

It was a strange conversation. I couldn't understand his fears. Mark and Jonny were absolutely solidly behind the band and it seemed that his paranoia was the only thing that would cause that to change.

The album itself had already been recorded, with the bulk of the tracks being laid down at VHF in Rugby. It had been cheap to record and it was sounding good. Jason then started mixing it, and, under pressure from the record company, he started to mix it at studios that weren't cheap. He was mixing down at Bath Moles for a while, and then we had booked a studio called Comforts Place down in Surrey, ostensibly to record 'Feel So Sad'. That single cost almost as much to record as the rest of the album. The high point of that recording, for me, was when a session singer had come down to do some female vocals.

She told us that she had been the voice of the 'Trio' adverts that had been pretty popular when we were children. She sang the Trio advert a lot more times than she sang 'Feel So Sad' that day.

Here I was getting into debt again, and there we were, in a hugely expensive studio which had tennis courts and a full staff to cook us breakfast in the morning and make our evening meals. There was a picture of the Bee Gees playing tennis on the wall. It was sort of glamorous, I suppose, but when you can't actually pay your rent that kind of glamour is more expensive than you can imagine. Especially if everyone isn't in the same position. And it seemed that we weren't all in the same position.

A mate of mine, an estate agent, had come up to me in a pub in Rugby where I had been having a pint and said, 'You must be doing pretty well for yourself?'

I half expected this to be another person in the pub asking me to buy them a pint because I had been on the telly, so I narrowed my eyes and said, 'What do you mean? I'm skint. Midland Bank is paying for this pint I'm holding. I can't even cover my rent.'

'Really?' he said. 'Because your bandmate and his missus were in my estate agent's the other day and they were looking to buy pretty big houses. They were talking about paying cash.'

Shortly after this I had been talking to Mark about the rest of the advance money that we had been promised. It was overdue, and I was complaining about it.

'There isn't any more advance money,' Mark said. 'Didn't you know? It's all been spent on recording and mixing.'

I hadn't known, and when Jason had offered to put me on a low wage as a retainer sometime later it had all fallen into place, and it didn't seem worth talking about, or trying to explain or understand. I made my decision quietly and then spilled my guts on that ferry ride back from Dublin. I still genuinely loved the band and I wanted them to do well. I wanted Pete to do well too. I wanted everyone to do well. Why not?

So as we got into the van and rolled it off the ferry for the drive back to Rugby I explained that I didn't want to leave them in trouble as far as any band commitments were concerned, and that I would do whatever had to be done until they could find a replacement.

I had done a fair amount of psychedelics during the previous year, and I was bit peeled and sensitive in some ways. They probably thought I'd lost my mind, and maybe I had in a way, but it wasn't the acid. I still turned up on time for every show and I had never blown a gig or been incapable of playing. I kept my shit together when I had to: music was always more important to me than drugs.

Later, we agreed that the last engagement I was to have with the band was to be the Peel session that was booked to take place in a couple of weeks. There was no bad feeling. No arguments. We just agreed, and maybe nobody was happy about it.

I didn't even feel bad when it came time to do the session. We all made our way down to the BBC studios in London, and the atmosphere was fine, if a little strained. Most of that session was laid down live in one take, with a few horn overdubs laid on afterwards. We knew how to play the songs by that point. Towards the end of the session, Doug D'Arcy turned up to cast his well-manicured opinion over the proceedings.

When Jason and I had first gone down to the Dedicated offices in London to present him with the final mix of 'Anyway That You Want Me' he had sat behind his expensive desk, smiled after listening to it, and said, 'I think it needs some more guitars.' That had surprised me a bit at the time, especially when Jason actually listened to him. We had been making music for quite a while by this point, music that had never been exposed to the creative opinions of a man who had never written a song or played in a band in his life. Regardless, Doug was in charge of the purse strings and he had also been fairly heavily stung off the back of the Spacemen 3 collapse, so maybe he owed it to his ego to have an opinion that we pretended to care about.

He'd gotten a bit more guitar and he had also gotten a picture off my wall for the sleeve of the record. Natty had given me a painting he had done that was an aquatic blur of oil pastel colours. I had given the picture to Doug under the express condition that I was to get it back at some point because it was my personal property. It never did come back to me, despite my increasingly irate protestations to Doug when he would turn up at shows. He just fobbed me off with his little smile and said he would return it. I later found out it was hanging, framed, in the BMG offices. Maybe it is still there somewhere.

Given all of this, when Doug D'Arcy appeared in the studio and walked into the control room to oversee what was to be my very last session with the band, I was not overjoyed. He was wearing an expensive-looking suit and he had on an unusual and expensive-looking pair of shoes which had little flowers embroidered onto them. Around the waist of his suit jacket was what looked to be a piece of garden twine. The piece of designer twine instantly took Jonny's attention. He barrelled over to Doug, laughed, and grabbed either end of the twine.

It wasn't actually garden twine, of course, but very expensive material that had been tastefully sewn into the very tasteful jacket so that it looked like garden twine. When Jonny grabbed both ends and pulled them tight, Doug's beautifully fitting suit bunched up in the middle, making him look very funny indeed. Jonny tied the two ends into a crude bow while Doug, very patiently and with barely discernible disgust, tolerated it.

'You look like a tramp, Doug!' Jonny said, laughing like a maniac. 'Did you find this jacket down at the allotment?'

Doug smiled his usual thin smile and patiently undid the knot that Jonny had so gleefully tied.

'This suit cost more than you will earn all year, Jonny,' he said, with a slightly more believable smile.

Doug sat down and cast his discerning ear over the proceedings while smiling the same money smile. I decided it was time to go and pack my equipment for the last time. My work was done.

As I wound my cables and packed the pedals away, I considered my choices and my reasons for them. I was fairly sure I was doing the right thing, even though nobody understood my reasons for leaving. It felt fucking awful, but it felt right.

I picked my old Gibson Thunderbird off its stand, laid it in its case, and closed the lid. As I was snapping the catches shut, Doug came up behind me.

'How are things with you then, Willie?' he said, in an affable and reasonable tone.

'Not too bad, Doug, thanks,' I said. I asked him if he had enjoyed Christmas.

'Yes, I did, thanks,' he replied. 'It was lovely. For the first time in ages we were all actually at our house in England. We have spent quite a few of them abroad in recent years, so it was really nice to have a good old-fashioned British Christmas at home for a change. How was yours?'

'Well, Doug, to be honest, it wasn't the best I've ever had. I am absolutely flat broke and I spent most of the holidays

carrying bricks at a slaughterhouse so that I could pay off some
of the rent I owe. You know I'm a vegetarian, right?'

He looked a little upset by the news, but nowhere near as
upset as I had felt when I had been slithering around in the
crap and mud carrying bricks on a freezing cold New Year's
Day at Midland Meat Packers.

'Oh dear,' he said. 'Sorry to hear that. We really should go
out for dinner sometime.'

'No thanks, Doug,' I replied evenly. 'Can I have my picture
back, please?'

And that was the end of that.

Part Four

Living on Nuts and Berries

Psychotic Reaction

I hate myself for loving you.
Written on a toilet door

The first time I heard Spiritualized playing without me, I was sitting alone in my flat next door. Jonny had been sent round to make sure it was OK. Because I had no doorbell, he threw some tiny stones up to my window to get my attention. I leaned out and he smiled up to me and said, 'Willie, we are gonna rehearse next door. Is that cool?' He was as friendly and enthusiastic as he always was and hopefully always will be. Despite my misgivings, I couldn't be a cunt about it. Being horrible to Jonny is like being horrible to life. What was I going to say?

I was hurting, because, with all my heart I had loved the band and the music we were making, but I had left of my own accord. 'Of course it's cool,' I lied, with a smile. 'Have a good 'un.' And then added some sarcastic comment about their recent publicity shot, where they were all wearing leather, trying to look rock and roll while lolling around in the back of a car. I was trying to make myself feel better. Jonny just laughed and I closed the window and sat down trying to prepare myself for what was to come. I told myself it was fine, made a cup of tea, rolled a cigarette and tried to relax.

It never occurred to me not to sit and listen, which was, perhaps, a masochistic move too far. Whatever. I had made my choice and I bore nobody any ill will. I certainly didn't want the band to suffer, but perhaps I couldn't go as far as wanting them to be as good as they had been when I played with them.

The first song started up and I heard it loud and clear through the thin fake wall that separated the two flats. 'If I

Were with Her Now', with its offbeat rhythm that Jonny and I had come up with in the back room of the Imperial not even a year before. The way I had felt playing it and the way I felt listening to the sound of the song coming through the wall as I sat and listened seemed to come from different lives.

It is a song of yearning, which contains the certain knowledge of redemption through the inevitable meeting of the subject and the object of their desire. The song talks about drugs being an unsatisfactory substitute for real love, and states as fact that the closeness of someone you love will change your state of mind for the better. Better than a hit. Better than a trip. Better than better itself. Being so close to the thing I had loved was like watching someone fuck the person you love as you stand helplessly behind a one-way mirror. I loved the music that band made, I loved being in the band, and now I had a ring-side seat for the grand betrayal that I had instigated by leaving. Everyone had told me I was crazy to leave, but I just had to. I knew what was coming and the least worst option had been to quietly turn away and take another path. Of course, love is not so easily broken and closely bound fates not so quickly un-entwined, so there I was, sitting alone and feeling lonely as my bandmates got ready for the honeymoon and the inevitable success of the album we had spent a year making and promoting, while I sat next door and listened to the party. Despite my own prickling self-defences and the disparaging voices in my head about the quality of the approaching bass playing, my heart was beating faster, and I was doing my best to stay calm. All of the contradictions I had felt on leaving the band were coming home to roost, and I was being forced to hatch the egg of my own choice whether I liked it or not. I was in debt, I wasn't in love, and I wasn't in a band any more. All of my dreams and ambitions for music were as threadbare as my bank account. My heart beat a little faster and my mind flickered between the choices I had made. I put a record on and tried to drown out the sound of the band I had been in with other music. *Kind of Blue* by Miles Davis unfurled like a ribbon of heavy smoke in the still room. It sounded resigned and steadfast, triumphant and defeated, and between each carefully measured note and beat could be heard stories of lost love, bum deals, hard times and hope. I couldn't hear any of it at the time. Even as I was trying to block out the sound of the music next door with the sound of Miles Davis I was still listening through the trumpet for the familiar sound of the love I had left. I knew that if I were in there with them, playing the bass, I would change. That, given the familiarity of that warm sound and the closeness of the band, I would feel better, safe and sure, but I also knew that *it* wouldn't change. The thing that had forced my hand and led me to resign was never going to change. It would only be ignored and postponed to a later time when it would be even more difficult to quit, like with any habit that refuses to acknowledge what lies beneath it. So there I was, getting ready for the kick and the withdrawal was going to be more brutal than I had imagined.

I pulled the needle off the record, sat back in the chair, and resigned myself to the inevitable, as the band started playing 'Run'. I took a grim pleasure in knowing that Sean wasn't going to nail the bassline. The familiar drumbeat started up. I knew all of the exact cues for the song and where I should have been coming in. The beat hits hard for threes and then skitters away for the same time like a boxer coming in for three jabs before dancing away again, while the guitars keep the forward momentum and stay on the heartbeat with the kick drum. The bass sounded disappointingly correct on the verses – missing a little of the easy groove that Jonny and I had found over the last two years maybe, but fairly tight for someone learning the ropes. It was the break that was going to trip him up, I knew that, and I moved into the kitchen to get a better earful of the mistakes I hoped were coming. I wasn't hoping for the band to fail – I was just trying to feel like I was worth more than I felt at the time, which was close to nothing. I had been replaced, like a punctured tyre or a broken window. Quickly and without mourning. At least that was how it felt. I would have done the same thing in their position, and I didn't expect them to do differently either.

The singing began and the familiar vocal refrain that had been borrowed from J. J. Cale and the Velvets drifted over the low frequencies that were coming through the wall. The lyrics talk about somebody on the run with nothing to carry and no soul. I guess I could relate to that in ways that were different now, even though I was in my own flat a hair's breadth from beating my head against the wall to drown out the sound I had loved only a few weeks before. I started to feel itchy. I scratched at myself distractedly, hardly recognising the fact, caught up as I was in regret, recrimination and self-loathing. I paced the kitchen floor and the song ploughed on as I made myself increasingly agitated by what I thought was the dumbest damn decision I had ever made. I considered going next door and taking the bass from Sean and explaining I had been wrong. Apologising. Then I imagined us all laughing about it like it had been a temporary madness on all of our parts and that everything was going to turn out fine, like it had just been a big joke and how could we even have thought such a thing? 'Hahahaha.'

Deep down I knew it was bullshit. It was over and there was no going back. I scratched myself and realised that I was feeling weirdly hot and that the insatiable itch was spreading. As I rolled up my sleeves to examine my own skin I heard the words, 'I love you,' come through the wall. My skin began to tighten and the itching started to burn. My mouth was dry and my lips felt like they'd been stung by nettles. I scratched at myself and ran my fingers over the raising rash of tiny bumps and blisters spreading across my skin. It was turning into a scene from *The Exorcist* and I was beginning to think that, this time, I was truly operating under a curse of my own making. I stripped my clothes off and examined my armpits. Sure enough, there the gooseflesh had turned a nasty shade of scarlet, and it was spreading fast. I could feel the prickling reaction running across my body and through my blood, raising angry points of flesh and turning me to fire inside. I scratched and scratched to no relief, as the music buried into me and my body reacted on a huge scale. I was going into anaphylactic shock and there were no obvious reasons why. I had experienced it once before as a teenager and I knew the symptoms well enough. My throat was growing tight and I was starting to swell up like a balloon, the skin stretching across every inch of me as my immune system started to go haywire and attack the rest of my body in defence.

This, at least, served to drag my attention away from what was going on next door. I knew I had to do something fast. Having neither a phone nor a car and with the emergency room of the local hospital too far away to walk, I decided to go round and see my friend Sheila, who lived just round the corner and who was a pharmacist. There was a part of me that was wondering if I had gone completely mad, because I had never ever heard of somebody having an allergic reaction to music before. As I got ready to leave the house the band started playing 'Anyway That You Want Me', which had been the first single we had recorded. *Am I loving you in vain?* I heard the lyrics but I was no longer listening to the quality, or lack of it, in the bass playing.

I was too concerned with getting some medical help and a second opinion on what I thought was an attack of psychosomatic madness. I dragged my coat on, ran down the stairs and locked the door behind me on the way out. I was now standing in the yard of the plumber's between the two flats, directly beneath the window where Spiritualized were playing. I stopped for a second, unable to resist the pull of the sound and heard the words, 'Am I loving you in vain?' Shaking my head and swelling by the minute, I turned my back on the weirdness of it all and ran for the small wooden door that led out of the plumber's yard filled with the pipes and pans of potential piss houses. I ran the hundred metres to Sheila's house, frantically rang the bell and knocked on the door while feverishly scratching at my body, which now felt like it was home to a nest of angry ants. Sheila answered the door and immediately looked concerned. 'What's the matter?' she said. 'You look awful.'

'Sheila, can you give me a lift to casualty? I think I am having an allergic reaction. Quick.' I stepped into the light of her hallway and after a quick look at my face, she ran back into the house, grabbed her car keys and we both ran to the car. When we arrived at St Cross, she parked in the place reserved for ambulances and we both ran into reception. She talked to the woman behind the desk, explained the urgency of the situation, and that she was a pharmacist. Within five minutes I was sitting in a chair in a curtained room with my shirt off while the doctor prepared two shots of adrenaline. I felt like my whole body was on fire and my face looked as though I had gone three rounds with a prizefighter.

As the first needle slid into the vein in my right arm and the doctor pressed the plunger I could feel the wave of relief spread through my body. The doctor checked my left arm and had a little more difficulty finding a vein. After the second shot was in I could feel the drug working instantly, cooling the angry heat in my blood as the furious itch began to subside.

Sheila stroked my arm and said, 'Are you all right, hon?'

I nodded and smiled and thanked the doctor and Sheila.

They watched me for five minutes to see that I wasn't blowing up like a zeppelin any more, and then they left me alone for five minutes. I could feel myself returning to normal. I was taking easy breaths again as the drugs did their work and the panic began to subside. I hadn't thought about the band once between leaving the house and starting to feel better.

I still don't know what happened.

Fame at Last

Eventually, things returned to something approaching normality. Spiritualized continued to practise next door now and again, but I had no further episodes with excess histamine and urgent trips to Accident and Emergency for shots of adrenaline. The agony was subsiding.

Despite the fact that Jason and Kate were my next-door neighbours, we no longer socialised, nor did we spend much time in each other's houses. It was like a dead relationship somehow and, although I bore them no ill will, we became increasingly distant. I read the overwhelmingly positive reviews in the papers when *Lazer Guided Melodies* came out, and then Spiritualized went out on the road to promote it. Sometimes I'd see them waiting in the van outside or bump into the rest of the band, and although it was a bit awkward, for reasons nobody really understood, it really wasn't as weird as it might have been.

I was still fairly heavily in debt to the bank, and I'd taken a few odd jobs to try to pay it off. My debt was still hovering around the three-grand mark and my sporadic window-cleaning job was not going to pay it off in a hurry. I was also signing on the dole and I had made an agreement to pay the debts off at a rate of ten pounds per fortnight with the bank. If I broke the agreement I was in big trouble. It would mean that I had defaulted and then they would have been within their rights to break my door down and take my stuff. When I had arranged the payment plan with the bank I had gone to see the nice bank manager who had looked through the music papers with me back in the hopeful days of Spacemen 3. I'd sat across the desk from him and explained the situation I was in. 'I feel like the vultures are circling,' I said to him.

'We're one of them, aren't we?' he replied, looking at me apologetically over his spectacles.

I think if it had been up to him, he would have let me off the debt there and then.

I was also starting to receive threatening letters from the bailiffs over a different unpaid bill. I had refused to pay my poll tax as a matter of principle and now the council was looking for me too. They couldn't legally kick the door in, but they could gain entry through an open window, or if I was stupid enough to let them in. It was a bureaucratic matter and before they could get to the point of legally kicking my door in, they had to make sure that they had a point of contact with me, which I was understandably avoiding. Life was becoming a bit of a cat and mouse game, where I would check outside the flat before leaving the house and always think twice before I answered the phone or the door. Not having a doorbell was proving to be a useful diversionary tactic. The bailiffs could stand around all day outside, ringing a bell that wasn't attached to anything for all I cared.

Rowley Ford visited me one day and offered me some good advice: 'Will, you've got to get your head out of your arse. You can't sit in this flat for ever.'

He was right.

It was getting close to Christmas when I heard the first stones against the window.

I was pretty sure that the bailiffs hadn't worked out which window to throw stones at yet. Anyway, it was nearly Christmas and even those wankers knocked off for Jesus's birthday. I looked out past the net curtains and saw a friend of mine looking up to my window from the street below.

What followed over the next few days was nobody's idea of festive fun. If the shit is going to hit the fan, it always seems to hit the fan at Christmas. It is a supposedly light and joyful time of year in the depths of midwinter when everyone is so intent on having a good time that you can't find serious help for love nor money. I guess it is no accident that the whole Jesus, Mary and Joseph story took place at this time of year.

That basic story, in case you are unfamiliar with it, is that a hugely pregnant woman and her husband visit a small town so that they can attend to some council census thing. Because it is Christmas, all of the hotels are full and they are unable to find a room for the night. The luckless woman is reduced to giving birth in a stable surrounded by barnyard animals. Let's just think about the realities of that for a second.

Anyway, it was Christmas and what neither I nor the young woman who I had let into my house knew was that she was about to go into a fully fledged psychotic episode, and I was about to unwittingly bear the brunt of it. I had once told her if she was in trouble she could come to mine. Maybe something in her remembered that. She stayed for two nights and during that time her behaviour became progressively weirder and more unnerving. She didn't eat, she didn't sleep, and she wouldn't let me sleep either.

At first she had seemed a little scared and ill at ease and I thought she just needed some rest and a place to hide out away from the party scene. After a while, it became evident that she had become fixated on me and had decided that I was either Brian Wilson, the devil, Jesus, or a combination of all three, which is a bit weird because I was only a bass player, after all. I had never been close to that kind of illness before and the ferocity and strength of her increasingly warped reality damn near threw me off my own axis. This hadn't become totally apparent until day two of her unscheduled stay, by which point she was screaming at me every time I went to sleep and alternating between sweetness and demonic rage every five minutes. In my innocence, I didn't know what to do about it. I didn't know what was happening, so I placated her, I humoured her, I brushed the strange behaviour off, and I explained it away to myself as I became increasingly unable to distinguish my reality from her delusions. It was only partly to do with the two nights of sleep deprivation and the overall creeping strangeness of the situation. By the end of the final night, I was a broken man. She would subject me to a torrent of abuse and I would just nod. If she had asked me to throw myself out of a window I would have done it without complaint. My initial concern for her and my subsequent unwillingness to throw her out, or draw the line, had proved to be a terrible mistake. She pointed at a large Silver Surfer poster I had on my living room wall and said, 'Is that who you think you are? The Silver Surfer?'

By this point if she had told me I thought I was a three-horned unicorn I would have meekly agreed.

'Hmmm,' she said thoughtfully. 'Do you mind if I cut some of your comics up?'

I didn't mind that either.

So she set to work, cutting up my comics, stopping only to shout at me every time I began to drift off to sleep.

By the morning, I didn't know if it was Christmas Day or Wednesday, and she was in possession of a brand new home-made badge. 'What do you think of it?' she said. 'Do you like it? Come and have a look at it.'

So I got a little closer. She had cut out a picture of the Silver Surfer in which he was being subjected to an unspecific torment on some cosmic electric rack. The Silver Surfer was uttering the words, 'She is draining me of all of my power.' It was certainly a striking badge.

'Do you like it?' she asked again. 'That's you, that is. We are going for a walk up town. Come on, Brian.'

I walked into town beside her, feeling like I was in a bad dream that I couldn't wake up from.

As we made our unholy promenade through town, we bumped into a couple of my friends who were buying the last of their Christmas shopping. It was Christmas Eve. 'All right, Will?' they said, seeming jolly and full of Christmas cheer. 'Merry Christmas.' They looked a bit concerned by my hollow eyes and lack of response.

'Do you like my badge?' my friend said, butting in front of me and holding her lapel out. 'Here, have a look. I made it myself. Does it remind you of anybody?'

And then she made them look at the damn badge.

My friends looked confused and they glanced between the two of us searching for some explanation.

I just looked away.

'Come on,' she said. 'Let's go shopping.' And we continued our little walk through town, stopping occasionally if we met someone we knew, so that she could show them the badge.

Sounds crazy, doesn't it? It was. She was in the grip of a fairly serious episode of mental illness and I hadn't worked it out. If you have become used to eccentric behaviour and occasional bouts of mania brought on by personal peculiarity, or temporary intoxication, it can be surprisingly difficult to tell the difference between unusual behaviour and outright psychosis. There is, however, a difference – an important one.

If you learn to recognise the difference, you might save someone's life, or your own some day. It might also stop you needlessly phoning the cops every time someone does something slightly outside of your narrow frame of normality. It's a delicate judgement call, and it is not one that I was in any way prepared to make at that time.

We parted in the town centre, and as she got further away it was as though a fog lifted from me. I began to go over the events of the previous night and none of it fitted together in ways that made any rational sense. I began to suspect that she had some very real and serious problems and that I hadn't even noticed until I had managed to put some distance between myself and her formidable manic energy.·

The more I thought about the situation, the stranger it became and the more convinced I was that she actually needed help. Despite my misgivings I was so tired that I didn't trust myself. I walked back to my house and immediately fell asleep.

Within an hour the phone started ringing. The first and second time I picked it up, I was greeted by a torrent of screaming weirdness. After the third time, I unplugged the phone and left the house. I decided to get a second opinion. I knew some members of her family so I made some phone calls to them, and made some general enquiries about her wellbeing and asked for their opinions on her mental state.

It was Christmas Eve. Nobody wants to hear that stuff just before Santa arrives.

Eventually, I managed to persuade her family that she might need some help. She was still at a point where she was able to keep a lid on her distress and to feign normality in some ways, so that when the priest came out to see her, or when the doctor finally arrived to pay a five-minute visit after endless phone calls, she smiled and acted surprised and when they had left, and only in front of me would she manifest that obsessive supernatural weirdness again. It was as hard as hell to get any help on Christmas Day. Her family said that perhaps she was in love with me, and that people sometimes act strangely when they are in love. Despite the fact that I had doubted my own sanity previously, I became convinced that this was a little bit more serious than that. I talked to another one of my friends about it.

'She's only a woman, man. What do you think she's gonna

do? Just tell her to fuck off,' he said. Over the next couple of days she made a point of hanging around outside my house, ringing me up, or appearing wherever I was. Whenever she did, things got weird. Telling her to fuck off was not going to work.

Between Christmas and New Year I was at my wits' end. She was everywhere I went, and her problems were becoming so obvious that other people were beginning to pay attention. A friend of mine gave me a lift down to my flat and I explained the situation to her on the way. We pulled up outside the flat to find angry mad writing scrawled all across the front of the plumber's windows and the door that led to my flat. Written in red, and in the desperate handwriting of the crazy, it said: 'William Carruthers is a worthless adopted bastard.'

My friend looked at me with sympathy and said, 'I'd get out of town for a bit if I were you, Will.'

The next day I was on a very long train ride away from Rugby. The further away I got, the better I felt.

People say you can't run away from your problems, but maybe they just haven't had the right kind of problems yet.

By the time I returned from my journey, I had missed a sign-ing-on date and my dole had been stopped. I had also missed a couple of payments to the bank and had therefore defaulted on my agreement with them, meaning they were going to send in the debt collectors and the bailiffs. Because my dole was stopped, I was also receiving no rent money, and that meant I was behind on that too. I moved out of the flat as quickly as possible and made arrangements to pay back the debt to my landlord.

I moved back to my mum's place and took a four-week job with a shot-blast gang up a canal tunnel. It was January and it was a dirty and difficult job. At the end of it, I paid the remaining rent I owed to my landlord, bought a British army sleeping bag and a good rucksack with my remaining cash, and then spent the last of my money on a bus ticket north to help a friend move house. From there I drifted wherever there was a spare room or a couch, moving up and down the country, hitchhiking, taking odd jobs, staying with family and friends, and working hand to mouth. I would return to Rugby occasionally, stay for a while then drift away again. I didn't feel safe staying in one place too long.

I had walked away from my debts. It was a move that meant I was no longer eligible for any housing benefit. It meant I couldn't see a dentist or a doctor. It meant I couldn't be on the electoral roll. It meant I couldn't rent a flat. It meant I couldn't pay utilities. It meant I couldn't get a bank account. It meant that I would have to scrape by in a world of cash-in-hand payments, with no visible social support network. It meant that I was on my own. I had become one of Margaret Thatcher's ideal citizens, with no recourse to state support, existing in a purely private world where everything had a price, and if you couldn't pay for it then you had to go without.

Of course, I didn't know any of that when I went. I just hit the fucking road. During the golden age of Britpop and 'Cool Britannia' I had somehow slipped through the cracks. I didn't play in another band for four years but I still carried a guitar with me everywhere I went.

There was a notable quote from one of the members of Tony Blair's government when they were first elected, after years of Conservative rule. An interviewer asked about the million men who were missing from the official census records. A million men, in my age group, had simply vanished from official government records around this time, and I had been one of them.

The interviewer asked the government official where he thought we had all gone. 'We think they've all gone to Ibiza,' he said, with half a smirk.

The social machine is a strange beast. In many ways you do not notice the way that it operates, or the scope of its operations, until you are in a position outside of it. As an outsider, I was made very much aware of the limitations of existence beyond the mechanisms of society. I found myself in so many catch-22 situations that there seemed to be no way back, and that only increased the sense of exclusion and, in a way, my determination to survive. It was a smooth slide out and a steep and slippery climb back in. Like a funhouse slide, with neither fun nor laughter.

If it had not been for the kindnesses of my family and friends and my own ability to adapt and make a living where I could, things could have gone very wrong indeed. I suppose sometimes they did.

I had a tooth abscess during this period. I couldn't find a free dentist and I had no money to pay for one. The tooth would infect and leave me in pain for a few days, then it would drain and eventually become reinfected. I wasn't using drugs at all, but I began to treat the pain with opium that I would make myself from plants I gathered on wastelands.

Abscesses hurt quite a lot, and I suffered with that one, on and off, for about a year, until one day it got so bad that I couldn't even open my mouth any more.

I rang a dentist and made an appointment without telling him that I had no money. When I went into his surgery he said, 'Please open your mouth and let me have a look.'

I said, 'I gan't oken my 'uckin outh. I need anti-giotics. I 'ot no 'oney. Lease gi me a grescription.'

He wrote out the prescription, but when he found out I had no money he never asked me back for further treatment.

Two Christmas Stories

Through every fault of my own I was living rent-free in my friend's back garden, in a small caravan he owned. A song thrush would perch in a nearby tree every morning and sing a song, and I enjoyed the sound of the rain on the roof. It was a really tiny living space, but it didn't leak and it was warm and cozy until the temperature dropped below freezing, at which point the Calor Gas heating pipes would freeze and, to avoid the same fate, I would retreat to my trusty sleeping bag, listen to the radio, and write while I waited for the thaw.

At the time, I was earning some money working with a man and a van doing house removals. He would come round and call to me through the big steel gates at the back of the property where the caravan was parked, and I would go and work for him for as long as he needed me. I worked for five pounds an hour. Sometimes he would employ me for half an hour. That was two pound fifty. I certainly learned the value of money. It was, I suppose, a subsistence existence. I was living hand to mouth but somehow I was quite content. It's surprising what you get used to.

As we got closer to Christmas the work became less frequent and I decided to try to sign on for a couple of weeks to get some money from the government. I had become pretty much invisible to society, which made signing on, or getting housing benefit, nearly impossible. So, cap in hand, I went down to the dole office, filled in the sheaf of paperwork they gave me and handed it back to them. After waiting two weeks, during which time I had visited them occasionally to make polite enquiries, I had still heard nothing regarding my claim, so I went in again to ask about it. They told me that I was expected for an interview at the big social security building nearby. Apparently there was a problem with my details.

I arrived at the featureless office block at the appointed time and date and sat down in a moulded plastic chair to wait for my interview. Eventually, I was told to go to another room. This particular room was about six foot by twelve, it had no windows and it contained a desk that stretched the entire width of the room, bisected by an unbreakable-looking clear screen that ran all of the way from the desktop to the ceiling. Effectively the room was divided into two and there was no way through from one side to the other.

There was another moulded plastic chair on my side of the screen, so I sat down on it and proceeded to read the graffiti which had been scratched into the wood of the desk. I recognised a few names. Eventually, the door on the other side of the room opened and a man came through and sat down on a moulded chair that was very much like the one I was sitting in. The man was middle aged and nondescript. He didn't return my smile, greeted me with no emotion and made it clear that he wanted to get down to business. I felt the same. I had been bored since I walked through the door.

'Mr Carruthers,' he began. 'We are having some problems with the details you have provided for us.' He was still as blank as the screen he was looking through. 'Specifically,' he continued, 'the part where you claim to have lived under a hedge and eaten nuts and berries for two years.' He looked at me sceptically over his glasses.

'What's the problem with that?' I replied with a serious, but not too serious expression.

'Our computer will not accept it,' he said, looking at me with the air of a man who was missing an urgent appointment with a cup of tea and a biscuit.

'In that case,' I reassured him, 'the problem would seem to be with your computer and not with my actual details, because, in fact, I did live under a hedge during the specified time and did sustain myself with nuts and berries during that period. If you have a problem believing me, I can show you the hedge and the nuts and berries in question.'

At this point, he betrayed a little irritation, laid down his notes, looked me in the eye through his protective screen, and uttered the immortal words, 'Mr Carruthers, what do you see your role in society as being?'

I began to realise why the screen was there.

I had never thought of myself as having any particular role in society. I suppose I liked to think of myself as being a little bit like the song thrush that turned up and sang next to the caravan every morning, but I wasn't about to try to explain that complex philosophical point to him.

I decided to go on the offensive instead. 'What's your role in society?' I said to him.

'I am a guardian of public funds,' he said indignantly, with a little too much emphasis on the 'I'.

He had started justifying himself.

'No you aren't,' I said, getting into the flow of it. 'You are a drain on public funds. What are you on? About twenty grand a year to sit behind your little plastic screen asking insulting questions of a legitimate claimant?'

'I am not here to answer your questions,' he spluttered, implying that I was actually there to answer his questions, and not just to get the money that I was legally entitled to.

He composed himself and continued. 'You claim to be of no fixed abode and yet you say that you live in a caravan in your friend's back garden. That is a fixed abode. Why haven't you given us an address?'

I was a little bit annoyed with him but I held my temper

and smiled reasonably. 'Well, the situation is this,' I explained, as you would to an idiot or a machine. 'I do, indeed, live in my friend's back garden in a small but beautifully arranged caravan. However, they do not want me to sign on from that address, so if I tell you where I live, I no longer live there. You see, if I tell you I live there, I don't live there, but if I don't tell you I live there, I do live there unless I tell you I live there, at which point I live somewhere else, so I wouldn't be living there and that would be wrong, wouldn't it? Do you follow me?'

He kept on laying the blank face on me so I knew I was making progress. I continued, 'Furthermore, if you do not give me the money to which I am LEGALLY entitled, I shall find out where you live, because I know you must come out from behind that screen sometimes, and then I shall go back to my non-fixed abode and I will grasp the tow bar with my own bare hands and roll my humble caravan, on its little non-fixed wheels, onto the road outside the house where you live. I will park it there over Christmas and when you and your family are eating your Christmas dinner, I will scratch, pathetically, at your window, weeping and moaning in a theatrical manner.'

The tone was generally good-natured, but I did get a little theatrical towards the end just so he knew I had it in me.

I looked at him as dispassionately as I could manage. It seemed to be the order of the day. Just keep it factual. No need for messy emotions on either side of the plastic.

He looked back at me through the protective screen that did not divide us outside of the room.

'Very well,' he said. 'We shall assess your claim.'

He left through his little door and I left through mine.

Two days later I got my money, my role in society still undefined.

He ate his Christmas dinner in peace, and I suppose we were both happy in our own little ways.

Or Something . . .

People who write and read and review books are fucking
putting themselves a tiny little bit above the rest of us
who fucking make records and write pathetic little songs
for a living . . . I don't get it. Booksellers, book readers,
book writers, book owners – fuck all of them.
Noel Gallagher

The horn beeped and I appeared out of some bushes, much
to the amusement of the driver. I must have been pretty tired
because the four measly hours of sleep had just flown by. I
brushed the dirt off myself, got in the van and rolled a cigarette. The van had dropped me off a few hours earlier and there
had seemed to be little point in getting comfortable, so I had
chosen to sleep in the garden at my mum's house, where I was
living at the time. We had finished late the night before and
the van had gotten a flat tire on the way back to Rugby. There
had been many dull hours spent beside the motorway, wondering why nobody had a fucking spanner that could remove the
wheel nuts. We had one tiny spanner that fitted the wheel nuts,
but there was no way anybody could get enough leverage on
it by hand for it to do its job. In the end, my friend Jürgen, a
German fellow who had somehow ended up in Rugby dodging
national service in his own country, suggested we lift a nearby
drain cover, slide that over our useless spanner, and then use
it to get the necessary torque to remove the wheel nuts. It had
worked, much to everyone's relief.

'Just beep the horn when you get here,' I had said as I'd got
out of the van in the early hours of the morning. So they had,
and there I was, sitting in the back of a minibus that smelled

like hashish, tiredness and yesterday's beer as we drove and picked up the other workers from all over Rugby. By the time we were all loaded up and ready to go it was fucking seven o'clock in the morning, or something unfriendly.

Nobody was communicating beyond essential grunting and moaning, so I just went to sleep as the van made its way onto the motorway that would somehow lead us to the grand stately home of Knebworth. I was woken up by the sound of somebody puking out of the van window. This was nothing unusual. There were more than a few alcoholics and drug addicts on the team. They were decent people, but they lacked ambition or something.

Go team.

Somehow our company had won the contract to work at one of the biggest concerts ever. It was that defining moment in history when everybody's stupid low-rent indie dreams were finally going to be blasted into the stratosphere. NEW LABOUR. BRITPOP. KNEBWORTH. OASIS. COOL BRITANNIA. It was a time of optimism and new beginnings, and somehow I was finally part of the future. I'd hit the big time. Well, when I say 'hit' it, I mean I had blundered into it like a person might walk into a glass door presuming it was open. Due to a combination of zero monetary ambition and poverty, I had fallen into another low-end job. It was probably day three of the load-in. The day before the big rock and roll show.

We arrived at Knebworth and found the other crews from various parts of the country, who were all in the same state as we were and who were generally looking like they wished they were somewhere else too. Most people were fairly awake by the time we all gathered to start work. Somebody with lots of tools attached to their belt gave out the orders. Some members of the crews had skills, like tuning guitars, or climbing, or rigging, or lights. I had no skills. 'OK, Will,' my gaffer said to me, 'you can dig in the cables.' He gave me a spade and walked me out into the field in front of the stage. When we got to the mixing desk he pointed out a big cable that stretched into the distance in about three directions. It looked like a big fat black worm. I had to cut the turf out, dig a bit of soil out, lay the cable in the trench, and then put the turf on top so no paying customer would trip over it and have a funny turn. My gaffer fucked off and I took a couple of ephedrine tablets from my pocket and swallowed them. I was still half asleep when I stuck the spade into the ground and made a start. There was half a fucking mile of cable to dig in. I dug the turf out, laid the cable into the little trench and then stamped it down with my boots. I looked at the stage and wondered why I was digging out trenches, and then I did a bit more half-hearted digging until the tablets kicked in. I channelled all of that bullshit energy into my trenching. I was like a maniac, digging and laying and stamping like it mattered to me. By tea break I had done a hundred metres or so. Because of the drugs I had hardly noticed my own exertions, even though they weren't really drugs because I had got them from a chemist. They were decongestants. They certainly decongested my doubts about why I was fucking bothering.

My mate Jürgen came over and we both went backstage to find the 'hospitality' tent. As we sat down I noticed a certain amount of unease within the tent and turned to look at what everyone else was looking at. Standing at the entrance were two high-ranking police officers. Lots of people in the tent were on drugs, or wanted to be, so the appearance of policemen attracted understandable attention. It was pretty much unheard of for any police to be seen in the backstage area anywhere at these events. The high-ranking officers surveyed the situation. They smiled and appeared to be benign. Nobody smiled back. I went back to the cables. Dig, dig, stamp, stamp.

It just went on and on like that until it was time to have a food break.

I wasn't hungry so I went for a little look around the backstage area. There was another big tent, with a massive toy-car track in it. I took two more pills and went back to the cables.

Dig, dig, stamp, stamp.

It was quite sunny, and everything was almost in place for the gig of the fucking century. I have to admit that I didn't feel like I was involved in history in the making. The PA started to make sounds, big walls of pink noise and the occasional burst of music. Somewhere in the distance, near the stage, I saw two white golf carts with people in them. It was the stars of the show pretending to be the Beatles, or something. They drove round and round and laughed. Their joy seemed neither convincing nor entirely convinced, or maybe I was just jealous. When Oasis had started they were like a punk rock Slade, and they were pretty good. After they got a bit bigger someone made the mistake of telling them they were like the Beatles, and, because they were popular and putting lots of cocaine up their noses, they believed that maybe they might even be better than the Beatles, a little bit. I was basically unmoved by my proximity to glamour. I kept digging.

They drove around a bit more, in what seemed to me to be an imitation of fun, or maybe an imitation of the Beatles pretending to have fun, and then, after they got bored of driving round in their little white golf carts, they went somewhere else. They were probably playing Scalextric, or doing drugs. To be fair, they were probably having more fun than I was, which wasn't really that difficult. Weirdly, I was not envious. Maybe the ephedrine was giving meaning to my life.

Dig, dig, stamp, stamp.

I didn't even know I was tired, even though I had dug in a quarter of a mile of cable. It was a battle between me and the drugs and the cable. None of us was winning. It was a nil-nil draw. There was still about a mile of cable left to dig in and I had a whole box of nasty speed pretending to be a cold remedy in my pocket. My nose was as clear as my conscience. I couldn't even be bothered to think about anything.

I looked around. My boss was walking across the field.

The boss had once sold the *Socialist Worker* on the streets of Rugby, but now he ran a job agency. He smoked a lot of cigarettes and looked quite stressed most of the time. It might have been work stress, or it might have been showbiz-sherbet stress, it was hard to tell. Every hour that we worked he got paid for. I liked him, but I couldn't resist taking the piss out of what I perceived as being the contradiction between his socialist beliefs and his current occupation as the head of a job agency, albeit a job agency employing the misfits who would have either been laughed out of (or would have laughed at) most of the other jobs available in our small town. My sarcastic nature and proclivity for wandering meant that my possibilities for advancement within the company were considerably diminished.

There was a fairly strict hierarchy within the crew. There were the roadies (people who were actually on the road with the band), all of the office people and organisers, and then there was us. The local crew of humpers and losers. The hierarchy was most evident in the type of drugs people took. If you were high enough up, you got to take cocaine, like the rock stars. If you were a low-end humper with no obvious skills, it was beer and hash. If you were a loser but had friends who weren't, you might be given the odd line. I worked at this job on and off for about a year and never even saw a line of cocaine. Anyway. Dig, dig, stamp, stamp.

A big old Luton van pulled up beside where I was working. I was so bored I stopped to look at it. The driver got out and rolled up the shutter at the rear of the van. About ten kids in their early teens piled out in a state of youthful excitement. They were feeling the glamour of being part of the rock and roll circus after having been cooped up with no seating in the back of a windowless van from Hull or somewhere. They had probably been promised free tickets to the gig of the century in exchange for a 'few hours work' and would most likely be flipping burgers and washing pots at one of the food vans while Liam was singing 'Rock 'n' Roll Star' or 'Champagne Supernova'. I guessed most of those kids hadn't drunk a lot of champagne, but at least now they *wanted* to. Cocaine lifestyles, golf carts, rock stars, big Scalextric. Dare to fucking dream. Dig, dig, stamp, stamp.

Oasis had been having a bit of a disagreement with another band called Blur. It was on the news and everything. Oasis hated Blur and the feeling was mutual. There was a battle for the number-one slot in the charts, a fight to see who would win. There could only be one biggest. It was survival of the most ambitious.

Blur had a song about a rich person moving to a country house and Oasis had a song about rolling with it. What 'it' actually was was never specified. Like all great advertising slogans it was vague but seemingly full of meaning. In the media the bands had been portrayed as being very different to each other, it was said that they were coming from different places in society. You know how the class system is in Britain, right? As soon as you open your mouth you get slotted into a sub-category on some tier of unbreakable class distinction. The funny thing was, both bands wanted the same thing, which was, of course, what everyone else wanted, which was to be the biggest, or the best, or something. It was neat divide and rule packaged as alternative culture and sold with mock disapproval and a vaguely patronising chuckle by the mainstream media. Can you imagine Crass doing it? Me neither. It was all about aspiration. Sadly, the aspirations in question were extremely fucking dull.

Dig, dig, stamp, stamp.

I aspired to stop digging. I was digging so that eventually I could stop digging. The only reason I did these shitty jobs was to earn enough money to stop doing them. Maybe that is why I kept on doing them too. At that moment the digging was the most interesting thing on my horizon. Speed is great like that. It narrows your perceptions until boring jobs make all of the sense in the world.

Dig, dig.

Stamp, stamp.

There was the sound of a big old self-important power chord from the PA. It was soundcheck time. There was a bloke onstage with a guitar. The guitar had a Union Jack painted on it, which completely failed to make my heart swell with nationalistic pride. The urchins from the back of the Luton van were fucking mesmerised though. This was probably the closest they were going to get to the gig of the century.

My feet were hurting a bit.

The bloke played some more chords, then John Squire from the Stone Roses came out and played a bit of guitar. His band could have been as big as the Beatles or as big as Oasis pretending to be the Beatles but they fucked it up. Or maybe they didn't. John Squire looked a bit uneasy. I liked him for that.

Dig, dig, stamp, stamp.

It was time to go home, thank fuck. My legs and my feet hurt from all of the speed-induced stamping and digging. I had played my part in rock and roll history to little fanfare and less applause. The cable was well and truly dug in. Nobody was going to inadvertently trip over that while wondering what a fucking wonderwall was.

I think I earned about eighteen quid for that five-hour shift. It was something like that anyway. I recalled a quote from the songwriter of Oasis. He had called for all members of the royal family and all Conservatives to be beheaded. I found that pretty funny. Fucking four-fifty an hour and I had to buy my own Sudafed. I wonderwalled how much the band got paid?

We all got in the van.

Everybody was much happier than they had been in the morning. Those of us who were not already drunk began to get drunk. There was a bloke from Belfast who worked on the crew. He had been chased out of his town by the local hard men because he stole the wrong car, or something. He brought out four cans of super-strength lager and drank them in about fifteen minutes. I never saw anybody get drunk so fast. He died of liver failure a few years later. He told me the best story once. He told me that when the bailiffs had arrived at his house with a policeman over some unpaid debt to the council, he had been forced to let them in. When the bailiff went to pick up the first of his belongings, Joe smashed it with a hammer before they could take it out of his house. He told me he smashed a lot of his own stuff that day and it was all completely legal. The police couldn't stop him smashing his own stuff.

I never got the call to work at the actual show, but I did get to watch it on telly. I was sat watching it at my mum's house after a night when I hadn't slept in the front garden. I saw the fucking golf carts. I had never been a big fan of golf. I saw the band driving the little white golf carts around backstage on the telly, like the Queen, or something. I looked at the people in the back of the golf carts on telly. I recognised someone I had once been in a band with. I hadn't seen her since. She had married a rock star and lived in a big house in the country somewhere. Her musical career had obviously been slightly more successful than my own. Oasis had a line in one of their

songs that said, 'Where were you when we were getting high?'
Well, I had been digging the fucking cables in. Any idiot could
have done it, but in a way I'm glad it was me.

A Very Strange Dream

Shortly afterwards, I had a strange dream. After the terrible conquering armies of Britpop had driven all of the shivering independent weirdos into the stadium for execution, the victors had moved to vast palaces in the countryside, decorated with the skulls of their enemies, to count their spoils and compose bloated rock operas and triple-album collaborations about the films of Michael Winner. It was like David Essex in *Stardust*, but without the glamour.

Kate and Richard were living in their shocking-pink mansion in the country, with Kate employing a cook to dish up all sorts of terrible avant garde meals for him. He was wasting away and Kate was noticing how fat the dog was getting. Richard smiled grimly around every forced mouthful and quickly spat it under the table to the dog, who was terribly constipated and prone to awful bouts of farting and explosive diarrhoea. Richard had to eat late at night in the music room and hide the Ginsters pasty wrappers from her, as he relived the glory days of the Verve on YouTube, while one of Oasis drove John Lennon's Rolls Royce into the paddling pool of tears that Chris Martin had shed on a crying jag after two glasses of champagne shandy and a crafty line of Lemsip. Then a huge booming voice crackled out over the psychic tannoy: 'Truly, success can be a greater curse than failure, especially if we must guard ourselves with robot snipers and surround ourselves with horribly fame-addicted Hollywood celebrities in order to bolster the fragile self-esteem that we used to get from . . . oh, I dunno, playing music with our friends.' Then a huge flaming banner appeared in the sky. It said, 'There is nothing quite as seductive and as disappointing as the things that we are told we should want and then do.'

Of course, this was merely the politics of envy, and it was only a matter of time until all of that wealth trickled down. Even in dreams.

No Lawyers, Only Longbows

Can you imagine what I would do if I did all that I can?
Sun Tzu

I had received the green bolt of yew as a gift for my birthday. It had come via a friend who worked in the medieval armoury at Holdenby House (a stately home close to Rugby and the resting place of the bones of Lady Diana). He had received the wood from a practising witch who worked as a seamstress there and who kept a garden filled with feared and forbidden plants. The fact that I had recognised a few of these plants by sight when I visited had impressed her in some small way, and she had given the seven-foot stave of yew to my friend to give to me. It was a peculiar birthday present, but it was what I had wanted. The yew tree is the oldest living tree on the British Isles, and it is rich with stories and mythology. The Fortingall Yew in Perthshire is thought to be one of the oldest trees in Europe. Estimates vary as to its true age: some say one thousand five hundred years, and some say three thousand years. Local legend claims that Pontius Pilate was born beneath the Fortingall Yew and played in its shade as a child. Yews are difficult to age. As the heartwood of the original trunk rots away the tree itself continues to sprout outside its own decay. No obvious centre means no rings to count, and therefore no definitive way to age the tree. Perhaps this is one of the reasons why the yew is traditionally associated with death, rebirth and the underworld. Many of the ancient yews of Britain are to be found in church graveyards, and whether the trees predate the churches, or the other way round, is sometimes a matter of speculation.

The friend who had given me the yew wood from the witch's

garden was named Peter Prince, a big man with an eccentric and occasionally darkly depressive nature, who hailed from the Black Country and who claimed gypsy ancestry. He couldn't read or write very well but he could make just about anything with his hands. Pete was a musician and an occasional shoemaker, who also liked weapons. He'd come round to the house where I lived and take me out to the country, where we'd shoot longbows or ride canoes, or fight with broadswords he had borrowed from the armoury. Once, he had proudly shown me two gleaming broadswords that had not yet been ground to a cutting edge, but which were big, heavy and extremely fucking sword-like. We went and drank a few beers and then decided to have a duel on the green outside the students' residence at Rugby School, which, as one of the most expensive and highly esteemed private schools in Britain, attracts the sons and daughters of politicians, diplomats, captains of industry and gangsters. We thought it might be amusing to conduct a loud mock battle involving clashing broadswords and obviously regional accents to show our future rulers that the fighting spirit was not quite dead in the peasantry. The steel clashed, ribald and disgusting insults were thrown, we didn't get arrested, nobody was seriously injured, and we thought it was funny. Anybody watching us probably thought it was another case of two drunk locals trying to kill each other again. There were always murders in Rugby.

Peter Prince spoke, in whispered tones, of a man who we shall refer to as 'Elron, the bow maker'. Elron was one of the original crew of Rugby hippies from the sixties who had a fairly formidable and mysterious reputation as a bit of a hermit and a traditional yew bowyer. The woman who owned the house where I lived knew Elron pretty well and had arranged an introduction for me. He had driven up from his remote and crumbling farmhouse in the Brecon Beacons in a car that ran on recycled chip shop fat. We bonded over a shared love of wild plants, and consequently I received some advice on the ancient art of bow making, none of it precise or scientific, but all of it invaluable. I never told him why I wanted the bow. I just listened and nodded as he explained about trial and error, the unique properties of yew, and the easily avoidable beginner's mistakes. 'Just work slowly and feel the way the bow wants to be made,' he advised. I went to visit him down at his farmhouse in a remote Welsh valley. Each corner of the tumbledown cottage was stacked with longbows of varying sizes and strengths. Knotted, horned, silky and gleaming, dark hearted and with a pale band of flexible sapwood along the front, each one was unique and lovingly handcrafted to pull evenly and fling arrows far and fine.

So, with my training from the eldritch bow maker and my bolt of rough green yew handed down from the witch through the master of arms, I was prepared for an epic revenge story of tragic proportions. I set about the task of making my weapon like a man quietly possessed. I felt wronged and thought only vengeance could make it right. I was going to settle a score. Any fool can pull a trigger without a second thought, but this was going to be personal. I was going to look somebody in the eye, and loose the arrow from a bow I had made with my own hands. My cherished hatred was preparing to flower into a bloody rose with a feathered stem. The sense of injustice had grown in me like a cancer, unseen and unacknowledged until I had begun to show symptoms of a disease which I did not recognise.

Murderous vengeance was not the thing I actually wanted, of course, it was a reaction to the things I felt were lacking from the situation that had provoked me. Fairness, decency and honour being absent, I had been forced into dealing with lawyers, and my lack of funds to fight a case of missing funds was a frustration that lead me back to the basics of the old snake brain.

I had begun chopping at the rough bolt of wood with my car-boot Bowie knife, carving off the bark and the first big chunks of wood until the basic shape of the weapon was made and it began to look less like a stick and more like a bow. I worked outside in the day and inside my small bedroom at night, becoming so fully absorbed in the task that I had little time for anything else. My bow was taking shape as the poison of the wood fed the fever that drove me on. My landlady, a woman of some sensitivity, did not ask too many questions, but occasionally I could see the concern in her. She had mentioned that there seemed to be 'a brooding presence' down towards the end of the corridor when I worked through the night. The small bedroom that I rented at the back of the terraced house was strewn with slivers and tiny scrapings of yew. They were in the bed, in my socks, and they completely covered the small area of floor space between the bed and the opposite wall of the room that I was sleeping and working in. This mess itself was invisible to me, focused as I was on the task in hand.

I visualised the final scene as the bow started to come to life. It was beginning to reveal its own shape and character and I knew every knot and contour of the wood by heart. I cut notches in the rough ends and strung it for the first time, bracing the wood against my leg and putting the first flex in it.

I come from a long line of warriors, but I hadn't known that at the time. My great-grandfather was an officer in the First World War. He was shot through the lungs in the Battle of the Somme and was pulled out bleeding but alive after laying in no-man's-land for some hours. He had spent years at the front. My grandfather was a commando in the Second World War . . . joined at seventeen, was posted to the Baltic Sea, came up the beaches at the D-Day landings and was then posted to Burma.

My father was a mercenary in the 'Belgian' Congo in the sixties, serving with ex-SS officers, and was a self-confessed 'National Socialist'. I was adopted at the age of six weeks into a family with no history of war. When they got me they knew only that my father had been a mercenary, which was strictly forbidden information. They were also told that the strange scarring I had on my knee was from a mysterious case of frostbite. Nobody seemed to know how a six-week-old baby might get frostbite, but there we are. My adoptive parents never ever told me that they knew my father was a mercenary. I guess in the early seventies it might have been considered somewhat glamorous and exciting to be a 'soldier of fortune'. They were aware of the realities of that only through films and the occasional news source. I imagine the truth was more squalid. Those mercenaries had been known as *'Les affreuses'*, the terrible ones. Regardless, they never told me what they knew of my roots. When I had asked my dad (adoptive) about my father (genetic) he had told me that my father had been an Irish musician. My dad was instrumental in guiding me away from war and into music. I had been keen to join the army at one point in my mid-teens, mainly as a way to avoid the drudgery and boredom of most of the working lives I was being offered, and partly because I craved adventure. He sat me down and said, 'Just remember, Willie, all that they are training you to do is kill people.'

Rather than trying to discourage me from joining the army, he encouraged me into music with praise and occasional support. He gave me the four hundred pounds to go and buy my Gibson Thunderbird when I joined Spacemen 3. I had taken that money with me and gone searching through the music shops of Birmingham. I tried a lot of basses until I finally walked into City Music on Colmore Row. As soon as I saw the Gibson Thunderbird I knew it was my bass. Playing it for the first time confirmed what I had known at first glance. It was love at first sight.

When I met my father for the first time, many years later, I had left his council flat in Chesterfield totally shell-shocked. He had talked to me about his admiration for Hitler and war all night as he smoked the hash he had requested I bring with me. I had sat on his sofa absolutely dumbfounded. The only thing I remember saying to him after politely turning down his offer of moving to 'a nice place he knew in South Africa where there were no black people' was, 'You don't know me very well, do you?'

The idea of a future filled with bad oompah music and inbred white supremacy really didn't sit well with my own worldview. The first thing I had done after the meeting was phone my dad. 'Hi, Dad,' I said. 'I just got back from meeting my father.'

'Oh, really,' he replied, keeping it light. 'How was it?'

'Well,' I said. 'Remember how you told me he was an Irish musician?'

'Did I?' he said, and then there was long silence.

'He wasn't. He was a mercenary. You knew that, didn't you?'

'Erm . . . ,' he said, searching for words, 'it's hard to remember. I can't remember saying that to you . . . maybe I did.'

'You did say that. Thanks, Dad,' I said. 'I'm glad things worked out the way they did.'

I had never been more grateful for having been told a lie in my entire life.

I didn't know all of that when I was sitting in my little bedroom with a bloodthirsty urge and a bedroom full of toxic sawdust. I fixed the string in the nocks for the fiftieth time and then braced the bow with my left hand, pulling the string back towards my open eye. I could feel the power in it and the potential. They say a longbow will pierce bulletproof glass with a steel bodkin point arrowhead. It hits the target, the point penetrates, the shaft of the arrow flexes and then kicks the arrow through with the recoil. It is a powerful weapon. A decent modern archer with a good pull should manage to fire an arrow over one hundred and eighty metres. An archer from the good old days of Edward III should have been able to reach a distance of three hundred metres and pierce a well-made suit of armour with a war arrow, regardless of the nobility of the prince inside it.

I began to consider the reality of the act I was preparing. I guess that the meditative task of actually making the weapon had cooled my bloodlust a little. I decided that I would now be satisfied with an arrow in the leg. Perhaps around the thigh. I guessed that anyone with an arrow in their leg would have good reason to consider the consequences of the actions that had lead to it happening.

'Yeah, just one in the leg and a pithy remark. That'll be enough,' I thought out loud, as I pulled the string back and took imaginary aim at my imaginary foe.

With the balance and pull of the bow correct, I began to sand and file the wood, taking it back to a smooth grain with finer and finer grades of sandpaper until it felt like silk in my hand. It was a war of attrition in more ways than one. When I was completely satisfied with the finish, I set about the decorative touches, inlaying two slivers of mother-of-pearl at the nocking point. Those two curls danced around each other like bright halves of the yin and yang symbol. I guess the darkness was all in me and I was prepared to admit no outward signs of it.

Finally, I chose a scrap of red leather for the handle, wrapping and cutting it precisely to fit, and then binding the top and bottom edges with green silk cord.

I strung the bow for the last time, gripped the handle, drew my left arm level with my face and drew the bowstring back to my nose with the fingertips of my right hand. I held it there for a few seconds, enjoying the tension, before returning the string to its resting position.

I was ready for the test firing, so I rang Peter Prince and we arranged to go out the next day for a little practise.

We arrived at the car park at Badby Woods near Daventry and unpacked the bows.

It was a bright summer morning and the dew was still light in the grass as we walked across the low hills beneath the old gnarled oaks and copper beech that stood at the edge of the forest. We found a place beneath the shelter of one of the trees and set up a target against the grassy bank in front of us so that no stray arrows would prang any unsuspecting dog walkers. We strung our bows and nocked up the first of the aluminium-tipped practice arrows.

Whap, whap, whap. The arrows buried themselves in the bank with satisfying force. It seemed like my bow could sing.

'Nice job, Willie,' Pete said. 'Not bad at all for a first attempt.'

I was pretty pleased with it too.

We fired a few arrows towards the empty beer can and then turned out towards the open fields for some distance shooting. The arrows looped away from us into the empty green fields and we followed them out, retrieving them from deep in the grass as we went.

I never used that bow for anything except entertainment.

In the end, I chose music instead of revenge, creativity instead of destruction, and something else instead of money.

The making of it had been enough to persuade me that blood, cold or warm, was not the cure for what ailed me.

It was only business, after all.

Thoughts on Being a Musician

As a musician, my greatest struggle has not been with the audience, or with poverty. It has not been with a reluctant muse, or addiction. The strange hours, the many miles, and the days spent working away in lightless, stinking rooms have not dented my resolve. My main problem has not been with illegal downloaders or dishonest managers, or with a greedy and rapacious industry and my own ability to make everything except money. My greatest challenge has been within myself. In the ways I have reacted to these situations. My greatest battle has been with my own bitterness and cynicism. There is nothing worse than bitterness. If you lose your love of music, they get you twice. It doesn't matter if you are right or if you were wronged, ripped off and left for dead by your companions at the side of the road.

Bitterness will get you nowhere. It will eat you, beat you and leave you washed out and burned up more than anything else ever could. It will lead you to see the world as a rotten place and your friends as enemies. It will sour every breath you take and leave you coughing ash at the walls of your self-made prison.

Did somebody take your idea and not give you any credit? Great. You've got another one, right? What are you going to do with it, lock it in the attic? You should be glad they took it. That means you can move on to the next one. Get out there, keep losing, learn from your mistakes, and move on. Remember why you started to play in the first place, and if that was for adulation and a Rolls Royce in a swimming pool then maybe you fell for the biggest scam of all. Just remember, reward and praise can be as much your enemies as privation and obscurity. Music is a grand tradition. We keep the night out, we sometimes quieten the angry spirits, and we breathe hope that we must first breathe ourselves.

Nobody said it was easy, but it gets a whole lot more difficult when you are carrying round a big sackload of grudgeful blame and hurt.

Remember what music has done for you? All those times a rhythm, a little melody and a few words helped you to understand that you were not alone? You are the crest of a wave, not some lofty pinnacle doomed to tragedy and worship. You are not there to have your arse kissed like a splinter off the deity, or to be kicked around like a dog. Ego trips are horrible and inevitable. Be part of the muck and mire, spread your grateful arms and pour it out. Remember the song that played when you fell in love. Remember when you were so damn angry, and when music turned that rage into a dance and a righteous howl that felt so much better than your mumbling, incoherent hurt.

This is a noble tradition. I am glad and honoured to have given back a little of what I got from it. I am glad to have given a little to someone who might give a little bit back to someone else someday. If you must lose, lose again, and at least lose gloriously. They don't call it *playing* for nothing. Grumpy old fuckers don't play, and nobody wants to play with them. Start from the end.

Thanks to the Ghostwriters

Most of this book was written in an attic room in Zagreb. The window allowed me a view of the whole city and, if I leaned out far enough, I could watch the sun rise and set. There was graffiti on the wall when I arrived that let me know I was in the right place. Written on the white chipboard that faced the bed were the words 'You can't kill me I was born dead'. There was also a drawing of a pyramid with an eye in it and the number 33 written close by. The person who had drawn them was not a fan of Spacemen 3.

I did not set out to write the book I wrote. I wanted to write a funny set of short stories drawn from nearly thirty years of playing in bands. I did not want to revisit some of the difficult moments of those first few years. This book dragged me in. It dragged me back to Rugby and the beginnings of the unlikely journey that led me to Zagreb and all of its heavy stories to live in an attic room in an apartment where an old lady had recently died of cancer. I wrote the bulk of this book in two months, snacking on cheese sandwiches, drinking red wine and mostly demanding to be left alone. I did not want to write about drugs, but then to write a book about Spacemen 3 without drugs in it would be absurd. The woman who lived downstairs was a methadone addict. The war had pushed her into addiction, as it had many people. War and painkillers go hand in hand. Pain and painkillers go hand in hand. Sometimes painkillers are so strong that you forget about what is causing the pain in the first place.

Many of the events that I describe in this book happened

over twenty-five years ago. Many of the people described here have changed in some ways. Some are dead. A couple died during the writing of the book. I guess everybody in the book is different these days.

It was a long road to Zagreb, to be sitting in the chair of a man who had kicked his own habit after enduring the siege of Vukovar and who then killed himself before he got a chance to meet his beautiful grandchildren. I wrote most of this book sitting in his old armchair. Although it was difficult to write some of it, and to revisit the past, I found that my attitude to the events I described changed as I wrote. I felt like it helped me put the past where it belongs. In the past. What I didn't like in it, I learned to accept and come to terms with. We were young and we all made mistakes. That's forgivable.

We can't really escape the past, and if we run from it . . . we'll spend a long time running. Sometimes the way through is to turn and face the things you are scared of, learn what you can from them, and then try to move on. Those noisy ghosts of memory only want to be heard, and sometimes they aren't as scary as they seem.

I had started the year with a painkiller habit I didn't want. It had caught me at a low point and I felt like I needed it. That old taste is difficult to forget sometimes. I kicked that habit in the spring (with the help of a good friend, a fine dog and a beautiful view). After that, I went out on the road and embraced the changes that I had resisted, with my final intention being to end up in Croatia and write a book. And that is what I did.

With Thanks to:

Baldvin Dungal, Kristina Mavar, Kruno Mavar, Don Santos, Iva Ilakovac, Tofa, Uli M. Schueppel, Tino, James Masson, Lee Brackstone, Hannah Bowen, Liz Carruthers, Carole Carruthers, Sue MacDiarmid, Michael Roumen, Bev, Kit and William, Oscar Van Gelderen, Craig Ferguson, Lorena Casal Iglesias, Anna Hiebsch, Mauer Park, Renata, the Pembrokeshire Coastal Path, Craig Bodsworth, the Druidstone hotel, Philip Wood, Sada Leigh, Sheila Sarup, Þingvallavatn, Gísli Pálmi, Hashi, Heidrun, Teddy, Nairi, Hannah Moorhead, Josh T. Pearson, Paolo Vizio, Greg Jarvis, the Thirteenth Floor Elevators, and everyone I ever played in a band with.

In loving memory of James Cruickshank, Natty Brooker, Sean Stewart, Rowley Ford and Bill Carruthers.